WALES: THE SHAPING OF A NATION

WALES

The Shaping of a Nation

PRYS MORGAN
and
DAVID THOMAS

DAVID & CHARLES

NEWTON ABBOT   LONDON   NORTH POMFRET (VT)

British Library Cataloguing in Publication Data

Morgan, Prys
  Wales.
  1. Wales—History
  I. Title   II. Thomas, David, 1931–
  942.9   DA714

  ISBN 0-7153-8418-X

Typeset by ABM Typographics Limited, Hull
and printed in Great Britain
by Redwood Burn Limited, Trowbridge, Wilts.
for David & Charles (Publishers) Limited
Brunel House Newton Abbot Devon

Published in the United States of America
by David & Charles Inc
North Pomfret Vermont 05053 USA

Contents

List of Illustrations   6

Preface   9

Chapter

1   LAND OF MY FATHERS   13

2   PEOPLE AND LANGUAGE   32

3   WALES AND ENGLAND   58

4   RURAL WALES   84

5   INDUSTRIALISATION   109

6   THE RADICAL TRADITION   134

7   CHURCH AND CHAPEL   155

8   THE DRAGON'S TWO TONGUES: LIFE AND LETTERS   178

9   LAND OF SONG, THE BARD AND RUGBY   195

10   THE GROWTH OF WELSH INSTITUTIONS   213

Appendices

I   WELSH NAMES: KEEPING UP WITH THE JONESES   231

II   COMMON PLACENAME ELEMENTS   237

Chronological Table   241

Bibliography   255

Index   263

List of Illustrations

PLATES

Upland Wales: unenclosed mountain land near
    Cwmystwyth, Dyfed   49
Raglan Castle, Gwent: one of the many guardians of the
    March, founded in Norman times but now dating mainly
    from the fifteenth century   49
The high street of a market town in the Welsh heartland:
    Lampeter, Dyfed   50
Claerwen Dam and reservoir in the Elan Valley: supplier of
    water to the West Midlands   50
Hill farm at Bodcoll, near Devil's Bridge, Dyfed   67
A prosperous valley farm at Betws Bledrws, Dyfed   68
Ruined buildings and spoil associated with lead workings
    near Cwmystwyth, Dyfed   101
Port Dinorwic, Gwynedd: once a prosperous slate-exporting
    port, now an equally prosperous harbour for pleasure boats   101
Lewis Merthyr colliery near Pontypridd, Mid Glamorgan:
    in the background are terrace houses stretching up the
    valley side   102
Treforest Industrial Estate, Mid Glamorgan: a government-
    sponsored development of the 1930s   119
Old but sound terrace housing, originally built for coal and
    iron workers at Dowlais, Mid Glamorgan: note the coal
    and ironstone workings at the end of the street   120
Llanwern Steelworks, Gwent: one of a number of new
    steelworks on the coast of south Wales   120
Park and Dare Hall, Treorci in the Rhondda Valley:
    a symbol of radicalism in the south Wales coalfield   153
The memorial to Aneurin Bevan, Tredegar Mountain, Gwent   153
The Anglican parish church of Peterston-super-Ely, South
    Glamorgan: an area of early Anglo-Norman penetration   154

An early Baptist chapel at Dolau, near Rhayader, Powys
(built in 1767)   171
Statue of Daniel Rowland, one of the leaders of Welsh
Methodism, Llangeitho, Dyfed: to the right lies the
Methodist chapel   172
The impressive façade of a Victorian chapel in Aberystwyth,
Dyfed   172
St David's University College, Lampeter, Dyfed, the first
university institution in Wales: the old buildings cut into a
motte (on the left of the picture) of Norman construction   205
University College, Cardiff: a more recent educational
establishment with an architectural style of very different
provenance   206
The National Museum of Wales, Cathays Park, Cardiff   223
The Welsh Office, Cathays Park, Cardiff   223
Robert Stephenson's rail bridge across the Menai Strait,
Gwynedd, now with an upper road deck   224
The most recent transport development in Wales, the M4,
now complete almost to Cross Hands, Dyfed: the
photograph illustrates some of the practical consequences
of bilingualism   224

FIGURES

 1 The traditional counties and county boroughs   10
 2 The new counties and districts, April 1974   11
 3 Major topographical features of Wales   14
 4 The geology of Wales   15
 5 The major regions of Wales *(after Emery)*   27
 6 Manors of Wales and the Marches in the fourteenth
   century *(after Rees and Bowen)*   42
 7 Independent Wales under Llywelyn I, 1234 *(after Rees
   and Bowen)*   44
 8 The Welsh-speaking population, 1901 *(after Pryce,
   National Atlas of Wales 3.1d)*   52
 9 The Welsh-speaking population, 1971 *(after Carter)*   53
10 Dykes of the Welsh borderland   59
11 Administration in the fourteenth century   63
12 The consequences of the Acts of Union   72
13 Turnpike roads, 1806   93

14 Enclosures authorised by act of Parliament, 1793–1815   96
15 Cropping regions, 1801   104
16 Distribution of iron works, 1750 and 1830 *(after Carter)*   115
17 Ports and port-feeders of the pre-railway and early
    railway age *(after Moyes)*   121
18 Coal types and National Coal Board collieries in south
    Wales, 1950 and 1975 *(after Humphrys)*   126
19 General election result, December 1910 *(after Madgwick
    and Balsom,* National Atlas of Wales *2.2a)*   143
20 General election result, 1945 *(after Madgwick and
    Balsom,* National Atlas of Wales *2.2b)*   147
21 General election result, 1966 *(after Madgwick and
    Balsom,* National Atlas of Wales *2.2c)*   149
22 General election result, 1979 *(after Madgwick and
    Balsom,* National Atlas of Wales *2.2d)*   151
23 Religious affiliation: nonconformist strength, 1971
    (after Williams, National Atlas of Wales *3.3b)*   174
24 Religious affiliation: Welsh-medium nonconformist
    strength, 1971 *(after Williams,* National Atlas of
    Wales *3.3c)*   175
25 Religious affiliation: Anglican communicants, 1969
    (after Williams, National Atlas of Wales *3.3d)*   176

Preface

As its title suggests, this book is in many ways a companion volume to Professor Gordon Donaldson's *Scotland: the Shaping of a Nation* (David & Charles, 1974), though the differences between Scotland and Wales give this book a rather different emphasis. We both contributed to *Wales: a New Study,* edited by David Thomas (David & Charles, 1977), and felt that there was scope for a concise volume on Wales, intended for the layman, which treated themes that were less overtly geographical or social and rather more historical. We have simply selected ten main themes (occasionally subdividing them further) which we consider the most important for an understanding of the make-up of modern Wales. It is not meant to be an academic or a specialised study, although we have drawn upon the work of many academic colleagues and upon the scholarly researches on which we are both engaged. Nor is it meant to be a complete guide to Wales and all things Welsh, for that would be an impossible goal in a book of this length.

Although there has lately been a great advance in the publishing of scholarly monographs, specialised studies and learned articles in journals on Welsh history and geography, the Welsh still lag far behind the English, Scots and Irish in producing concise general surveys for the use of the layman. We hope that this book may do something to fill the gap. We have listed a number of the more specialised studies in the bibliography, and in compiling these lists we have had in mind the more accessible volumes, generally published after 1945 and written in English, although we have in many cases based our chapters on books published earlier, and (as for example in the chapter on 'Church and Chapel') on works published in the Welsh language.

Inevitably in a book dealing with historical themes, problems of nomenclature arise following the sweeping changes in the names and boundaries of Welsh counties and districts in April 1974. While the changes are described in some detail later in the book, we use both the old and new names of administrative units so frequently that it is helpful to define our territorial reference at the outset. Fig 1 therefore illustrates the traditional counties, which had served almost unchanged from the sixteenth century, and Fig 2 the new units dating from 1974.

Fig 1 The traditional counties and county boroughs

10

We have received ready assistance from a number of people to whom we express our gratitude. Several academic colleagues have made suggestions for improvement which we have been glad to accept. They shall remain nameless lest our imperfections be visited upon them. We thank also those who have allowed us to redraw and use maps that they originally devised. Their names appear in the

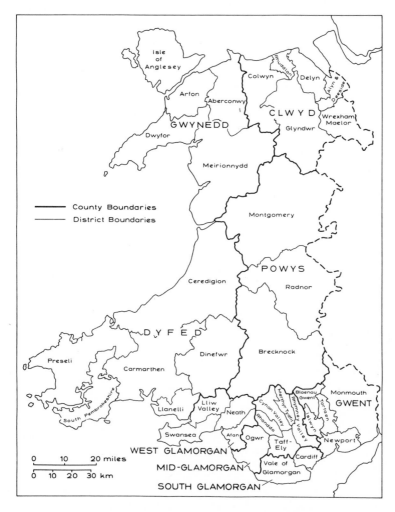

Fig 2 The new counties and districts, April 1974

figure titles. Particular thanks must go to the secretaries who transformed our drafts into readable text, to Ron and Mark Swift who travelled far to take the photographs which enhance our work, and to Tim Grogan, whose cartographic skill is well in evidence in our maps. Finally, we wish to thank the publishers for their resourcefulness and enthusiasm.

PRYS MORGAN
DAVID THOMAS

CHAPTER 1

Land of My Fathers

The land of Wales, revered in the national anthem, has been a critical and formative factor in the shaping of the nation. The hills and valleys, the resources of geological time, the weather and climate, the contrasting quality of the soil, have not in themselves determined the course of human affairs, but the land has certainly contributed more to the story of Wales than mere stage scenery to a play.

The central massif of Wales, the Cambrian Mountains, forms the heartland of the country (Fig 3). It stretches from the rugged uplands of Snowdonia (Eryri) in the north-west to the smoother outlines of Blaenau Morgannwg, brooding over the coalfield in the south-east; from the moors of Mynydd Hiraethog and the Clwydian Range in the north-east to the barren peaks of Preseli in the south-west. It is a fastness and barrier. Yet from this upland core radiate river valleys which provide not only a green, agricultural contrast with the harsh wastes at higher elevation, but also lowland corridors that have eased movement throughout the whole period during which Wales has been peopled. To the north, but particularly to the south of the mountain heartland, from the Vale of Glamorgan, through Gower and into the lowlands around Milford Haven, lie the coastal plains which have given access from the east and in turn have allowed influence from lowland England to penetrate to the western fringes of Wales. The mountain-backed, protected coastal plain of Cardigan Bay, on the other hand, has developed quite a different character — isolated, often looking more to the sea than the land, and preserving its native traditions more tenaciously than other coastal regions.

Add to these broad and varied influences the diversity which stems from the geological benefactions of stone and mineral, from the considerable contrasts in climate ranging from the mild, early-growth parts of south-west Dyfed to the wild, cold, wet and inhospitable areas of central and north Wales, and from soil quality varying from the very best in parts of Gower and in the Vale of Clwyd

13

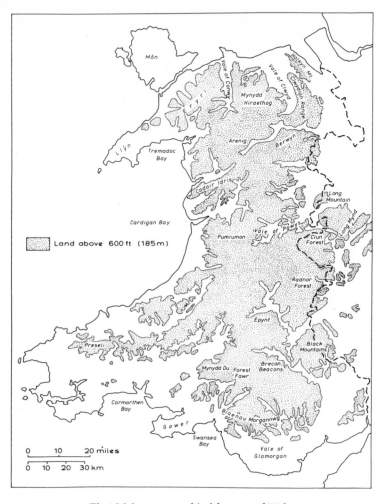

Fig 3 Major topographical features of Wales

to the worst ill-drained and stony land in the hills, and it is clear how it is possible to arrive at a paradox. In a complex and contradictory way, the land of Wales serves both to unite and to divide its people. Such has been its historical importance that it rewards closer examination.

Structure and landform

Most of Wales is composed of old, hard rocks (Fig 4). Nearly all the country is built of rocks more than 200 million years old, but in parts

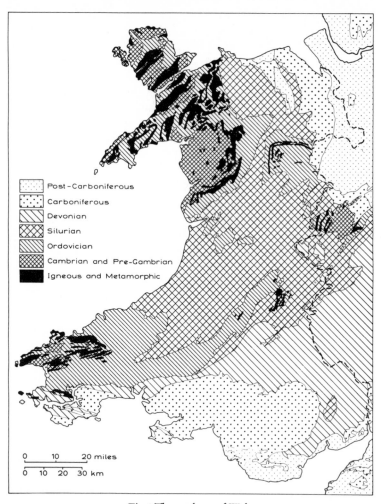

Fig 4 The geology of Wales

of Anglesey some rocks may be as much as 650 million years old. It is no chance that a number of the oldest of the geological periods, for example, Cambrian, Ordovician and Silurian, take their names from Wales and are used internationally. In relatively recent geological times these rocks were uplifted, above what is now Cardigan Bay to the west and the lowlands of the English border to the east. Their resistance to erosion and their elevation provided the basis of the present upland core of Wales. Geological structures are highly complex and of several different ages. For example, among the higher

15

areas, Snowdonia and Blaenau Morgannwg are dominated by basin or syncline forms, while Berwyn and Pumlumon are essentially structural domes. In some areas, hard volcanic rocks form the imposing peaks, for instance in Snowdonia and Cadair Idris, but elsewhere, such as in the Brecon Beacons, resistant sedimentary rocks provide the mountain crests. Much younger rocks appear in the Vales of Clwyd and Glamorgan, and in the northern part of the border country, where they contribute to the lowland nature of those areas.

Geology, of course, provided Wales with much more than the foundations of its mountain heartland and peripheral vales and plains. It yielded resources which were to play a key role in the human landscape and economic development of the country. Most of the important themes are considered at greater length throughout the book. But consider, to take only a few examples, how the ready availability of local stone in most parts of Wales influenced the nature and even colour of the traditional farmstead, how it has helped determine the nature of field boundaries — stone or stone-based banks in many parts of the country — and how local stone together with the widespread use, until well into this century, of roofing slate derived from Snowdonia, the Cadair Idris region and the Preseli Hills, has given a special character, some might even say a drabness, to the older sections of Welsh towns and villages. Likewise, the extractive and mineral industries were important, not only in terms of economic development, but also in their effects upon the landscape and settlement of the areas in which they were pursued — slate quarrying in the regions just mentioned, coal and ironstone mining in the north-east and south-east of the country, lead mining in north Wales and in northern Dyfed, and limestone quarrying for both agricultural and industrial purposes in many parts of the country.

When the geological outcrops of Wales are viewed in greater detail, an interesting and important point emerges. It is that the regional landforms fashioned upon and with the rocks, older or younger, are much the same. This strongly suggests that the detailed sculpturing of the physical landscape postdates the geological events so far described, and so it is generally held. Landforms of two main kinds appear.

First, one of the universal features of the Welsh landscape is what might be termed the 'upland plains'. While high and rugged peaks

16

certainly exist, particularly in Snowdonia, Cadair Idris and the Arenig range, most of the Welsh uplands are characterised by long and largely uncluttered skylines. These upland surfaces or plateaux are remarkably consistent in elevation from place to place, and are seemingly indifferent to geology, often cutting across rocks of different type and resistance, and through major structural features. They occur at many heights, ranging from little above present sea level to the highest points in Wales. In some areas, such as northern Dyfed, a succession of plateaux can produce an almost staircase effect; large, level treads being backed by steeply sloping risers. The lower plateaux, now and in the past, have provided flat areas for agriculture. The higher exposed plateaux have more usually been devoted to woodland or to moorland and rough grazing. Both low and high surfaces are plainly the result of the processes of erosion which have undertaken their work in relatively late geological times.

There is little debate over the origin of the lower or coastal plateaux. Those lying below 700ft (210m) are almost without exception regarded as of marine origin. That is, they are thought to have been formed in the same way as the present-day, wave-cut, rock platforms around our shores, though of course when sea levels relative to the land were much higher than now. The higher plateaux are more contentious and have given rise to controversy among geomorphologists. In the absence of confirming evidence, largely because of the greater age of the higher surfaces, one group has taken the view that all are the result of marine planation; another group that the distinctive landforms stem from the action of rivers together with associated weathering and mass movement on slopes, in other words, subaerial erosion. Even within the second group there are differences of interpretation, but the majority tend to the view that the plateaux are essentially fragments of what were once very large, almost featureless, river basins.

Associated with and dissecting the plateaux are the major streams of Wales. They provide another source of discordance; that is, a lack of adjustment to geological structures. Broadly, the main drainage lines radiate from the centre of the country and, like the plateaux, cut through outcrop and structural features. The marine plateaux school of thought has little difficulty in explaining this: the streams were initiated at the highest levels and as the sea level fell, relative to the land, plateaux emerged and the streams found their way seawards across successive surfaces oblivious of geology. The subaerial school requires a now-vanished cover of younger rocks lying above those now remaining, upon which the drainage was initiated and then superimposed onto the present landscape. The debate cannot be satisfactorily resolved, but it is worth noting the opinion of a recent writer that the fashioning of the plateaux and the alignment of the streams we observe today has in all probability happened within the relatively short period of the last 20 million years.

One further important consequence of the changes in sea level which, one way or another, created the plateaux and discordant streams, is upon the stream long-profile. Many Welsh streams are characterised by a step-like steepening of gradient. This may be due to past uplift of the land, perhaps to harder bands of rock, or possibly to a combination of the two. Certainly, these steps or 'knicks', because of their association with swifter-flowing water, became an attraction for early water-powered industry. There are many examples in Wales of such sites being utilised. Along the Teifi valley, for example, particularly in its lower tributaries, many woollen mills were established in the early years of the Industrial Revolution. In two adjacent settlements, Dre-fach and Felindre, forty-five mills were in operation between 1840 and the end of the century, though between one and five woollen factories per settlement was more typical.

The second set of major landforms in Wales results from the work of ice. Between 1.5 and 2 million years ago, at about the same time as the first appearance of the *Homo genus* elsewhere in the world, the climate of northern and western Europe deteriorated to the point where it was akin to that of the Arctic today. Cold, harsh conditions did not persist without interruption. Evidence for at least two major phases has survived in Wales, each preceded by a warmer interglacial period, but it is likely that there were many more than just two of these sequences. During the cold periods, each lasting many thousands of years, ice sheets, nourished in the uplands of Wales but also moving southwards along the Irish Sea, spread over most of the country, while valley glaciers, guided by the former river valleys, edged downwards into the lowlands. The result was that the physical landscape was considerably modified.

Ice has enormous erosive power. Former river valleys were deepened and widened to form the broad, clean-cut valleys of today. Streams have become re-established in these troughs but are frequently and obviously too small to have cut the valleys they now occupy, while tributaries are left 'hanging' on the valley sides. In a few places, mainly in Snowdonia, glacial overdeepening has led to the formation of ribbon lakes. Elsewhere, many of the lower portions of valleys, such as those of the Mawddach, Dyfi and Tawe, have been eroded with rock basins below sea level, and would now be fjord-like were it not for subsequent infill with superficial deposits. At higher levels, ice, snow and frost have combined to etch knife-edge ridges or massive armchair-shaped basins, known as *cirques*, to provide the only really rugged scenery in Wales.

What is eroded, however, must also be deposited. Haphazard, unsorted material, known as *till* or *boulder clay*, mantles much of Wales. It is thicker in the valleys and lowlands than at higher elevations, and it sometimes occurs in characteristic forms. Ice-margin ridges, known as *moraines*, are found frequently, as at Margam and Orleton, where they delimit the extent of the last glaciation. In other places, moraines may indicate temporary ice margins or ice re-advances, such as near Wrexham. The five major Sarn features of Cardigan Bay, the low submarine banks partly exposed at low tide that figure so largely in Welsh folklore, are also morainic ridges. Occasionally, in areas of low relief, for example in northern Anglesey and near Hirwaun, thick till is formed into gently rounded mounds called *drumlins*, and popularly known as 'basket of eggs topography'.

The depositional features so far described are those largely of active ice. The last glaciation was at its peak around 18,000 years ago, but within 4,000 years, with catastrophic haste judged by the standards of geologic time, deglaciation had been completed. The dramatic change in climate released large quantities of water previously imprisoned in the ice sheets, and this fashioned glacial drainage channels in till and bedrock, and deposited sorted sand and gravel in many forms. The channels are now often without streams or carry streams that bear little relationship to overall river patterns. They were formerly thought to be exclusively the result of overspill from glacial lakes, and indeed some may have been, but many are now interpreted as meltwater channels created by streams flowing over, alongside or under dead ice. They are particularly numerous in the Conwy valley and in the lower Tywi basin. Temporary lakes were impounded by ice or glacial deposits. These have contributed their own lake sediments, but more marked in a number, such as in the former Lake Teifi, are the delta fans along the edges of the present

19

valley, now often the flood-free sites for small settlements. In the outwash areas at and beyond the retreating ice front, sands and gravels were widely deposited, and these sometimes took the form of mounds or *kames,* long sinuous ridges or *eskers* and ill-drained depressions or *kettle holes.* Such features are common in the lowlands of south Wales and in the northern section of the border country.

The final phase of the Ice Age, between 11,000 and 10,000 years ago, was marked by another very cold period but one in which the land was largely unglaciated. Frost was severe, though daily or seasonal thaws would have been common; yet only a little below the surface the land remained permanently frozen. While such conditions had undoubtedly existed earlier, and on several occasions, the evidence has been destroyed by subsequent erosion. It is only this final phase that has left an appreciable imprint on the land. Frost shatters rocks, and during thaws more moisture penetrates the rocks to facilitate later weathering, while at the same time water also aids the movement of material downslope, particularly over a frozen subsurface. Many upland screes were formed during this period, but more important in areal terms are the vast stretches where eroded materials, rock and soil, are sludged down to form the deep mantle of superficial deposits so characteristic of Welsh upland valleys. Often these deposits have been further moulded by streams into terrace-like forms which, in addition to frost-fashioned fragments, contain resorted glacial materials.

And so to the present interglacial period, if such it be. Climate has ameliorated and one of its most obvious effects is evident along the 600-mile (1000km) coast of Wales. During the previous interglacial period, some 125,000 years ago, a high sea level created by global deglaciation established the main outlines of today's coast and left a series of raised beaches, notches or steps in the coastal rocks, up to 50ft (15m) above present sea level. The passing of the Ice Age has meant that once more sea levels have risen, and that marine erosion upon both bedrock and glacial deposit has been renewed. So it is possible to argue, as one author has done, that the coasts of Wales alternate between rocky shores and lowland drift coasts. The resistant rock outcrops mostly yield coastlines with cliffs, while the recent, unconsolidated materials not infrequently generate dune systems. In some places, such as Milford Haven, former valleys have been drowned and now provide water access well inland. In others, and particularly in Cardigan Bay at the mouths of streams such as the Dyfi, sand and shingle spits have grown across estuaries, aiding the development of saltmarsh and river deposit on their landward sides. The coast of Wales, just as the land it defines, presents both easy access and impenetrable barrier; it both encourages and deters movement and economic development and, as does the remainder of the country, it offers a range of opportunities to those who choose to come and go by water rather than by land.

Weather and climate

The variety of the landforms is matched by the variations in weather and climate. Weather — the day-to-day experience of rainfall, temperature, sunshine and so on — is, of course, fickle. Wales is a battleground for air masses from ocean and from continent, from polar and from tropical sources. The relatively cool, maritime influences from the western quarter predominate, but never for too long at one time. The short-term changeability of the weather is further emphasised by the relief of the land and its orientation in terms of the air mass movement. Lower areas almost always experience the more clement weather, but there is no certain rule. When the warm moist south-westerlies blow in summer, the uplands certainly receive more rain than the lowlands, but western and southern coastal fringes get more than the north coast plain and the border country, which are in the rain shadow of the mountain core. Yet in winter when cold continental air brings snow, the east frequently suffers more than the west. Western coasts experience more gale-force winds and a warmer winter; eastern lowlands more fog, particularly in autumn and winter, and more summer thunderstorms. Put together over a considerable period, these varied conditions constitute the climate: a long-term generalisation of the weather.

Possibly the most marked feature of the Welsh climate is its wetness. Precipitation increases sharply with elevation and, because of the strong westerly component in the wind pattern, tends to be lowest in the northern and eastern lowlands. Annual amounts range from 160in (4000mm) in Snowdonia to below 30in (750mm) on the north coast and in parts of the borderland. Very substantial parts of the country receive more than 50in (1250mm). Differences in rainfall can be quite localised. Longer periods of rain or more intense rainfall can be triggered by any appreciable windward slope.

Temperatures, while never extreme, also vary considerably over the country. In the uplands, the effects of altitude combine with the increased cloudiness and lower amounts of sunshine to depress temperature levels. In the lowlands, temperatures may be 3-4°F (2°C) higher in both summer and winter. Along the coasts, where a limited maritime influence is experienced, onshore breezes during the warmest months may reduce daytime maximums by a degree or so, but would also tend to increase the amount of sunshine; moderating sea temperatures delay the summer maximum temperatures usually attained in July to the following month, while in winter the relatively high sea temperature creates a narrow mild zone, particularly evident in south-west Dyfed but to a more limited extent in the westernmost parts of Gwynedd. Here air frosts are minimised, little snow falls or lies upon the ground, the growing season is long and plant growth is encouraged. South-west Dyfed is more favoured climatically than any other place in the United Kingdom, with the exception of the south-west tip of Cornwall and the Isles of Scilly.

Compared with rainfall, temperature and sunshine, the other elements are comparatively insignificant. They create only minor contrasts or are limited in effect. Perhaps one only is worth further mention here: windspeed. Gale winds cause damage to crops, livestock and buildings, and can greatly inhibit movement by sea. In Wales, strong winds are experienced mostly in the uplands, where livestock have been given protection by the planting of timber stands, shelterbelts and hedgerows, and on the coasts, where man-made or planted shelter is also used, but where agriculture and settlement have frequently adapted by seeking sheltered sites.

Within Wales, therefore, the climate creates contrasts in which the extremes are represented by, on the one hand, the highest, wettest, coldest, most cloudy and most exposed areas occupied and used by man and, on the other, coastal, rather dry, warm, sunny, but also somewhat exposed, areas where the living is easy. The importance of such differences for the development of agriculture and other human endeavours can hardly be overstressed.

So far, the discussion has concerned regional variations in present-day climate, but plainly there have also been variations over time. Over long periods, such as during the thousands or even millions of years in which the Welsh landforms were created, very substantial climatic changes took place. However, there is plenty of evidence to suggest that less sweeping, though quite important, alterations in climate have occurred within shorter time-spans, and influencing the prehistoric and historic periods. For example, it is possible today, in the raw and treeless parts of the country at heights of near 2000ft (600m), to find tree remains — birch, oak and mountain ash — preserved within peat bogs. At one time trees must have grown at far higher elevations than they do now, and at some subsequent period climatic conditions must have been such as to encourage the widespread growth of peat. Or, to take a more recent example, in medieval times, vineyards were common on the borderland, particularly in the area around Ross-on-Wye. It has been suggested that, calculating on the basis of the northern limits of modern commercial viticulture in Europe, vine cultivation could only have occurred if average summer temperatures in this area were 2.3°F (1.3°C) higher than today.

A good deal of detective work, using a wide variety of different types of data, has been undertaken into postglacial climatic change. Throughout, one must visualise that regional and altitudinal differences would have persisted. After the rapid rise in temperatures that brought the end of the Ice Age, gradual amelioration of conditions continued until the postglacial 'climatic optimum' was reached between 6500 and 3000 BC. Temperatures were roughly 4.5°F (2.5°C) above present, rainfall was abundant and forest spread rapidly up the hillsides, probably to well above today's treeline. As the ice sheets disappeared, Palaeolithic man became established in Wales, living precariously, and certainly disagreeably by our standards, in caves, but later, as climatic conditions improved, Mesolithic peoples with more advanced tools of stone, flint and bone settled themselves on open ground. In many parts of Britain, the upland areas above the thickening forest were favoured, but in Wales the coastlands of the south and west seem to have been attractive. Indeed, it is probable that these coastal areas formed part of a routeway stretching from the south of present-day France, along the western seaboard through Brittany and Cornwall to the western part of Scotland and the Scottish islands.

At a number of periods, one about 5000 BC and another from about 900 to 450 BC, a particularly wet and cool climate was experienced with mild winters. The conditions retarded tree growth, but were ideal for the formation of peat. Many waterlogged hollows developed considerable thickness, but the distinction between the earlier and later periods is often clear. Sometimes the boundary horizon is marked by the preserved stumps of trees, which indicate the dominant vegetation between the two highly maritime epochs, when a somewhat drier climate allowed trees to flourish. These vicissitudes of climate were endured by the Mesolithic food gatherers and by the peoples introduced by subsequent invasions, the Neolithic farmers and the makers and users of bronze and iron. It was not until the Iron Age that people first began to move from the Celtic homeland in central Europe towards Britain, and it was as late as 300 BC that the main wave of Celtic immigration reached Wales, thus establishing the roots of present Welsh population and culture.

The Celts were greeted by a drier period, but one with many severe winters, which must have made their hilltop settlements very uncomfortable. Following the Roman conquest, summers particularly became warmer and this allowed the development of agricultural estates, though there were few in Wales. The improved conditions were harbingers of a second climatic optimum in the early medieval period. Summer temperatures rose at the peak between AD 1100 and 1250 to more than 1°F (0.6°C) above those at present, while they were more than 2°F (1.1°C) higher than those of the seventeenth century. Summer rainfall was probably of the order of 10 per cent less than now. Winters were frequently moist yet mild, temperatures being fractionally above those of today. Little wonder that the 'Domesday Book' in 1086 could record thirty-eight vineyards in England in addition to those of the crown.

Inevitably, there came another significant change in climate. In the later Middle Ages, increasingly maritime conditions persisted in which rain-bearing westerly winds brought a return of wet, cool summers and colder winters. There was a period of partial recovery between 1450 and 1530, but thereafter the trend of deteriorating climate was re-established; summers were progressively more cool and damp, and winters dry but very cold. Such was the severity of the climate that the period 1530–1700 is often referred to as the 'Little Ice Age'. Glaciers in Europe reached their most advanced positions since the Ice Age proper, and in the late Tudor period particularly, frost fairs on the Thames were a frequent diversion. Wintertime in upland Wales must have been especially difficult. There would undoubtedly have been heavy losses of livestock, and in many summers cereals cannot have ripened properly. But on the credit side, the plagues which had troubled Britain in the Middle Ages were now virtually eliminated from Europe north of the Alps.

After 1700 another general change led to higher temperatures in both summer and winter, though occasional cold spells were still experienced. Rainfall tended to increase in winter and decrease in summer. This final phase of amelioration appears to have reached its peak in the 1940s and 1950s.

Soils and vegetation

Both the soils and vegetation of Wales are, to a large degree, the product of its geological and geomorphological history, its past and present climate and the activities of man and his animals. The uplands and the lowlands are again strongly differentiated. In upland Wales, high rainfall, low temperatures, exposure and the pasturing of animals are the chief features. Where slopes are very steep, no soil or perhaps very thin, badly developed soils occur. But widely elsewhere, the high rainfall, together with a vegetation cover which creates an acidic litter, have produced a characteristic soil known as a *podzol*. The downward movement of water through the soil, by mechanical and chemical means, washes out some of the minerals and deposits them at greater depth leaving a bleached surface horizon, often grey in colour, that can be identified in many mountain districts. More frequently, particularly where soils are very thin, peaty materials disguise the effect and darken the surface layers. In other parts of the uplands, waterlogged conditions, often partly created by impervious substrata, lead to *gley* soils. These again have a greyish colour, though peat growth tends to conceal this, but are distinguished by a marked mottling in the subsurface horizons. Where drainage is greatly impeded, hill peats develop, though many of the thick and extensive tracts derive from times when rainfall in the uplands was even higher than that of today.

Plainly, the soils described are unattractive to tillage, and where used for agricultural purposes have tended to provide pastureland, sometimes improved, but more likely rough grazing. Such natural vegetation as Wales possesses is therefore concentrated in the uplands, though if grazing animals were removed it is clear that presently restricted species — trees, bushes and flowers — would spread quite rapidly. But under existing conditions, grass moorland is dominant, with coarse grasses, such as white bent and purple moorgrass, occupying the higher ground, and more palatable types, such as common bent and sheep's fescue, together with patches of gorse and bracken, the less elevated positions. The bog areas are mainly moss-covered, but tussocks of coarse grass and cottongrass are found on the fringes. Only when sheep are absent does heather moor occupy large areas. Over the past few decades the uplands have experienced a major vegetational transformation as a result of the widespread introduction of conifers by the Forestry Commission and by private timber-growing concerns.

In lowland Wales, by contrast, less extreme rainfall, higher temperatures and better drainage have produced extensive stretches of a soil known as *brown earth*. Its nature varies somewhat from place to place, depending on the parent material (for example, the brown earth derived from the Old Red Sandstone of Brecknock is deep red in colour), but it is not leached nearly as strongly as the podzol and has a high humus content as a consequence of its long history under grass. The soil provides a sound basis for agriculture. Soils developed on limestone material obviously have a high calcareous content, and attract lime-loving plants and distinctive cropping patterns. However, at only marginally higher altitudes, these soils are shallow and are often uncultivated. In very wet, waterlogged parts of valleys, lowland peats can develop while at the coast, bog-land sometimes occurs and leads to an intermixture of peaty and alluvial deposits. As indicated earlier, coastal dunes are also extensive, and where colonised by plants or reclaimed have yielded dune soils which warm readily and encourage early spring growth.

Other than the very wet areas, where bog and saltmarsh species dominate, or on the uncultivated dunes where marram grass is close to ubiquitous, there is little even semi-natural vegetation in the lowlands. The influence of man and his animals, from Mesolithic times onwards, has been too great. He has tamed the pasture for his grazing stock, he has deforested natural timber for fuel, building, industry, and to create agricultural space, he has enclosed the waste and drained the marshland. As time has passed, progressively more of the lowlands have been occupied until today improved grassland and arable predominate. Evidence of former natural vegetation exists only in isolated patches and in the hedgerows.

Regional contrasts

The paradoxical assertion with which we began this chapter, that the land of Wales contributed both unity and diversity to the story of its

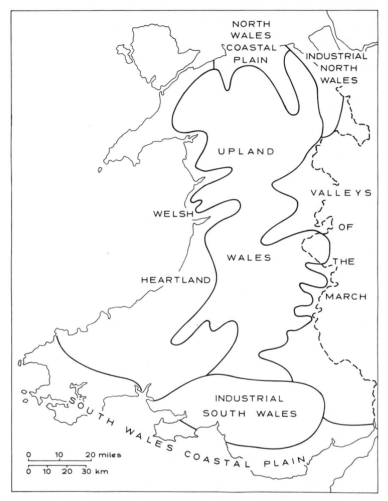

Fig 5 The major regions of Wales *(after Emery)*

people, can now be explained. The unity stems largely from the existence of the mountain core and of its reasonably coherent peripheral regions; the diversity, from the contrasts of upland and lowland, but also from the substantial differences which exist between adjacent lowland regions. While both unity and diversity have their origins in the land, they have, of course, been greatly consolidated by the use to which man has put the resources at his disposal. It is useful to review the traditional regional areas of Wales and

27

to examine their distinctiveness (Fig 5).

As always, one must begin with the hills, the features that make Wales so obviously distinct from England. Upland Wales is a region of extremes. Its hills are steep and its valleys deeply etched. Its climate is harsh and its soils are poor. It is largely deficient in resources, and when from time to time its meagre minerals and rocks have been exploited, it is always the lowlanders who have profited. Upland Wales is a place for folk who can, or are obliged to, survive in unfavourable conditions, remote from centres of economic and political power. Little wonder that it is thinly peopled and that it has suffered seriously from out-migration over a very long period. Lack of substantial inward movement of people has meant that it is traditionally a region of cultural continuity. The Welsh language and Welsh society have been vigorous over much of the region up to quite recent times, though they are now both being eroded in some eastern parts, and in particular where major river valleys give easy access into the mountains. If the proportion of the population able to speak Welsh is an adequate index, a substantially anglicised wedge has now virtually severed the Welsh speakers of the northern and the south-western sections of upland Wales, where typically between 70 and 80 per cent of the population still speak their native tongue. Contrasts between upland Wales and the adjacent peripheral regions are considerable, though the differences are not always in respect of the same characteristics.

To the west of upland Wales, and protected by it in many senses, lies what has been termed the Welsh heartland (or in Welsh, *Bro Gymraeg*). Here the land is kinder. It is less elevated, river valleys and the lower coastal plateaux provide flat areas where pastoral or mixed farming can prosper, the climate is windy but mild, and soils, while not always the most productive, are adequate to sustain very profitable agricultural use, mainly with milk or milk products as the marketable goods. Along the coast, from Conwy, Bangor and Caernarfon in the north to Cardigan and Fishguard in the south, towns have grown up to fulfil varying needs at different times, but they have long provided services for a rural population now with a relatively high average density of over fifty persons per square mile (nineteen persons per square kilometre). Its protected, isolated situation has enabled the region to maintain its essentially Welsh character up to the present, and because, by the standards of rural Wales, it is densely peopled, it is logical that the region is viewed as

28

le Pays de Galles. Threats to its custody of the native traditions are keenly felt and readily become political issues. While over most of the region more than 70 to 80 per cent of the population is able to and usually does, speak Welsh, the towns are frequently more anglicised than their hinterlands, and this is particularly so where they have become centres for the holiday industry or have attracted a retirement population. The towns around the estuaries of the rivers Dyfi and Mawddach have been especially favoured by English visitors and this has resulted in a number of adjacent administrative districts in which Welsh speakers are either in, or are rapidly approaching, a minority. Little further decline in the Welsh language is needed for this area to amalgamate with the Severn valley wedge and so not only to divide this region into two, but also to isolate Welsh-speakers in Wales as a whole into two distinct groups, those of the north and those of south-west Wales.

Where access to the English lowlands has been easier, English influence is of long standing, as in the north and south Wales coastal plains. Throughout historic time the coastal plains have provided the most direct corridors to the west by means of which the country could be both conquered and colonised. In addition, they are among the naturally most-favoured regions. The coastal plateaux and open river valleys, particularly in south Wales, are easily traversed and readily cultivated; the climate is mild and most suited to arable working, soils are good and in Gower, south-east Gwent and in the Vale of Clwyd among the best in the British Isles. In north Wales, of course, the coastal plain peters out at Conwy, beyond which the mountains of Snowdonia reach the sea. Incursions began with the Anglo-Norman settlement of the late eleventh and early twelfth centuries, but they have continued intermittently, though in different forms, in subsequent periods. There are two main consequences. The first is that the coastal lowlands provide a contrast with upland and heartland Wales in the amount of Welsh spoken. Normally below 20 per cent of the population speak the language and often less; in eastern parts the figure may be as low as 1 or 2 per cent. Where the coastal lowlands abut dominantly Welsh-speaking areas, the divide is usually quite sharp, and nowhere more so than between the northern coastal plain and Mynydd Hiraethog, and between south Pembrokeshire and Mynydd Preseli, where the classic regional division, the *Landsker,* now as in the past, marks the boundary. The second consequence provides equally pronounced contrasts.

Incoming, non-Celtic peoples brought with them their own cultural and social systems which have imposed upon the land a quite distinctive man-made landscape. While in upland and heartland Wales the rural scene is dominated by scattered farmsteads serving small farming units and set within the irregular hedgerows of a small-field system, the coastal plains, particularly where they were occupied by the Anglo-Normans, are more reminiscent of the English Midlands. Compact villages, not uncommonly containing farms, and often with a castle, church, village green and sometimes even traces of open-field agriculture, serve a system of farms, larger in scale and more orderly in their distribution than anything the individualistic, land-owning Welsh system could have produced. Even the village names — St Bride's Major, Michaelston-le-Pit, Peterston-super-Ely — occasionally betray their antecedents.

In much the same way, influence from lowland England penetrated the eastward-flowing valleys of the March. The rivers Dee and Vyrnwy, but especially the Severn, Wye and Usk systems, offered means of penetrating the upland core. The progress of anglicisation may have been slower than on the northern and southern coasts, but progress there was as is testified by the virtual absence of Welsh-speakers in all but the westernmost parts of Powys today. Plainly the uplands blunted these thrusts and this contributed to the survival of the heartland as a distinctive region.

The most intrusive factor of all, however, into the traditional rural life of Wales was the large-scale mining and manufacturing which heralded the Industrial Revolution. Rural and scattered industries had existed in many parts for many centuries, but the concentration of the metal industries upon the coalfields of both north and south Wales, from whence they derived both power and raw material, created what now may be identified as industrial Wales. The northern and southern regions share in common their geological base, their rapid industrialisation in the late eighteenth and nineteenth centuries, their attractiveness for rural population as mining and industry developed, their close industrial communities and their unemployment and related problems of the twentieth century. They are dissimilar in their landscape and their economic orientation. The north Wales coalfield is largely lowland and has always had close links with Merseyside and Lancashire. The south Wales coalfield is largely upland and has always had close links with Bristol and south-east England. Perhaps because of its upland nature, but certainly as a result of the inflow of Welsh-speaking population from mid and west Wales in the early period of industrial development and of its tightly knit working-class society, the south Wales coalfield has resisted anglicisation for longer than the adjacent lowland. Up to 1951 at least 20 per cent of the population of much of the central (Mid Glamorgan) part of the coalfield were able to speak Welsh, and in the western section of the coalfield, between Llanelli and Ammanford, the figure exceeded 80 per cent. But only thirty years later the position of the language had deteriorated substantially. In the centre of the coalfield, the Welsh-speaking population barely exceeded 10 per cent of the total and even in the west considerable anglicisation had occurred. Even so, such is the density of population in the coalfield and industrial regions — often over 1200 persons per square mile (460 persons per square kilo-metre) — that the number of Welsh speakers in absolute if not rela-tive terms is the equivalent of that in the heartland, though plainly they are sufficiently diluted culturally to be unable to sustain with any widespread success the Welsh-language institutions so common on the west coast. But whatever the composition and character of its population, and whatever its economic future, industrial Wales, with its urban manufacturing landscape, provides perhaps the starkest of all contrasts with the surrounding rural regions. It illustrates, as well as any other region, the strong influence of land and place upon the development of society and economy that this chapter has aimed to stress.

CHAPTER 2

People and Language

That the inhabitants of Wales have problems of identity should surprise no one. Their very name, the *Welsh,* was one bestowed upon them by the Anglo-Saxons and means, simply, *foreigner.* To themselves in their native tongue they are *Cymry* or *fellow country-men.* Their forbears were Iron Age peoples, Celtic in origin, at least some of whom spoke a language ancestral to modern Welsh (or *Cymraeg*). Though heavily latinised and stemming deep in its history from the Indo-European and Old European languages, modern Welsh now bears little resemblance to the Germanic group of languages which yielded English and many other European tongues. While the language originally gave Wales its character and unity, subsequent influences and waves of immigrants, as seen in Chapter 1, have pushed back the linguistic frontier such that the Welsh heartland is now a beleaguered cultural core around Cardigan Bay and less than one in five of the inhabitants of the country speaks the language. The identity crisis that results may help to explain why national consciousness at the moment is apparently most strongly focused when fifteen men in red shirts play with an oval football in one of Wales's most anglicised towns, its capital, Cardiff.

The coming of the Celts

There is abundant evidence in Wales of its peopling from the Ice Age onwards. Palaeolithic man survived in wretchedly cold conditions, hunting ox, reindeer and other wild animals with primitive stone weapons from his limestone cave dwelling, or later, as the climate grew warmer, from an elemental man-made shelter. The indications are that in Wales, Palaeolithic folk were sparsely distributed and cul-turally impoverished, certainly when compared with contemporary groups in France or Spain, where cave art of very high quality flourished. As the climate improved and forests and swamp spread over much of the lowlands, with trees stretching up the hillsides to nearly 2000ft (600m), Mesolithic hunters and gatherers moved into Wales bringing with them a technology well in advance of that of the Palaeolithic people. Mesolithic folk were able to fashion simple tools from stone, bone and particularly flint, which was used to form microliths, sharp cutting flakes that were hafted in wood and bone. With modest tools, Mesolithic man found the forest difficult to clear and tended to confine his activities to the coasts and to the exposed regions above the treeline. In Wales, if we are to judge by his remains, he mainly chose the former. The commitment to flint, which is not found in any geological stratum in the country, restricted Mesolithic man to coastal areas, where beach flints derived from Irish Sea glaciation provided the raw material.

Fresh waves of settlers brought new and improved technologies. Cultivation and the domestication of farm animals had evolved in the Middle East around 9000 BC. Techniques diffused by a number of routes, but most influential in Wales were those which passed through the Mediterranean basin, along the coasts of Atlantic Europe, and entered the country, like the Mesolithic cultures, by means of the western seas. They may have taken 6,000 years or so to arrive, but gradually, improved stone axes, massive stone-built tombs, and indications that animals were being herded, all herald the steady onset of the Neolithic Age. It is not possible to say at what date farming of the land first took place in Wales, but it cannot have been long before the original metal workers, smiths and traders known as Beaker folk, after the distinctive pots they made, brought their bronze tools and weapons into Wales. Later during the Bronze Age, after about 1000 BC, improvements in bronze working greatly increased the number and variety of metal tools. Bronze became plentiful and many distribution points have been identified in Wales. The use of timber for smelting may, indeed, have initiated the process of deforestation, and it is clear that a considerable increase in population took place. Today, the vigour and technical development achieved by Bronze Age peoples is marked by the many standing stones, stone circles and burial chambers (cromlechau) scattered throughout Wales. Of course, throughout these changes, earlier cultures survived and were subsequently modified by the incoming technologies.

Up to the Bronze Age, which stretched roughly from 1800 BC to 500 BC, Wales had been a receiver of different cultural influences, at

33

times being subservient even to Ireland. It had not yet begun to evolve a distinctive culture of its own; nor is it possible to discern at this stage the origins of what was to become the Welsh people and society. But with the coming of the Iron Age that was to change. During the Late Bronze Age in Britain, the Celts and their fore-runners spread across Europe from their homeland in the central part of the Continent along the Rhine and further east into western Europe. They had acquired the techniques of iron working and carried with them improved methods of farming, including a two-ox plough with iron ploughshare which could cope with land hitherto uncultivatable. They reached lowland England by 500 BC and began to settle and establish a culture known in Britain as Iron Age A. The main wave of Celtic immigrants, identified as Iron Age B, followed in about 300 BC. They entered Britain from Gaul, mainly into the western parts of the country using the sea routes and estuaries. In some areas they created lowland agricultural villages, but in Wales they are best known for the many hillforts which they built, particu-larly along the west and south-west coasts and in the borderland, on the summits of the lower hills, mainly at or below 600ft (180m) in height. A final wave of Celtic people (Iron Age C) came into south-east England after 100 BC, retreating before the advancing Roman legions which were in the process of conquering and pacifying Gaul.

It is clear that it is to the Iron Age B peoples that we must look for the roots of Welsh life. While their lowland cousins may have had a substantial concern with the cultivation of crops, including cereals, it is likely that in Wales a more pastoral economy developed, based upon the herding of cattle, sheep and pigs, with limited cultivation only on favoured hillslopes or perhaps more widely where better-drained and sheltered land occurred. Certainly wheat, barley and flax were grown in small irregular fields as a supplement to the herd-ing activities and there is abundant evidence of other domesticated animals, such as horses, pigs, dogs and chickens. It is not certain whether the Celts lived in their hillforts, or whether only a few took residence within the defensive banks while the remainder spread more widely to tend their crops and stock, gathering for protection in the fort, with their animals and belongings, only during what must have been the frequent bouts of strife. Their material culture was relatively advanced. Smiths forged iron and bronze implements — tools, ornaments, swords, shields — and the ornaments, weapons and pottery were often decorated with abstract designs of

34

high artistic quality. It would be wrong to think that the colonisa-
tion of Wales by the Celts was as straightforward as this summary
account may make it appear. Some Celtic elements — pottery and
even the technique of hillfort building — may have preceded the
arrival of the Celts in Wales and may date to the Late Bronze Age.
It must also remain an open question whether a high proportion of
the Welsh population on the eve of the Roman conquest in the first
century AD was Celtic, or whether there were substantial numbers of
pre-Iron Age peoples, whom the Celts had subjugated and upon
whom they had imposed their culture and language.

Again, it is tempting to believe that the first Celts brought with
them the language that is ancestral to modern Welsh. It may have
been so, but the story is not without its intricacies. In their homeland during the first millennium BC, the Celts had probably originally employed a more or less universal language that is now known
as Common Celtic. Before they arrived in Britain that language had
divided into two main but related groups. Goidelic or q Celtic
(the q derives from the hard initial sounds that some words have)
and Gallo-Brittonic or p Celtic (because the softer p replaces the
q in equivalent words). When the Iron Age people reached the
British Isles we know from classical writers that they spoke Celtic
languages. Broadly speaking, Goidelic occupied the western outer
arc in Scotland, the Isle of Man and Ireland, while Brittonic formed
an inner arc in Wales, England and southern Scotland, but there
must have been considerable intermixture. Goidelic may have been
spoken in limited parts of Wales from the earliest Iron Age, but it
was greatly strengthened, or reintroduced, by considerable Irish
settlement in both north-west and south-west Wales in the
immediate post-Roman period. That the language of Wales today
derives from Brittonic is partly, at least, a result of the arrival from
southern Scotland, where the two forms of Celtic were also mixed,
of a group of p Celts, known as the Sons of Cunedda. It is not certain
whether their move was made voluntarily or under pressure, but
they very quickly ousted the Irish q Celts from north Wales, and
eventually, over several centuries, pushed out the Goidelic speakers
of the south-west, thus consolidating the hold of the Brittonic
language over Wales. In the sixth and seventh centuries the Celtic
speakers of Wales were cut off, certainly by land, from their fellows
in Cornwall, northern England and Scotland by Anglo-Saxon pressure westward. Brittonic speakers driven from Cornwall and the

35

west of England by Anglo-Saxons crossed the Channel and settled in north-west Gaul forming the nucleus of the Breton nation. From that time Welsh, Cornish, Breton, Irish Gaelic, Scots Gaelic and Manx began to emerge as separate languages. Written Old Welsh first appeared in the late eighth century; it evolved into Middle Welsh in the second half of the twelfth century, and a recognisably Modern Welsh emerged in the fifteenth century.

The Roman conquest

Compelled to secure the north-west frontier of the Empire and stimulated by the likely prestige to be won, Emperor Claudius invaded Britain in AD 43. While strongly resisted in some areas, within five years the Roman legions had subdued most of southern England, which was ultimately to contain the major civil settlements, both urban and rural. By shortly after AD 70 the Romans began construction of the fortresses which were to provide the permanent bases for the legions and to form the pivots from which the military zones in Wales, Scotland and in the north of England were to be controlled. The building of both Deva (Chester) and Isca Silurum (Caerleon) was begun in AD 74 and thereafter they served as the major garrison towns of Wales. Within the military zone, small forts, by no means always consistently occupied through the Roman period, were linked by roads, some of which were carefully surveyed and engineered while others were of lower standard. Many of the fort sites in Wales now carry the element *caer* (castle or fort) in their present placenames, as in Caerhun, Caersŵs or Pen-y-gaer, though of course not all castles or forts in Wales, and hence not all placenames including *caer,* are of Roman origin.

Though the conquest of Wales presented difficulties to the Romans, it was relatively swift and was accomplished by AD 78. Life for the Celtic peoples, however, must have carried on much as before the Romans came. There is evidence that some tribes, for example the Silures in south-east Wales, were moved out of their hillforts into newly constructed towns of the Roman pattern, but many of the smaller groups were left to pursue their traditional way of life. But more than three centuries of occupation cannot be without influence. Not only did the legionaries and their followers add a new element to the population of the country, but they also brought a limited amount of improved agricultural practice, especially in the Vale of Glamorgan where several villas were established, they introduced greatly advanced mining technology in their search for minerals, particularly for gold at Dolau Cothi, for iron in the Forest of Dean in the southern border country and widely elsewhere for copper and lead, and they strongly influenced Celtic vocabulary by ensuring that large numbers of Latin words entered everyday speech. When pressures in other parts of Europe forced the withdrawal of the legions from Wales late in the fourth century, hillforts may have remained occupied or have been reoccupied, and life may have reverted to the pattern established before the Roman conquest. But an indelible mark had been made upon the people and the landscape.

Post-Roman influences

The advancing barbarian tribes of Germanic peoples which had pressed so hard on the northern frontier of the Roman Empire and eventually, with other groups, led to its contraction, soon entered Britain. The Anglo-Saxon invaders settled first in the east, but after the fifth century pushed westwards and northwards and isolated the Celts of Wales from the other Celtic peoples. Wales as we know it first emerges in this period as a coherent, territorial unit. The Welsh were hemmed in and under pressure. In the eighth century King Offa of Mercia caused an earthen bank to be constructed to mark the frontier between the Celtic Welsh and the Germanic Mercians, what has been termed 'the boundary line of Cymru'. In Offa's Dyke, Wales had acquired an eastern frontier, both physical and political, stretching from the estuary of the Dee to that of the Severn, one not greatly different from the present national boundary.

The pagan Anglo-Saxons were largely converted to Christianity by missions from Rome in the seventh and eighth centuries. In Wales, Christianity developed earlier and independently of this movement. It has been argued that as early as the fifth century three facets are identifiable. First, the remnants of Romano-British Christianity, surviving only in the non-pagan lands not conquered by the Anglo-Saxons, contributed an episcopal tradition stemming from imperial days. Secondly, the Church of Gaul had absorbed ideas from the Middle East that emphasised the eremitical tradition, the importance of withdrawing from the world and living the life of a recluse. It is thought that these notions were brought to Wales

37

along the western sea routes by Gaulish refugees who fled from their native country in the immediate post-Roman period in advance of the barbarian invasions. Finally, Ireland had become converted by Britons, such as St Patrick and others, and in the early fifth century the island emerged as a vigorous source of religious energy which was re-exported to Wales. These separate traditions fused in the evangelical, yet ascetic wandering missionaries known as the Celtic saints.

Alone, or with a band of followers, the Celtic saints travelled through their part of Wales, preaching and converting to the faith. Where they achieved particular success, they would establish a church, perhaps a temporary building only at first, and surround it with an earthen embankment, thus defining a religious enclosure or *llan*, a word which later transferred its meaning to the church build-ing. Often the dedication of the church commemorated its founder or the founder's patron. By using original dedications, it is possible to trace the sphere of influence or cult-area of each saint. While most churches would have been established originally in isolated loca-tions, many have since attracted settlement and have contributed one of the most common placename types in Wales, namely *Llan* followed by a saint's name, as in Llanddewi (*Llan* plus *Dewi* [David]; there are at least 14 such placenames concentrated in south and west Wales), Llanbadarn (*Llan* plus *Padarn;* there are at least 7 such placenames concentrated in mid Wales) and Llanilltud (*Llan* plus *Illtud;* there are at least 5 such placenames concentrated in south-east Wales).

Most influences reached Wales from the south and east, but an exception is provided by the Norwegian Vikings, who by the eighth century had settled in the Orkney and Shetland Islands. During the course of the following century, drawn southwards largely by the growing wealth of the Irish monasteries, raiding parties moved by way of the Isle of Man and the Irish Sea to influence the Welsh coast. There is little archaeological evidence, except for a ship burial at the mouth of the River Usk, but placenames indicate that the north and south Wales coastlands proved attractive, though settlement may have been lighter than was once supposed. The largest Welsh settle-ment today to carry a Norse name is Swansea (*Sveinn,* an Old Norse personal name plus, perhaps, *ey,* Old Norse for an island), and it is thought to have been a Viking trading post.

The Anglo-Norman conquest

The vicissitudes of political control in medieval Wales, its squab-
bling princes, its occasional and brief periods of unification under
such as Hywel Dda (Hywel the Good) in the early tenth century,
Gruffydd ap Llywelyn in the mid eleventh century or Llywelyn II
in the late thirteenth century, together with the story of the
emergence of administrative units, territories and counties, must be
considered at greater length later (see Chapter 3). It is sufficient here
to note that through the period of Anglo-Saxon pressure Wales, as
a geographical entity, remained intact, it developed its own system
of land holding and law and it possessed a flourishing native cultural
life in which music and poetry excelled. Above all, it had its own
language which in the long term provided a more unifying force than
anything the princes could muster.

The last major, successful invasion of the British Isles, came in the
late September of 1066, when William of Normandy, with 5000
Norman knights and a few thousand others, landed in southern
England. From their base at Pevensey they moved to Hastings
where in mid October they met and defeated Harold's forces within
a few hours before proceeding to bring south-east England swiftly
under control. It was William's intention to establish a strong centralised government, and in order to secure the flanks of his new
kingdom he allotted critical border territories to powerful followers,
earldoms in which the King's representative was given considerable
power of action. The three main areas perceived to be at risk were
the Channel coast, the north of England and the Welsh Marches.

In preceding centuries the Welsh had not been content to remain
quietly on their own side of Offa's Dyke. The temptation of easy
plunder in the rich English lowlands had proved too strong and
raiding parties were common, sometimes with devastating effects.
Hereford and Gloucester suffered particularly, and not least in the
eight-year period, up to his defeat and death in 1063, when
Gruffydd ap Llywelyn dominated the whole of Wales. Ironically his
fall preceded the Norman conquest by three years and was followed
by a return to local rule by intermittently warring princes, whose
power often depended upon temporary alliances with others, on
their own but also on the English side of the Dyke. Wales was in no
condition to face the Norman challenge, though the invaders did not
necessarily realise the strength of their position. However, it does

39

help to account for the rapid progress made by the Normans in the early years of their conquest, certainly up to 1095, and why it needed the emergence of Welsh leaders of outstanding ability to check the Norman advance at a later stage.

Along the Welsh frontier the Normans had a clear plan. The castles and county towns of Chester, Shrewsbury, Hereford and Gloucester were to be the pivots of the invasion. The conquest was not to be engineered by an organised campaign with an army in the van, but by gradual encroachment by raiding parties acting on instruction from the Marcher lords. Typically, if a successful expedition expropriated land, and if it was felt to be capable of being held, a temporary castle would be built on a man-made earth mound and protected by a wooden palisade. An outer court at ground level might provide security for a small garrison, store and animals. Such a 'motte-and-bailey' castle thus became the centre of a new lordship and, if blessed with continued success, would be replaced by a more substantial stone structure, though not necessarily on precisely the same site.

The Norman agricultural system was quite alien to Wales. The Welsh had evolved a tribal organisation in which blood relationships were very important. Society was composed of bondsmen and free tribesmen, who existed side by side in a mixture of small nucleated and also scattered settlements. The freemen worked limited patches of arable land, usually in small irregular fields, which could be inherited by all male offspring, and depastured stock on the open upland moorland, often practising transhumance (see Chapter 4). The Normans, in contrast, operated a feudal organisation based upon the manor. It required open fields, tilled in an annual rotation, and was therefore more suited to areas where land was flat, soil was fertile and the climate mild and reasonably dry. These are the conditions, as we have seen in Chapter 1, which pertained in the Welsh lowland, the very areas which the Norman cavalry found easiest to traverse and subdue. To service the agricultural area, to assist in control and to provide centres of administration, the Normans built small fortified towns constructed on a grid-iron plan and known as *bastides*. They would eventually attract traders and craftsmen and form the nucleus around which an Anglo-Norman population could develop.

Penetration into Wales was thus very swift in the valley lowlands of the March and along the south Wales coastlands, led initially by

William fitz Osbern based at Hereford and Roger of Montgomery at Shrewsbury. The valleys of the Severn, Wye and Usk soon acquired a succession of motte-and-bailey castles which were quickly followed by stone fortresses. In south Wales, movement westward was also swift but progressed further. The Vale of Glamorgan was quickly engulfed and led the Normans on to Gower and south-west Dyfed. Eventually they moved up the west coast to Aberystwyth, though many of the west-coast settlements must have been supplied from the sea in troubled times. In south Wales some very substantial stone castles were constructed, such as those at Brecon and Cardiff (since rebuilt), testifying to the richness of the land and to the success of the occupation. In north Wales progress was far more difficult. The terrain was unhelpful to the Normans, but in turn assisted the Welsh of the ancient principalities of Gwynedd and Powys. The Normans thus held and colonised the lowlands of south and mid Wales, while north Wales and the uplands elsewhere remained substantially in Welsh hands. Where Norman lordships spread into the uplands, the low-lying areas around the castle and boroughs were often administered manorially as Englishries, while the Welshries on higher ground retained their native practices, though under Norman supervision. The distribution of manors in the fourteenth century (Fig 6) makes clear the areas in which the Norman system supplanted that of the Welsh.

At the junction of the two cultures there was plainly conflict, as we know from the many accounts of bloodshed during and after the period of conquest; but there were also most profound differences in people and landscape. Contrasting with the traditional Welsh ways were the Anglo-Norman or Normanised-Welsh population, enmeshed within a feudal system, cultivating open fields from compact villages or perhaps living in small towns — a completely foreign form of settlement — and practising a form of Christianity that owed much more to Canterbury and Rome than it did to the Celtic saints. The remnant patterns of some of the open fields survive and so do over fifty stone castles in various stages of disrepair, together with traces of many hundreds of motte-and-bailey sites. But most lasting has been the influence of the non-Welsh population introduced into eastern valleys and into the lowland of south Wales.

The incomplete conquest was plainly unsatisfactory from an Anglo-Norman standpoint. It left a core mountainous area in Welsh

41

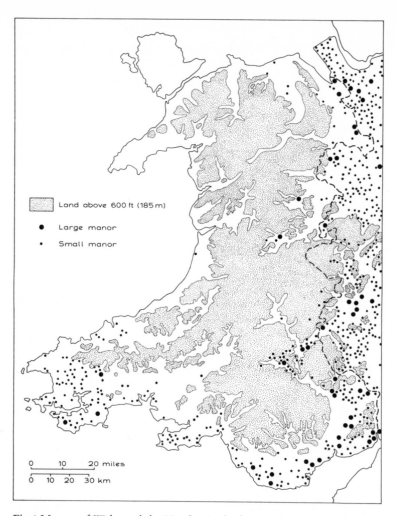

Fig 6 Manors of Wales and the Marches in the fourteenth century *(after Rees and Bowen)*

hands, a base from which by treaty, marriage or other alliance, principalities could associate, as they had done in previous centuries, to create far more effective resistance than when they acted independently. While Powys in the north-east and Deheubarth in the west had sometimes taken the lead, their geographical positions were weak, and it was the north-western kingdom of Gwynedd, from its Snowdonian fortress and with its secure agricultural base in

Anglesey, that had so often been at the heart of such associations, and was to be so again in the period 1100–1282, sometimes referred to as that of the 'Welsh resurgence'. It was a time in which military alliances were forged between the princes of Gwynedd and those of Powys and Deheubarth, but it was much more than that. It was also a period in which the arts and scholarship flourished, in which the Celtic church was given support, in which the Welsh laws were codified in both Welsh and Latin, and in which the folk legends were collected and preserved. At no time was the resurgence stronger than under the greatest and last princes of Gwynedd, the two Llywelyns.

Llywelyn the Great (Llywelyn I, 1194–1240) and his grandson Llywelyn the Last (Llywelyn II, 1246–82) were not only accomplished military commanders, they were also very shrewd men who had learned a great deal from their Anglo-Norman foes. Step by step, they both absorbed other Welsh territories (Fig 7) to unite substantial parts of the country and to form a feudal state policed by stone castles, as for example at Cricieth, Dolwyddelan and Deganwy in Gwynedd, Dinefwr in Deheubarth, Dolforwyn in Powys Wenwynwyn, and Dinas Brân in Powys Fadog. It will be noted that neither feudalism nor the use of stone in building was traditional in Wales. Further, as part of a deliberate policy, they arranged marriages with members of the royal family (Llywelyn I married Joan, natural daughter of King John), but particularly into the families of the powerful Marcher lords in order to strengthen their dynasties. They began to pose a considerable threat to the English crown. Llywelyn I had to contend with a relatively weak English king, Henry III, and in the early part of his reign, Llywelyn II achieved his greatest success when England was divided by the barons. In 1267 under the treaty of Montgomery, he came to control nearly all of Wales and was recognised by Henry as *Princeps Wallie* (Prince of Wales). But on the accession of Edward I he encountered the most powerful of the English medieval monarchs, who determined to subdue Wales and bring it firmly and finally under the English crown.

The Edwardian conquest was planned and decisive. After a short period of consolidation around the core stronghold of Gwynedd, Edward himself led the move into north-west Wales. Llywelyn II had been killed in 1282 in a chance encounter in mid Wales, and though his brother David put up stiff resistance in their homeland, the defence was quickly overcome by Edward's armies, while his

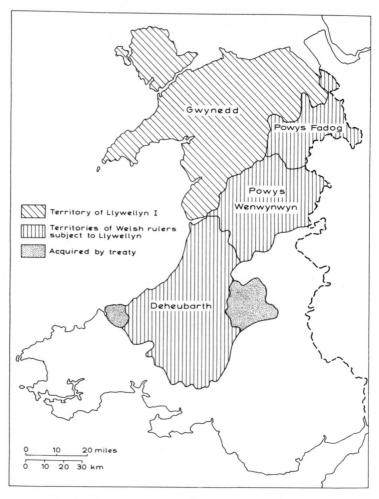

Fig 7 Independent Wales under Llywelyn I, 1234 *(after Rees and Bowen)*

control of the sea ensured that supplies from Anglesey were to be denied to any who contemplated continued resistance. To secure his conquest, Edward built a chain of castles at Rhuddlan, Conwy, Beaumaris, Caernarfon and Harlech, all on defensible waterside sites so that they could be supplied, if necessary, by sea. Other formerly Welsh castles, such as those of Cricieth and Dolwyddelan, were rebuilt or extended by him to control critical areas. Edward also established boroughs, usually enclosed within substantial walls and of the bastide type, in which English craftsmen, merchants and other settlers could be given protection. The military conquest of 1282 was confirmed in the Statute of Rhuddlan two years later. It led to the creation of an English principality, in which the eldest son of the English king was to be Prince of Wales, to the establishment within the principality of five new shires on the English model — Anglesey, Caernarfon, Merioneth, Cardigan and Carmarthen — and to the strengthening of the grip of Canterbury over the Church of Wales. With the exception of a number of scattered and unsuccessful plots against the English crown, and the romantic yet tragic Glyndŵr revolt of the early fifteenth century, it was the end of armed Welsh resistance, as the bards of the time were quick to note, but it was also the end of migration into Wales carried through by force of arms. Henceforth, the pressures on Welsh culture, society and language were to be largely social, political and economic.

The Welsh language: early development to 1890

The culture and society of any nation, open to outside influences, is very difficult to isolate and define. So-called traditional ways of life frequently undergo modification through time as alien features are absorbed and modified; and yet often there persists a sense of cultural distinctiveness peculiar to that people alone, recognised by themselves and by others. This is certainly true of Wales. Since it lost such political independence as it once had early in its history, the cultural and social identity of Wales and the Welsh has not unnaturally been closely associated with the survival of the Welsh language. It does not follow that those who do not speak the language lack national feeling or patriotism, as will quickly emerge, for even Welsh-speakers rarely use Welsh on all occasions. It does, however, suggest that shifts in allegiance to the language mark a cultural change which in turn has helped to create the sense of 'two nations', now at the heart of the crisis of national consciousness in modern Wales.

The Anglo-Saxon pressure of the sixth and seventh centuries, as has been noted above, cut off the Welsh from their fellow Celtic speakers in other western parts of the British Isles and encouraged the development of Welsh as a separate language. Welsh had already borrowed large numbers of words from Latin and was to continue to develop as a language by absorbing further vocabulary, principally from Anglo-Saxon, Norman French, and from both medieval and modern English. To give a very few examples: *pont* (bridge) and *ffenestr* (window) have clear Latin origins; *betws* (small chapel), like *pont* a frequent element in Welsh placenames, is derived from the Anglo-Saxon *bead-house; cnaf* (knave) is of medieval date; while an *ambiwlans,* frequently seen on Welsh streets, is a modern borrowing from English, first recorded in 1911, though, of course, English had derived the word from French and Latin. While the language evolved, the areas over which it was spoken remained surprisingly stable over many centuries. Both Offa's Dyke and the modern political boundary, when it was created by the Acts of Union in 1536 and 1543, had isolated some Welsh-speakers on the English side of the line, principally in Herefordshire and Shropshire. But communications were poor and communities largely self-contained, and there the Welsh-speakers remained until their numbers were gradually eroded by English influence in more recent times.

It has been said that in Wales proper, up until the middle of the sixteenth century, Welsh was used for all purposes save religion (in which Latin was employed), and since that time for religion and little else. The statement is a sweeping generalisation, but it encapsulates an important truth. The Acts of Union proscribed Welsh as an official state medium, whereas previously it had been widely used for local administration. It led to the gradual replacement of Welsh by English for most public purposes, other than religious, where the use of Welsh in the Protestant church was encouraged by the Tudors, and certainly assisted greatly in sustaining the language in this aspect of life. As late as the middle of the eighteenth century, Welsh was still the language used in most parish churches in Wales, except in the extreme east of the country and in the Vale of Glamorgan, Gower and south Pembrokeshire, all areas of early English influence. Though even here, in the Vales of Glamorgan and of Powys, for example, many churches were bilingual. There were also a few bilingual churches in the extreme north-west corner of Shropshire.

While Welsh survived strongly into the eighteenth century it was being used for fewer purposes. It was also ceasing to be a universal language among all groups in Welsh society. The upper classes, gentry and merchants adopted English more swiftly than others. There were very strong practical and economic motives for doing so. There thus emerged a fairly sharp distinction between this small anglicised group and the workers and peasants, who continued to speak their native tongue because they had no good reason to change. Over the next century economic pressures built up and bilingualism spread. In Wales, bilingualism is often regarded as a stage in the process of anglicisation; if this is true, then the Anglican church visitation returns of the mid nineteenth century tell a sorry tale. Everywhere the bilingual zone had encroached into what a century before had been dominantly Welsh-speaking areas: the south Wales coastal plain was bilingual or wholly English in speech, considerable westward penetration had occurred in mid Wales, and isolated patches of bilingualism had appeared in the resort towns of the west coast, but significantly also in an extended stretch of the upper Vale of Tywi. By the middle of the nineteenth century religious nonconformity had taken a firm grip in Wales, and it may be that a higher proportion of the more anglicised middle and upper class groups adhered to the Anglican church, thus introducing a slight bias in the returns. Even so, the language of church services provides the best information available before the first census attempt to establish linguistic statistics in 1891, and it plainly chronicles the beginning of the decline of the Welsh language.

It is sometimes suggested that it was the Industrial Revolution which initiated the decline of the Welsh language in the nineteenth century. Certainly the commercial importance of English cannot be denied, and it is clear that the coalfield population of both north and south Wales grew by in-migration. But it should be remembered that the encroachment of English speech had already begun in rural areas before the onset of major industrial development and that in the early years of industrialisation in the coalfields, much of the influx of population came from Welsh-speaking rural areas in mid and west Wales. In consequence, until well into the twentieth century, the coalfields of Wales contained a higher proportion of people able to speak Welsh than many of the surrounding rural districts. Of course, migrants also came to the new industrial regions from England and Ireland. This movement introduced bilingualism which in the past four or five decades has rapidly converted regions of Welsh-speaking population into areas where monoglot English-speakers dominate.

When in 1870 the Education Act laid down that English should be the medium of instruction in schools, and children were actually punished for speaking Welsh among themselves, the proportion of

47

the population able to speak Welsh declined still further. It was perceived by many that economic and social success could only be achieved by fluency in English, and for some the ability to speak Welsh became a sign of inferior social status. Neither educational prejudice nor social stigma persisted, however, and indeed today both the educational system and social status operate to a large degree in favour of Welsh, but at this important period bilingualism became widespread. English was spoken throughout the country in many spheres of life, and the scene was set for the Welsh language tragedy of the twentieth century.

The Welsh language: 1891–1971

At no time before the nineteenth century had the population of Wales been large. Estimates suggest (they can do no more for the period before the first population census was taken in 1801) that numbers reached a quarter of a million at about 1500, and had crept slowly up to half a million by about 1775. The first census revealed a population of nearly 590,000, distributed broadly throughout the country but lying most densely in the richer agricultural regions. Essentially the distribution may be visualised as a thinly peopled mountain core surrounded by a penumbra of more thickly populated, largely rural areas strung along the coasts and borderland. The industrialisation of the coalfields had already begun with the establishment of metal manufacturing plants, but as industrial growth gained pace, two important changes occurred. First, the population rose rapidly. By 1831 the population of Wales was close to one million and was to rise to two and a half million before the outbreak of World War I. Secondly, major shifts in population took place. Rural areas had always lost surplus population to the towns, but generally natural increase more than kept pace. In Wales, all counties continued to return increased population figures in the censuses up to 1851, but in the mid nineteenth century there was a major turning point. Thereafter many rural areas lost population to the coalfields and industrial regions in such numbers that total population actually fell. Rural depopulation was thus initiated and has remained a feature of almost all of rural Wales until quite recently. It is a process fuelled by rural deprivation and by the prospect of improved economic and social conditions in the urban–industrial regions of both Wales and England.

48

Upland Wales: unenclosed mountain land near Cwmystwyth, Dyfed

Raglan Castle, Gwent: one of the many guardians of the March, founded in Norman times but now dating mainly from the fifteenth century

The high street of a market town in the Welsh heartland: Lampeter, Dyfed

Claerwen Dam and reservoir in the Elan Valley: supplier of water to the West Midlands

At the date of the first census to record Welsh-speakers in 1891, the effects of those changes were becoming apparent. In the course of the nineteenth century the distribution of population had altered dramatically. By 1891 the near-empty heartland contained even fewer people, the higher density peripheral distribution in the richer rural areas was still in evidence though now a series of towns with both market and tourist functions had become much more important, partly at the expense of their rural surrounds, but completely outstanding were the massive populations of the two coalfields, where by the end of the century coal mining had come to dominate the metal industries. Early migrants to the coalfields had been largely supplied by nearby rural areas, but as time went on the demand for labour increased and the net was more widely cast. A study of the birthplaces of the residents of the Rhondda valley, using the census of 1891, shows clearly that while the single largest element in the migrant population derived from elsewhere within the county of Glamorgan, a substantial proportion came from the still largely Welsh-speaking areas of mid, south-west and western Wales. Significantly though, a sizeable contingent originated in Gloucestershire and Somerset.

That only 54 per cent of the population of Wales in 1891 was shown to be able to speak Welsh caused little concern. No one knew accurately what proportion had been able to speak the language in previous periods, and it was not generally regarded as an important issue. The new University of Wales, first established in Aberystwyth in the 1870s, had not initially even intended teaching Welsh, and when it did, certainly at first, it did so through the medium of English, rather as one might teach Latin or Greek. Not far short of a million Welshmen spoke Welsh (over half of them claiming to speak no English), while in England, America, Patagonia and elsewhere, unenumerated in any census, there were many thousands more. In the coalfields, where traditional Welsh ways of life had been disturbed and replaced by an equally close but industrial society, Welsh-speakers continued to be dominant. Over most of the southern coalfield more than 50 per cent of the population spoke Welsh and in the western anthracite region of the field the figure frequently exceeded 90 per cent. Even in the coal-mining valleys of Monmouthshire up to 40 per cent of people were Welsh-speakers. In the north Wales coalfield it was virtually the same. In many areas over 50 per cent were able to speak Welsh, and around

Hawarden, close to the border and within 10 miles (16km) of Merseyside, over 20 per cent spoke Welsh. Whereas the anglicisation of the coalfields was only just starting, other urban centres had long served to introduce an English-speaking population into dominantly Welsh areas. The seaside towns are obvious examples, but market towns, with their emphasis on commercial activity, now

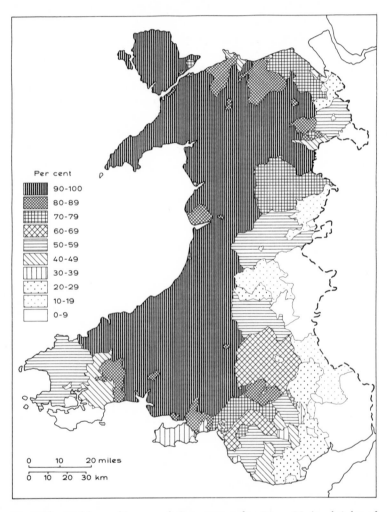

Per cent

▓	90-100
▓	80-89
▓	70-79
▓	60-69
▓	50-59
▓	40-49
▓	30-39
▓	20-29
▓	10-19
▢	0-9

Fig 8 The Welsh-speaking population, 1901 *(after Pryce,* National Atlas of Wales *3.1d)*

played an increasingly important role.

So it was that by the beginning of this century, the English bridgeheads had been established (Fig 8) and the swift decline of the Welsh language began. At first, as population continued to grow, the *absolute* numbers of Welsh-speakers rose and reached one million, but their position *relative* to total numbers was always

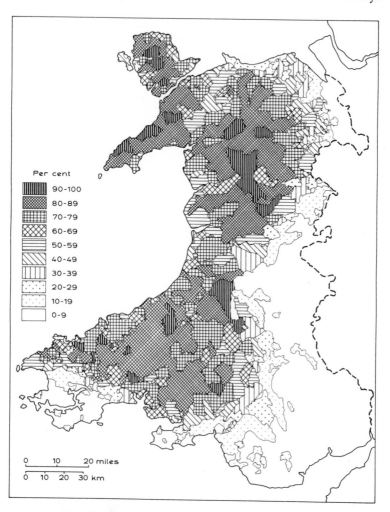

Per cent

	90-100
	80-89
	70-79
	60-69
	50-59
	40-49
	30-39
	20-29
	10-19
	0-9

0   10   20 miles

0   10   20   30 km

Fig 9 The Welsh-speaking population, 1971 *(after Carter)*

deteriorating and absolute numbers were soon to follow. The census showed that in 1901 50 per cent of the population of Wales were able to speak the language, 44 per cent in 1911, 37 per cent in 1931, 29 per cent in 1951, and in 1971 it revealed that there were 540,000 Welsh-speakers (20 per cent of the total population). The number of monoglot Welsh-speakers declined from 15 per cent of the total population in 1901 to 1 per cent in 1971. Fig 9 shows the distribution of Welsh-speakers in 1971, and should be compared with Fig 8 to gauge the scale of change during the course of the present century.

The origins of the linguistic anglicisation of Wales are plain, but an intriguing question remains: after a period of very slow, almost imperceptible decline up to 1850 followed by one of swifter retreat in the nineteenth century, why did the Welsh language suffer such a setback in this century? How could it be that over only seventy years and at a time of largely increasing population that the numbers of Welsh-speakers fell from a million to half that number, and that their relative strength fell from a half to one-fifth of the total population? The explanation is not straightforward; no single factor was respon-sible, but there were several which all tended in the same direction. First, society became far less local in character. The railways had already allowed easier movement to other parts of the British Isles and abroad, but in the 1920s and 1930s motor transport by road greatly increased mobility. English became not only commercially more important but rapidly acquired an enhanced social function. This was greatly assisted by the enormous expansion in the avail-ability of the mass media to people generally. With increased literacy in English, newspaper readership expanded and as the century pro-ceeded, the radio, the cinema and eventually the television intro-duced English speech into local communities and, even more signifi-cantly, into the home. The economic depression between the wars also had its impact on the position of the Welsh language. Depressed markets and slackening international trade ensured that rural depopulation continued, but they also introduced new features into Welsh life. The coalfields and industrial regions which had become the source of much of Welsh prosperity in the nineteenth and early twentieth centuries now, in common with the older coalfield regions elsewhere in the British Isles and indeed in Europe, experienced sharp economic decline. No longer could the north and south Wales coalfields attract rural population, who therefore in increasing numbers moved instead to the anglicised market towns or to

England. In addition, quite new migration streams were initiated from the coalfield to destinations which were typically in the English Midlands or in the London region, where the newer consumer goods industries flourished and labour was short, or in the already anglicised coastal areas of Wales where towns were still expanding and where the most prosperous elements of the metal industries were by then located. The movements not only anglicised those who migrated, but also created a 'backwash effect' as the non-migrant residual population came to terms with the English-speaking sections of their families. Finally, an important element in the decline of the Welsh language stems from the scenic quality of the Welsh landscape: fine mountainous districts lying conveniently inland from a coastline with a pleasant combination of sandy beaches and cliffs or rocky headlands. In Welsh-speaking areas the tourist industry introduced monoglot English, the areas became bilingual and then frequently dominantly English in speech. In the coastal towns, already partially anglicised, the process took place quite rapidly — from Prestatyn in the north to Barry in the south — and though slower to develop in rural areas, it happened here also, as in Snowdonia and along the Cardigan Bay coast. In more recent years, the anglicisation of these tourist areas has been assisted by their ability to draw second-home owners and a retirement population. Rural depopulation left a somewhat generous housing stock, and old cottages ripe for renovation sold cheaply at first, but property has now become more expensive with increasing demand. Numbers of newcomers are such that recent censuses have revealed that overall depopulation has been checked, and many districts, for the first time in a century, have an increasing population. Of course, these figures disguise the differences in both population and language trends between the more popular anglicised coastlines and uplands, and their Welsh-speaking hinterlands.

The Welsh language today

The rapidity with which the Welsh language declined in this century converted the comfortable majority of Welsh who spoke their native tongue in 1891 into a small minority within less than a hundred years. It also converted the passive acceptance of the decline, among some at least, into active, sometimes vociferous and politically orientated channels. Youth, language and housing societies arose, each having as part of its rationale the need to sustain the Welsh language, seen as the principal repository of culture, tradition and nationhood. In addition, official support has been given by both local and central government. Welsh-language medium schools now exist in most parts of the country; Welsh is widely taught to English-speakers; radio, television and other means of communication employ Welsh as widely as is thought to be acceptable in a country where four-fifths of the population are monoglot English; and the Welsh language has been given official status and safeguarded by Act of Parliament. Doubtless these measures together must have retarded the decline in the use of Welsh — there is no sure way of knowing — but they certainly have not eliminated the decline. In the recently published census of 1981 only a little over half a million people are shown as able to speak Welsh, 19 per cent of the population.

Inevitably there is another side to the coin. Passivity among the majority group, the monoglot English-speakers, most of whom also firmly regard themselves as Welsh (in the same way as English-speaking Scots or Irish feel attachment to Scotland and Ireland), has given way not so much to militant advocacy, but to a certain sense of resentment. It is not universally felt or expressed, any more than pressure to extend the use of the Welsh language is universally supported by Welsh-speakers, but it is distinctly detectable. There is an irritation that Welsh-language speakers receive too much attention, that they are allocated too many of the limited resources available, that they divert attention away from more pressing economic and social issues, that they have too much television time at peak viewing periods, that they may be regarded as better qualified for employment in prestigious posts because they are bilingual and that they practise a linguistic snobbery (quite the reverse of the one perceived only a hundred years before). It is significant that in both popular and academic circles, Wales can be thought of as being composed of two quite distinct territories: Welsh Wales (*Bro Gymraeg* or *Cymru Gymraeg*) and Anglo-Wales (*Cymru ddi-Gymraeg*).

Welsh Wales, the *Bro Gymraeg* or alternatively the Welsh heartland, as it was described in Chapter 1, is the area where the Welsh language is still strongly entrenched. In general, 80–90 per cent of the population speak the language, but Welsh speech in the area as a whole is becoming fragmented by the towns, both coastal and

56

inland, by the holiday areas and by the wedge of English-speakers across mid Wales. The latter has divided the three main centres of Welsh speech in the north — Anglesey, the Llŷn peninsula, and inland Meirionydd and parts of adjacent districts — from that in northern Dyfed to the south of the wedge. It has been estimated that Welsh Wales contains 57 per cent of all Welsh-speakers, the remainder being widely spread among the monoglot English-speakers of the often more densely peopled sections of Anglo-Wales. The former county of Glamorgan, in percentage terms now heavily anglicised, contains a quarter of all Welsh speakers. Of the Welsh-speakers in the four core regions identified above, well above half are in the northern Dyfed area, which must therefore be regarded as the single most important Welsh-speaking region. Here, Welsh-speakers divide more or less evenly between the rural dwellers of Carmarthen and Cardigan districts, and the primarily industrial population of the western part of the coalfield.

While in the anglicised buffers between the four Welsh-speaking regions numbers of Welsh-speakers fall to about 50 per cent of the total local population, the dividing line between Welsh Wales and Anglo-Wales is very sharp indeed. Within a very short distance the proportion able to speak Welsh falls from around 80 per cent to below 20 per cent or even below 10 per cent. The narrow transition zone has an interesting and important characteristic, revealed for the first time in 1971. In that year the census recorded not only those able to speak the language, but also those able to read and write it. It emerged that roughly a quarter of those who could speak Welsh were unable to write it, and that these were clustered most strongly in the transition zone. Lack of literacy may have a number of causes, but the consistent regional distribution firmly suggests that in Wales it is principally a feature of language decline. Further inroads into Welsh Wales are therefore to be expected. With such sharp differences in attitudes and numbers able to speak Welsh, it is plain why consideration of the language has become central to so many of the cultural and social questions posed in Wales today.

CHAPTER 3

Wales and England

The last chapter dealt largely with the peopling of Wales and with the cultural and social consequences of the successive waves of invaders and other influences from outside the country. One aspect, mentioned early in passing, now needs further elaboration. It concerns what might be thought of as the evolving political geography of Wales: the changing institutional framework within which culture, society and economy develop.

In Welsh life there has often been a divorce between territorial consciousness and the political–administrative structure. At the national level, it has been stressed by one writer that while Wales, of all the Celtic units that form part of the United Kingdom, is the one which possesses in greatest measure the attributes of nationhood, it is also the one which had progressed least on the road to statehood. Belfast and Stormont, Edinburgh and Holyrood had until quite recently no Welsh equivalents. Cardiff was not formally declared capital of Wales until December 1955. Indeed, it is arguable that there was no real need for a capital before that time since there was no administrative function for it to perform; the first post of Minister for Welsh Affairs was not created until 1951, over sixty years after the equivalent post in Scotland, and then it was a part-time appointment. It took thirteen more years for the first Secretary of State for Wales to be named and for the Welsh Office to be founded. The reason for the slow development of the political–administrative framework must be sought deep in history.

Offa's boundary line

After the fifth century, the Welsh princes came under increasing pressure from the incoming Germanic peoples. However, while the Celts of Wales were separated from their Celtic fellows of the north-west and south-west of Britain, few inroads were made by the new-

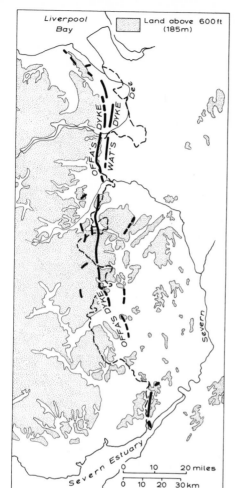

Fig 10 Dykes of the Welsh borderland

comers into the Welsh peninsula itself. In the mid-eighth century, King Offa the Great of Mercia constructed an earthen frontier dyke to mark the border between the territories of the Mercians and those of the Welsh. For the first time in history, Wales had a defined eastern boundary line (Fig 10).

It was once supposed that Offa's Dyke was intended as a military, defensive work, created to hold back the raiding Welsh. It was an easy-enough mistake to make: the earthwork is still very impressive in some sections today and must have been formidable when built well over twelve centuries ago. Now it is thought to have been a frontier based upon compromise, and therefore to delineate an agreed boundary line. It was thus not only a physically defined border, but also a territorial, political and cultural divide.

The precise alignment of the Dyke is of interest. Broadly speaking, it follows the eastern margin of the Welsh massif, roughly the line along which one would have expected the Mercian advance to have ground to a halt. But in the south the Dyke crosses the Hereford basin and reaches the Severn estuary by following the course of the River Wye. The Dyke, of course, did not long remain as a political and cultural divide. With the decline of Mercian power the Welsh moved eastwards again, and there is no difficulty in explaining why at later stages in history considerable numbers of Welsh-speakers were (and even today a few still are) located to the east of Offa's boundary line. It has been observed that in its course from Prestatyn in the north to Chepstow in the south, the Dyke over long stretches is followed by the present-day political boundary. In broad terms this is true, though the two boundaries are rarely coincident. They diverge most in north Wales, where Offa's Dyke and its more easterly predecessor, Wat's Dyke, run to the west of the present boundary, and in the south, where the Dyke cuts through the western part of Herefordshire and therefore lies to the east of today's line. In its central sections, the Dyke and present border nowhere diverge to any great extent. Of course, the two boundaries have no direct connection, one with the other; they are alike in alignment because they result from geographical and historical processes which are themselves very similar.

Behind Offa's Dyke, Welsh native society had developed a distinctive territorial and administrative character. A number of major tribal areas or *gwledydd* constituted unstable political regions under nominal dynastic rule: Gwynedd in the north-west, Powys in mid and north-east Wales, Deheubarth in the south-west and Morgannwg and Gwent in the south-east. The *gwlad* were sometimes subdivided, for example, Powys into Powys Fadog and Powys Wenwynwyn, sometimes united. Within each *gwlad* were the *cantrefi* (or hundreds), subdivided into two or often more *cymydau* (commotes). It was the commote which, by the time of the codifying of Hywel Dda's laws in the tenth century, had emerged as the chief unit of administration, whatever had been the custom previously.

Within the commote, law and order was maintained by a local lord who owed allegiance, though sometimes this was no more than tenuous, to his prince. His court was located in some central place and typically near this spot would be the township in which dwelt the bondsmen, who gave service to the lord, tilling his land and tending his cattle. Their settlement was known as the *maerdref*. The free tribesmen, on the other hand, were organised in family groups and widely scattered through the commote, where they owned and worked their own land. Each family group occupied a *gwely* (literally a *bed*) which was composed of a number of homesteads or *tyddynod*. On the death of a freeman, the land and property were divided equally between all his sons, under the system of inheritance that was known to the Anglo-Norman lawyers as *gavelkind*. It led, of course, to the continuous subdivision of land and to smaller and smaller holdings, each with its own *tyddyn*, and produced the dense, but dispersed, rural settlement pattern so characteristic of Wales to this day.

While there must have been many variations to this pattern of administration within a country that had rarely known political unity, the system was quite different from that introduced following the Anglo-Norman conquest.

Edwardian administration

At the time of the Norman invasion Wales was far from united. Norman penetration of Welsh territory across the line of Offa's Dyke was achieved not by an organised campaign led by an army, but by the gradual encroachment of raiding parties based upon the firm control of the major borderland towns. At first, as they subdued the lowlands of south and mid Wales by planting temporary wooden, then more permanent stone, castles, there may have been little change in administration. The Norman lord supplanted his vanquished Welsh equivalent and assumed the privileges which thus accrued. It has been noted by some writers that, for example, the boundaries of many of the Welsh commotes became, with little change, those of the Norman manors which succeeded them, and because of this, some commote boundaries, particularly where they used natural barriers such as rivers, have persisted to the present day. But as time went by, Anglo-Norman feudalism was established in all its forms, and thus began a process of change which, eventually, brought important administrative economic and social changes to Welsh life.

By the thirteenth century, Norman law and customs were widespread in the lowlands of south and mid Wales, under the influence of the Marcher lords. There had been marked changes also in agricultural practice and in the nature of urban settlements. In the north and west, Welsh administration continued, though under Llywelyn I and his grandson, Llywelyn II, these areas became the core of what was increasingly, as it expanded, also a strong feudal state. The need to remove a dangerous rival led to the Edwardian campaign of 1282, which brought Wales firmly under the English crown. The conquest was confirmed in the Statute of Rhuddlan on 3 March 1284, a settlement which speeded up the process of change already underway and modified the native social organisation. In a real sense, the Statute initiated the evolution of the present-day political map of Wales. The territory held by the Marcher lords continued to be administered under the pre-conquest system. The remaining areas of conquered land in the north-west and west were reorganised into shires on the English model.

Five new shires were established: Anglesey, Caernarfon, Merioneth, Cardigan and Carmarthen (Fig 11). Together these formed the Principality of Wales, which in 1301 became, nominally at least, the area to be ruled by the monarch's eldest son, thus establishing a tradition by which the male heir to the throne is known as the Prince of Wales. In some ways, Edward's approach was conservative. In constructing the new shires he grouped existing native hundreds and commotes. The four northern counties were formed entirely in this way. Carmarthen in addition contained Marcher land and therefore had a distinction within it in terms of administrative origin between a Welsh north and an English south. Both the counties of Cardigan and Carmarthen had already experienced a form of shire organisation. Now these arrangements were formally recognised. Flintshire was created out of three tracts of land previously having little association, save that they had all once been part of Cheshire. For this reason it was not designated as part of the Welsh Principality. Pembroke and the Lordship of Glamorgan, with territories substantially smaller than the counties that came to acquire these names, had long been settled by the Anglo-Normans and were already subject to English-style shire administration.

Each of the new counties was in the charge of a sheriff, but for general legal and other political supervision a regional grouping of counties was devised. Anglesey, Caernarfon and Merioneth were

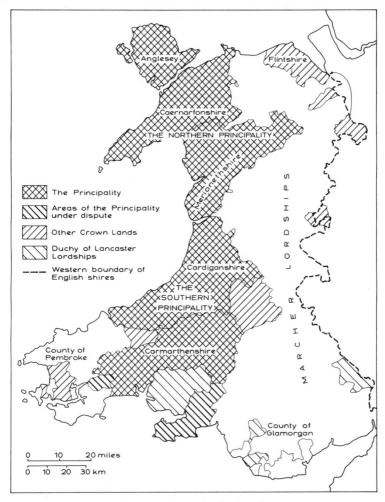

The Principality

Areas of the Principality under dispute

Other Crown Lands

Duchy of Lancaster Lordships

Western boundary of English shires

Anglesey

Flintshire

Caernarfonshire

THE NORTHERN PRINCIPALITY

Merionethshire

Cardiganshire

THE SOUTHERN PRINCIPALITY

Carmarthenshire

County of Pembroke

County of Glamorgan

MARCHER LORDSHIPS

0   10   20 miles
0 10 20 30 km

Fig 11 Administration in the fourteenth century

placed under the Justicular of Snowdon, based in Caernarfon Castle; Flintshire was made subject to the chief officer of the neighbouring county, the Justicular of Chester; while the counties of Cardigan and Carmarthen were already organised for administrative purposes under the Justicular of West Wales at Carmarthen, and continued to be so. By this means the English crown came to exercise a firm control over Wales, and especially of those former tribal *gwledydd*, Gwynedd and Deheubarth, which had been the major areas of native resistance and menace. As a second line of defence, Edward had also secured the routeways into England with stable and well-established administrations in the north and south Wales coastal plains, and with the buffer of Marcher lordships along the border county, though these small, semi-independent, private kingdoms were often in the future to prove more threat than protection.

Glyndŵr's revolt

Following the Edwardian settlement, the Welsh by and large settled for their lot. From time to time, rebellions against the crown were supported by the Welsh gentry, at least some of whom were descended from the families of the native princes, but revolts were highly sporadic in occurrence and invariably unsuccessful. Generally, the Welsh came to terms with their new rulers. Some saw benefit in active support for the new order, though few Welshmen achieved posts of any importance until well into the fifteenth century. Most suffered a hard, even an unpleasant, life through the later Middle Ages. Wales was not united with England in 1284 and the Welsh were not intended to be regarded as equals. Much of the administration was in the hands of Englishmen, and of course there was misuse of largely uncontrolled authority. The Welsh were also disadvantaged economically as the English grasped control of trade and were more than able to compete with them in the acquisition of land. Discontent became widespread. By the mid fourteenth century it had reached high levels, and in addition, the plagues and social frustrations common too in England, fuelled the feelings of oppression. The Welsh had not forgotten their champions of old. The bards sang of triumphs past and dreamed of political and economic success in the future. They awaited the saviour who would deliver them from the English yoke.

Open revolt needed only a leader of stature and the right opportunity. When a leader emerged in the form of Owain Glyndŵr, he must have seemed to his fellow countrymen the very fulfilment of the bardic prophecy. Born in 1354, he was of noble native lineage, an important advantage among a people who value family history so highly. On his father's side he was descended directly from the royal house of Powys, and on his mother's from the royal line of Deheubarth. He could also claim descent from the royal family of Gwynedd. What is more, he understood English ways, having served as a court official in London before settling in Wales. The trigger of revolt was less worthy of prophecy. As the holder of a small Welsh lordship, Glyndŵr had a private dispute with his neighbour, the great Marcher Lord Reginald Grey of Ruthin. The quarrel deteriorated to armed conflict and almost unintentionally sparked off an insurrection that was eventually to spread to the whole of Wales.

The speed with which a relatively minor local squabble turned to a national uprising is, of course, indicative of the standing of Glyndŵr as a leader and of the feelings of discontent rife in Wales. But there were other contributory factors. An important element was certainly the reaction in Wales to political events in England. The English civil wars had led to the triumph of the Lancastrians in 1399 and the removal and murder of Richard II. This caused alarm. If the Welsh leant in any direction, it was towards the royal family of York. Henry IV of Lancaster was plainly a usurper, a king against whom revolt could be justified and possibly successful in an unstable period. Within Wales Glyndŵr was able to give coherence to the many kinds and sources of problems of the Welsh. As old economic and social bonds disintegrated, he was able to emphasise that the mainspring of most causes of discontent was an alien disruption of the proper and natural order. In short, he provided the Welsh with a target for their pent feelings, namely, the English. Consistent with these ideas was Glyndŵr's attempt to give practical expression to the incipient feelings of nationhood that appear to have been emerging at this time. It is wrong to judge early fifteenth-century nationalism by present-day standards, but Glyndŵr certainly attempted to give Wales those attributes of nationhood that were important in his period. He was crowned Prince of Wales in the presence of envoys from elsewhere in the British Isles and Europe. He attempted to set up a royal house and to create a civil service with members derived from two proposed Welsh universities, one in the north and another in the south. He summoned parliaments in Machynlleth and Harlech, bringing together men from all commotes of Wales, adopted seals of state and used the coat of arms of the Gwynedd royal house. He proposed ecclesiastical reforms which would have led to an independent Welsh church, centred on St David's, with clergy educated at the two Welsh universities. And finally, he outlined a national territory which would have included substantial portions of the English border counties, the homeland of a nation state wholly independent of England. While writers of the nineteenth and twentieth centuries have given the Glyndŵr story romantic and patriotic overtones which it may not warrant, it is undoubtedly true that, after the Llywelyns, he came the nearest to founding a unified Welsh state and may well deserve the title he has been given, 'father of modern Welsh nationalism'.

Glyndŵr never achieved his wider aims, but at the peak of his power he commanded the support of the whole of Wales. His campaign began in north-east Wales late in 1400, and after Ruthin his forces attacked Denbigh, Rhuddlan, Flint and Hawarden. In the following year he moved southward through the border country into the south Wales lowlands, and in 1403 consolidated his hold on the south-west. As he grew stronger, in 1404–5, he established himself in the north-west, in the mountain core of Gwynedd from which so many earlier Welsh champions had sought to control the national territory. From this base he attempted to institute the reforms and national institutions for which he is now famous, though Glyndŵr was not only a far-sighted political figure, but also a talented military leader.

The English crown could plainly not tolerate such developments, and it needed only time to assemble superior forces before the inevitable suppression of the rebellion occurred. The repossession followed a familiar pattern: penetration of the lowlands by the English while the Welsh retreated into the fortress of Gwynedd. The taking of Anglesey by the English in 1406–7 was crucial; it deprived Glyndŵr of his granary. By 1410 he had disappeared and was probably dead within five years.

The consequences of the defeat were very different from what might have been if Glyndŵr had been able to maintain Welsh unity and to resist the English forces. In the course of the revolt much land had gone untended and there was widespread destruction. Old scores were settled and not least upon the English-dominated towns. There was severe disruption of economic life. But instead of a period of reconstruction and reconciliation, the return of Lancastrian government to Wales brought greater humiliation than hitherto. Not only were the lands of the rebels seized by the King, and severe fines imposed upon an already impoverished people, but

Hill farm at Bodcoll, near Devil's Bridge, Dyfed

discriminatory legislation was enacted which greatly limited the freedom of the Welsh. If they had previously thought themselves to be second-class citizens, now they were legally so. Welshmen were not allowed to bear arms or armour, to hold unauthorised gatherings, to be appointed to responsible public office, to engage in the trial of an Englishman or to acquire land within even a Welsh borough. An Englishman who married a Welsh woman suffered the same disabilities. In the border towns, in order to strengthen defence, Henry IV's government forbade the Welsh to be citizens and gave powers for the confiscation under certain circumstances of Welsh goods in retaliation against the theft of English property. While it is true that these punitive laws were not often enforced, their very existence yielded a sense of national grievance that could be exploited by any future leader anxious to enlist Welsh support.

Wales subsequently underwent one of its most lawless periods. Some of Glyndŵr's followers survived by becoming outlaws, a few even achieving local reputations akin to that of Robin Hood. To these, as the fifteenth century proceeded, were added soldiers returning from the wars in France, skilled in bloodshed and pillage, and the many survivors from the battles of the Wars of the Roses, in which considerable numbers of Welsh became involved on both sides. Wales must have been well ready for the coming of Henry Tudor, perceived as Welsh prince and saviour, to deliver the country from tyranny and disorder.

The Acts of Union

Henry Tudor's Welsh connections were strong. His grandfather, Owen Tudor, was of pure Welsh stock and had married Catherine, the widow of Henry V. He also had noble English blood in his veins, particularly through his mother, Margaret Beaufort, who was in direct line to John of Gaunt, the third son of Edward III. He was born in Pembroke Castle, and spent his first fourteen years in Wales, mainly in Pembroke and Raglan. His next fourteen years were spent in impoverished exile in France. While his claim to the English throne came through his mother, it was his Welsh ancestry on his father's side which assured him support in Wales. In August 1485,

A prosperous valley farm at Betws Bledrws, Dyfed

he returned from Brittany, landing with a small force in Pembroke-shire. He gathered support on his march through mid Wales, and within the month triumphed over Richard III at Bosworth, where he fought under what was assumed to be the red dragon standard of Cadwaladr. Superimposed upon the green-and-white livery of the house of Tudor, the emblem has now come to be accepted as the national flag of Wales. Wales had finally conquered England and a Welshman had assumed the English throne — or so it must have seemed to many in Wales.

Henry Tudor, now Henry VII, was certainly generous with his favours to his Welsh supporters. High offices were showered upon his closest allies, many of them Welsh, and London became a mag-net for countless ambitious Welshmen seeking to advance them-selves at court, in the administration and in the professions. The Welsh, indeed, became very unpopular as a result of their privileged status. But apart from patronage to individuals, Henry seems to have done very little to redeem his promises in Wales more gener-ally. The policy of the Tudors in Wales is a hotly debated issue, but a fairly strong school of thought holds the view that the Tudors made use of their popular support in Wales to strengthen their hold on the throne and to further their other interests, rather than to bring any substantial benefits to Wales itself. Reforms, when they came, tended to be legal and administrative. For example, the statutory disabilities imposed by Henry IV were gradually removed, notably during the first decade of the sixteenth century by Henry VII, but the major administrative reform was undertaken by his second son, Henry, who succeeded to the throne in 1509.

On the accession of Henry VIII, Wales was still in turmoil. Law-lessness was still prevalent, and the imposition of control from London was greatly hampered by the very untidy administrative framework. In the west and north the Principality had a shire organisation with English-style local government machinery to conduct the affairs of each county. In theory, English criminal law prevailed, but in practice there was much variation. Civil law relied heavily upon local customary practice. In addition, there were three Counties Palatine, Pembroke, Glamorgan and Flint, which were governed directly by the sovereign, again nominally according to English practice. Elsewhere, the lordships of the March were ruled with their own officials and machinery. A large number of the lordships had by this time become crown property, but some were still in private hands, a few of them Welsh. To some degree the Marcher lordships had been controlled by the formal establishment of the Council of Wales and the Marches, in 1501, based at Ludlow, to enforce law and order in the border country and to prevent wrongdoers moving from one lordship to another to escape punishment, but such policy as existed was ineffective and inconsistent. A radical and standardised approach was needed, and this was essentially introduced, under some pressure, by Henry's government in what later became called the Acts of Union in 1536 and 1543.

In more recent times, particularly since the late nineteenth century, the effects of the Acts of Union have been re-evaluated. They are now frequently seen as the beginning of the end of Wales and the Welsh. They undermined the dominance of the Welsh language by proscribing it for many official and almost all legal purposes; they replaced the laws of Hywel Dda, where the traditional legal system still persisted, by English law; they led to a widening of the social division between the Welsh gentry, rapidly becoming anglicised, and the ordinary folk; they encouraged the decline of Welsh cultural life, replacing it with a London-based culture; and, administratively, they virtually abolished Wales as a separate entity. At the time, while not unopposed, the Acts seem to have been generally welcomed. For Welshmen finally to have achieved full equality before the law with their English neighbours must have more than compensated for any disadvantages that were perceived, and the new administrative and legal arrangements, though they devalued the native tongue in the pursuit of efficient management, at least held out the hope of a more stable and peaceful life, and at best offered the opportunity for individual advancement in the new unified state. Many of the consequences of the Acts of Union, especially in the social and religious aspects of life, will be discussed later in the book; here, attention will be directed towards the legal and administrative provisions.

The 'Act for Laws and Justice to be Ministered in Wales as it is in this Realm', as the measure of 1536 was titled, though hurriedly drafted and later to be modified by some minor legislation and by the major Act of 1543, had a clear intention: to incorporate Wales within the English state by extending to it all the English governmental systems. The administrative difficulties from which Wales had suffered were to be resolved quite simply. The troublesome Marcher lordships were abolished as semi-independent units and

assigned, with crown land, to a reorganised shire structure. Some
were allocated to existing Welsh or English border counties.
Cardigan, Carmarthen and Merioneth were enlarged, and the
ancient Counties Palatine of Glamorgan and Pembroke were considerably reshaped. The shires of Gloucester, Hereford and Shropshire were those to benefit within England. The remaining Marcher
lordships, some owned by the crown, were blocked together to

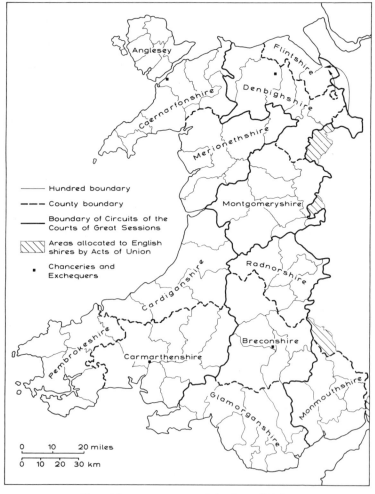

Fig 12 The consequences of the Acts of Union

form the five new counties of Brecknock, Denbigh, Monmouth, Montgomery and Radnor (Fig 12). The Act of 1536 remained faithful to the boundaries of the Marcher Lordships when outlining the new county territories. It was therefore the land ownership of the Marcher lords and of the crown which was paramount in dictating the new county boundaries, and not any feature of the natural landscape. Occasionally, where the lordship boundaries happened to follow even older tribal divisions, the latter were perpetuated and appeared in the post-union political map. An often-quoted example is the boundary between the two new shires of Denbigh and Montgomery, which is coincident with the divisions between the two parts of Powys, namely Powys Fadog to the north and Powys Wenwynwyn to the south. Minor adjustments to boundaries were made by the Act of 1543, but again the former townships tended to remain intact, and the reasons for transfer, where known, certainly have no basis in physical or human geography. Quite a number of the later transfers were made between the Welsh and English shires. For example, the Archenfield region passed to Hereford and quite large tracts to Shropshire, including the Lordship of Clun. These changes introduced into the eastern boundaries of the Welsh counties even greater sinuosity than before, and ensured that the division between Welsh and English counties was even less appropriate as a linguisitic frontier. Considerable numbers of Welsh-speakers were left in south-west Hereford and in north-west Shropshire. Of course, the line between the Welsh and English counties subsequently came to be regarded, and eventually to be used administratively, as the Welsh border. But this was not the purpose at the time. The Acts of Union were intended not to divide, but to unite.

However, Wales was not fully absorbed, particularly in legal affairs. It was allowed, largely as a matter of convenience in an area so remote from Westminster, to retain its own system of law courts, already established in the older shires, but which were now introduced, with one exception, into the new counties. The country was divided into four circuits for the Courts of Great Sessions, with three shires in each circuit. Regional chanceries and exchequers were established at Brecon and Denbigh, while those already in operation at Caernarfon and Carmarthen were confirmed. This special Welsh system of law courts lasted until 1830. Monmouthshire was omitted from the arrangement, perhaps because it broke the symmetry of the system, but certainly because it was regarded as accessible to Westminster. For many centuries as a consequence it was to hold an anomalous position. For legal administration it was within England; for ecclesiastical purposes and most, though not all, legislation it was firmly in Wales. But in the mid sixteenth century there was no reason for anyone to give thought to such difficulties.

The Acts of Union did more than create a new political and legal map of Wales. Within the counties they set up the machinery of administration and representation. Each shire was prescribed a county town, all of which, except for New Radnor, developed as an administrative centre. Within the shires, hundreds on the English pattern were identified for more local administration, those of the old Principality in the north and west following the medieval, tribal commote boundaries, but those of the new counties created in 1536 being largely freshly devised by a special commission. Each hundred was composed of parishes, but these did not become civil units of administration until after the Reformation. Hitherto, except for the parliaments of Edward III when forty-eight Welshmen attended, Wales had been unrepresented in Westminster, even at the parliament which passed the Act of 1536. Now each Welsh shire was to be represented by one elected knight and by one burgess, not two as in England, from every borough which was a shire town. There were two exceptions: Monmouthshire was to have two shire members, while the county town of Merioneth was to be unrepresented. The lower representation in Wales than in England, and the small differences within Wales itself, were presumably a response to different levels of population and prosperity.

The Council of Wales and the Marches, which had been formally re-established by Henry VII, was also given new life under the Act of 1543. It was composed of the Lord President and his deputy, together with twenty-two members, all nominated by the crown. The Council acted both as a court of appeal and as an administrative body responsible for such things as ensuring the implementation of acts of Parliament, and the appointment and supervision of the senior officers of the shires, including sheriffs and justices of the peace. The second became its more important function. The authority of the Council extended not only over the thirteen shires of Wales but also to the five English border counties of Cheshire, Hereford, Gloucester, Shropshire and Worcestershire. In the late sixteenth and early seventeenth centuries these border shires sought to break away from the jurisdiction of the Council, and in 1604 the Westminster courts decided in their favour. The Council was supported by the crown, but after a long wrangle the Council was suspended in 1641, revived in 1660, and finally dissolved by statute in 1689.

So it was that between 1536 and 1543 the political framework of modern Wales was established. There were to be many changes of emphasis as time passed and also some changes in administrative boundaries and functions, but there can be no doubt that the mid sixteenth-century legislation established patterns which were to persist and caused momentous changes, many of which the Tudors could not reasonably have foreseen or perhaps intended. It was a truly formative period in the development of Welsh institutional systems, and for England it initiated the process that eventually brought the whole of the British Isles under a government based in London.

The power of the shires

It was the intention of the Acts of Union that the new political framework should be strong, stable and durable. And so it came to be. The shires, the chief units of administrative and legal control, acquired boundaries that were to persist, little modified, until the 1970s, while their authority, though often changing, continued to be augmented as the demands made upon local government increased.

The chief administrative officer of the shire, and representative of the crown, was the sheriff. He was chosen annually by the Council of Wales and the Marches and held wide powers. Initially, at least, he was responsible for most legal administration outside the courts themselves; he was both assessor and collector of taxes; he acted as returning officer in parliamentary elections; and he also had an important military role, for it was his duty to defend the shire against the king's enemies. Perhaps the sheriff was given too much power; many soon developed formidable reputations for dishonesty. In time, their duties were assumed by other officers, particularly by the justices, and their activities became purely formal.

The establishment of justices of the peace in Wales was an exceptionally shrewd innovation of the Tudors. It granted important legal and administrative powers to local laymen, drawn from families 'of good name', and thus made more palatable the enforcement of the sometimes harsh English laws in Wales. Eight justices were to be chosen for every shire, each having an annual income from property of at least £20 a year and being familiar with the laws of the land. In a poor, sparsely populated and often inaccessible country, the number of justices per shire was frequently exceeded and the personal qualifications waived. Nevertheless, the justices appear to have performed their very broad judicial responsibilities reasonably well. Acting as individual justices, or in their quarter sessions and special sessions, they tried and sentenced offenders ranging from non-attenders at church, vagabonds and petty thieves, to those engaged in plots and rioting; indeed, all persons whose offences did not require a jury. To the justices must go much of the credit for the fairly swift improvement in the observance of law and order after the Acts of Union. In addition to their judicial duties, they carried heavy administrative loads. They were responsible for the maintenance of bridges and gaols; they oversaw the setting of wages; they inspected weights, measures and the quality of goods; they licensed and controlled ale houses; and perhaps most onerous of all, they supervised the provision of poor relief.

The justices were not without their critics. While the majority may have undertaken their duties with propriety and thoroughness, it is certainly true that some misused the new and largely un-monitored powers that had been placed in the hands of what were part-time and amateur officials. The records of the Council of Wales and the Marches reveal that more than a few were partial in their legal judgements and were slow to take administrative action which might be contrary to their own advantage. But it is difficult to know, in respect of the complaints made at the time, how many of these were triggered by self interest or family feuding. And in any event, in the sixteenth century, to make the best of one's personal good fortune in achieving office might not have seemed so strange: concepts of democratic responsibility had not developed to any degree in local affairs, and indeed it was not until the nineteenth century that the governance of the shires was given over to the selected representatives of the people.

As the shire gained more powers, so the number of its officers multiplied, and also so the pressure grew for some devolution of responsibility to smaller units in order to achieve more efficient control and to ensure the provision of public services. Following the union, each shire had been divided into hundreds, after the English pattern. In the shires of the ancient Principality, the old Welsh commotes were pressed into service as hundreds, but elsewhere, the new shires of 1536 were subdivided into hundreds by a specially appointed commission, established under the Act of that year, which seems to have paid little regard to the older boundaries. Each hundred was under the care of a resident justice, who was responsible for appointing constables: a chief constable of the hundred and at least one other for each township. By the mid nineteenth century the hundred had become virtually obsolete as an administrative unit, except for a few minor matters and as a census division, and even these functions were soon to disappear.

Far more persistent and ultimately more important as a local government unit was the parish. No mention is made in the Acts of Union of administration within the parish, which of course had been a means of ecclesiastical management; but after the Reformation the parish quickly came to be used as the smallest unit of local government. To the Tudors, the union of England and Wales and religious changes were clearly inter-related, both representing steps towards the emerging, unified, sovereign state. The adoption of the parish in civil administration also had the advantage that it diverted power away from the manorial courts of the troublesome feudal lords. As early as 1555, in the reign of Mary Tudor, the parish became responsible for the purely secular task of the upkeep of highways. The church wardens, elected by the parishioners, in addition to continuing with their supervision of church affairs, now together with the constables of each parish were required to elect annually two surveyors of local roads and to recruit unpaid labour for highway repair, a particularly unpopular duty. The parishes later acquired further civil responsibilities, such as the control of vermin, but perhaps their most difficult task came under Elizabethan legislation, which greatly extended their duties in the relief of the poor. The church wardens had for long organised the collection of charitable alms on Sundays and holy days; under the new poor laws they became responsible by statute with a number of other householders of the parish for giving assistance to the sick, poor and aged, for putting the able-bodied poor to work and for apprenticing pauper children. All these poor law activities were financed by a compulsory poor rate which the church wardens and other overseers were responsible for collecting and distributing, subject to the justices of the peace.

The system served Wales well for several centuries, but industrial urbanisation first, and later, demands for more broadly representative local government, brought about changes not only in responsibilities, but also in structure. The parish, particularly, it became clear, was a unit too small to cope with the changed circumstances of the nineteenth century. Gradually its powers were assumed by larger districts. The Highways Act of 1862 empowered the aggregation of parishes, long the custodians of the local road network, into more effective blocks, while the 1870 Education Act did much the same in its field. The establishment of urban and rural sanitary districts was achieved by Acts of 1871 and 1875, but it was a measure of 1888 which made most impact. The Local Government Act of that year reconfirmed the county as the superior local government authority and established popularly elected county councils, to which most of the administrative work hitherto undertaken by the justices of the peace passed. A few years later in 1894, another act consolidated the arrangement and, further, created the next lower tier, namely, the urban and rural districts. It also constituted the civil parish, as a third tier, now without any ecclesiastical links. In the same period, Cardiff and Swansea were nominated as county boroughs, and later, Merthyr Tydfil and Newport were added. In effect, they had the powers of a county, independent of the county in which they fell, but retained the borough form of government. The revised system of counties, county boroughs, urban and rural districts and civil parishes remained intact for nearly a hundred years. But in the 1950s and 1960s, new thinking on the organisational efficiency of this pattern raised questions which were to lead in the 1970s to a substantial revision of the county system that had lasted since 1536, and some of it since 1284.

Recent reorganisation of local government

While the extractive and manufacturing industries of Wales suffered a setback in the period between the wars, continuing industrialisation provided a stimulus to the long-established drift of population from the countryside to the towns and cities. The trend was further emphasised by the growing importance, as living standards rose, of the urban-based tertiary industries, those activities which had as their end product a service to the community rather than goods. Consequently, as the twentieth century wore on, towns and cities became more and more the economic and social foci of the areas in which they were located. These were changes, experienced as much in England and Scotland as in Wales, which caused growing dissatisfaction with the local government framework and gave encouragement to those who advocated a reform of the system.

A number of deficiences had been identified. First, it was clear that the local government areas no longer fitted the pattern of modern life which had become dominantly urban. As further economic, social and technological changes occurred, it seemed that the mismatch would increase. Both theoretical and practical studies had emphasised the interdependence of urban areas and the tributary zones they served. They led to the concept of the city-region, to an administrative area which would unite what the urban and rural districts currently divided. Some writers went so far as to advocate a unitary, all-purpose urban local authority. The second difficulty arose from the fragmentation caused by the present system. In 1972, Wales had 13 counties, 4 county boroughs, 32 non-county boroughs, 73 urban and 57 rural districts. The counties and county boroughs exercised totally independent jurisdiction, subject to national control, over environmental services, such as land-use planning, transportation and other major developments, as well as over social services, such as education, health and housing. Each was able to delegate some of these responsibilities to lower-tier authorities, but did so in different measure. Add to these difficulties the atmosphere of hostility that often existed between adjacent authorities, and particularly between counties and their county boroughs, and it will be plain how troublesome integrated planning had become. Finally, a major concern had arisen over the size of local authority areas. Many local authorities were too small in territory and in revenue, and too deficient in highly qualified manpower and technical equipment, to fulfil their responsibilities. Population migration had also left many rural areas sparsely peopled and therefore with high *per capita* costs for service provision. Modern transportation and improved accessibility obviated the need for small and very local administrative areas, and consequently there was nothing to prevent the creation of more efficient units.

After years of discussion, the reforms of local government in Wales were first announced in a consultative document, but, following opposition from the political parties and other groups in Wales, were revised before given effect by the Local Government Act of

1972. While many of the English counties survived substantially intact and often with their traditional names, a sweeping reorganisation took place within Wales. No single county remained with unchanged boundaries, and no single county's name survived unaltered (Figs 1 and 2). The new system was two-tiered. In the first tier there were eight counties, most carrying names which were derived from the roughly comparable tribal divisions of Wales. In the north-west, Gwynedd was composed, in greater part, of the former counties of Anglesey, Caernarfon and Merioneth. In the north-east, Clwyd was made up of the counties of Denbigh and Flint, together with the small section of Merioneth around Corwen. In mid Wales, Powys emerged from the counties of Montgomery, Radnor and Brecon, while in the south-west, Dyfed was constructed from the counties of Cardigan, Carmarthen and Pembroke. The former county of Glamorgan was split three ways into West, Mid and South sections, and only Monmouthshire, of all the Welsh counties, continued with more or less its former territory as the new county of Gwent, the only boundary changes being rather minor alterations to its western edge. The new counties were subdivided into a total of 37 lower-tier districts, 23 of which were granted borough status. Several districts in the rural areas were as large as the traditional counties, but in the densely populated parts of the three counties of Glamorgan and in western Gwent, the districts were quite small.

While the changes were considerable, they were less than totally radical, and plainly did not embrace in its entirety the thinking that had led to the changes. The new two-tier system was certainly more balanced in terms of population; it was less fragmented; the units of local government were larger than their predecessors; and they did not differentiate between town and country. On the other hand, the new areas did not really approach the city-region principle, and in a number of instances appear to have disregarded it completely. When former county boundaries followed rivers, such as the Teifi, the county or district often used the same line, thus perpetuating the administrative divorce of socially and economically integrated settlement. The Conwy valley, now wholly within Gwynedd, is an exception. In other parts, regional affiliations were ignored. Ystradgynlais, for example, is essentially a settlement of the south Wales coalfield yet was allowed to remain in Powys, a county which it shared with towns as distant as Machynlleth and Llanfyllin, both formerly in northern Montgomeryshire. Presumably such anomalies continued because of the various compromises between county councils, pressure groups and other bodies, necessary to gain acceptance of what at times were highly contentious proposals. Quite what stimulated the tripartite division of Glamorgan, originally to have been only into East and West Glamorgan, other than purely party political considerations is hard to tell. The Act of 1972 established a Local Government Boundary Commission for Wales as a permanent body to keep under review the local government and election areas. It is possible that some of the anomalies may in time disappear as a result of its activities.

The revised county and district boundaries came into being in April 1974 (Fig 2, page 11). Since the recommendations for the reform of local government in England were undertaken over a slightly different timescale and by a different procedure, the proposals for England and Wales evolved to a large degree independently. The Welsh border as defined by the shires created under the Acts of Union thus was not under consideration and remained as it was.

Alongside and sometimes as part of the debate over local government reform was the discussion of regional devolvement of central government functions. In England, the discussion revolved largely around the responsibilities that should be devolved and the administrative convenience that would result. In Wales, and also in Scotland, the debate took quite a different form.

The Council for Wales and Monmouthshire had been established as early as 1948 as a consultative body. It was distinguished by the singular lack of attention governments of either political complexion paid to its proposals, and therefore by increasing frustration through its eighteen years of life. Its importance was that it provided a focus for those who demanded a popularly elected, national parliament with real powers, a vehicle for the expression of national consciousness that would be in stark contrast to the ineffective Council. Early concessions from Westminster were regarded by the devolutionists as derisory: a part-time Minister in 1951, a Minister of State to assist the Welsh Minister in 1957, and a Ministry which came to be perceived more as a means for implementing unpopular government measures in Wales, rather than as a body that would mainly be concerned with serving Welsh interests. The creation by the Labour government in 1964 of a Secretary of State for Wales, working through a newly established Welsh Office based in Cardiff (formally the Welsh capital city since 1955) was welcomed by most. But there were still nagging doubts over whether the Labour party, now the dominant political party in Wales, had a deep commitment to fast-growing Welsh national expectations.

In July 1966 the unexpected happened. Gwynfor Evans, president of *Plaid Cymru*, the Welsh Nationalist party, won a parliamentary by-election in Carmarthen at the expense of the Labour Party. Home Rule for Wales was not a major issue in the election — the government's economic performance and local dissatisfaction with the Labour Party were probably more important — but the result gave *Plaid Cymru* an impetus which allowed it to prosper as never before. In 1967 and 1968 it achieved exceptionally good results in the Labour strongholds of the south Wales coalfield, in two parliamentary by-elections coming within one or two thousand votes of taking the seats. The first town council to come under *Plaid Cymru* control was that of Merthyr Tydfil. A new mood of nationalism was widespread, undoubtedly assisted by the politically more radical stance of *Plaid Cymru*, now much more professionally organised than hitherto and under pressure from militant groups of Welsh-speakers such as the Welsh Language Society *(Cymdeithas yr Iaith Gymraeg)*, but also by the weakening hold of the Labour Party over the urban–industrial areas. The economic plan for Wales in 1967, the last regional plan in England and Wales to appear, was not highly regarded as a solution to Welsh industrial problems, and even the recently founded Secretaryship of State for Wales, and the Economic Council which had taken over from the old Council for Wales and Monmouthshire, were proving disappointing. It was the high point of nationalism and of the electoral success of *Plaid Cymru*. After 1970 the party contested all parliamentary constituencies and while it achieved a number of victories (it gained seats in Caernarfon and Merioneth), these were in solidly Welsh-speaking areas. Overall its electoral success was limited. In the four general elections from 1970 to 1979, in only 10 of the 36 Welsh seats did the party's average vote exceed 12.5 per cent.

While the fortunes of *Plaid Cymru* have waned, the jolt its electoral gains gave particularly to the Labour Party persisted. The impact was the greater because very similar voting trends were evident in Scotland. After a further period of active debate, it was decided to put the issue of Home Rule to a public referendum. The Wales Act of 1978 proposed the establishment of a Welsh Assembly with executive powers, to be based in Cardiff. A building was even selected as the Assembly House. Implementation of the Act was to be made conditional upon acceptance by a 40 per cent vote of the registered electorate. At last, no more than public endorsement was needed for Home Rule over most domestic matters. But times had changed. A severe industrial depression was underway, focusing attention away from political and onto economic affairs; the tide of nationalism was ebbing from its high point around 1970, especially as more militant nationalist groups began to alienate the monoglot majority; questions had arisen over the wisdom of creating an extra, perhaps expensive, tier of government that would interfere with the freedom of local authorities; and very possibly, though the effect is difficult to measure, the old suspicions between *Cymru Gymraeg* (Welsh Wales) and *Cymru ddi-Gymraeg* (Anglo-Wales) had been re-established. Welsh-speakers feared that the new Assembly would be dominated by the Labour Party for ever more, relying upon the massive support it could secure from the Anglo-Welsh of the south Wales coalfield. The monoglot majority feared that bilingual speakers would be given preference, especially when new public sector jobs came to be filled.

When the country went to the polls on St David's Day 1979, the proposal to set up a Welsh Assembly was soundly rejected. Only one-fifth of those who cast their votes was in favour of the implementation of the Wales Act. The referendum was conducted on a county basis. While individual districts may have polled a majority of votes in favour of Home Rule, no county even approached that number. In Gwynedd and Dyfed, the core of Welsh-speaking *Cymru Gymraeg*, well below 35 per cent of those voting were in favour, and in more anglicised parts of Wales the figure was typically around 15 per cent. It is likely that the referendum result does not provide the end of this particular story, but it does illustrate how complicated and interwoven are the strands of Welsh national consciousness, in which a clear distinction is drawn between self-awareness and self-government, between nationhood and statehood. These are distinctions which reflect a level of social and political sophistication that will be explored further in following chapters.

CHAPTER 4

Rural Wales

When Giraldus Cambrensis (Gerald of Wales), a native of Dyfed and a famous scholar and topographer, travelled through Wales in the twelfth century, he made a special point of noting that the majority of the inhabitants of the country lived not in towns or villages, but in scattered homesteads. Population was widely dispersed and by present-day standards small in number, probably less than a quarter of a million.

In those areas where native society dominated, tribal groups of both bondsmen and freemen occupied land, owing allegiance and providing dues and service to a local lord (see Chapter 3). The free family groups owned and worked their own land, which was subdivided under a gavelkind inheritance system until individual holdings were barely sufficient to sustain one family. Farm units became smaller, settlement spread and standards of living could have been little above subsistence level. The system did not encourage arable working, neither did the relief and climate of tribal Wales. Undoubtedly in favourable areas there were patches of land under the plough, but generally pastoralism prevailed. Giraldus writes: 'The people almost without exception live upon meat, oatmeal, milk, butter and cheese. They eat great quantities of meat, but bread somewhat sparingly . . . most of their land is used for grazing, a little for tillage, less still for gardening, and for the growing of fruit trees hardly any at all.'

In lower areas, especially where highly prized water meadows existed, grassland was of good quality, but in the uplands and on steep slopes, rough pasture and forest were normally the major land uses. As pressure of people upon these slim agricultural resources built up, it became the practice to depasture stock upon the upland wastes, usually regarded as common land. In one sense, this led to a rural economy that was semi-nomadic. At first cattle, but in later centuries sheep, were moved in summer months to the upland pastures in search of grazing. This *transhumance*, employed also in other upland areas of Europe, became established as part of a seasonal round. It was customary for animals to winter in the more sheltered lowlands on the permanent grassland or on the limited but consequently valuable land set aside for summer crops. As soon as spring planting was possible, but also in order to conserve lowland pasture, the animals were moved from around the homestead, often known as the *hendre* (old home), to the fresh upland grass. Traditionally, the transfer took place on *Dydd Calan Mai* (May Day). In the uplands a temporary, but perhaps later a permanent, dwelling was constructed, often known as the *hafod* or *hafoty* (summer house) or sometimes as the *lluest* (cottage or shieling). But once the lowland crops were harvested and before the onset of winter, the stock was returned to the lowlands, customarily on or before *Dydd Calan Gaeaf* (a November festival). In the higher elevations it is likely that the summer season on the upland grazing was shorter than tradition has it.

The Norman conquest of Wales, a rapid but piecemeal process of land acquisition along the coastal plains and in the east-facing river valleys, consolidated later by the Edwardian campaign of 1282, introduced a quite different agricultural system. The Norman lords who assumed control of the territories of Welsh chieftains, initially did little more than acquire the services and dues which were previously the right of their vanquished predecessors. In the remoter areas of many Norman lordships the traditional Welsh agricultural practices and customs continued (these were the Welshries referred to in Chapter 2), but in lowland areas where land was flat and fertile, and the climate mild and dry, the feudal, manorial organisation that the Normans knew so well was introduced into the Englishries. On each manor there were free tenants, who had the right to sell land and move elsewhere if they wished, but the majority of the people were serfs, and bound to the lord of the manor for service and dues. Among other services, they cultivated land for their lord on his demesne, but they also engaged in arable and pastoral activities on their own account. The cultivation was in communal, open fields, tilled in an annual rotation. The manorial system flourished in those areas most readily secured by the Normans. Both the system, and the regions in which it could most effectively be pursued, ensured that arable working and its produce were much more common on the coastal plains accessible to England and in the valley lowlands of

85

the March. As it was subject to centralised control and focused upon open arable fields, the system developed nucleated village settlement around castle and church, and eventually market towns, quite unlike the dispersed settlement pattern of tribal areas.

Both the native Welsh system and Norman feudalism, which supplanted it in parts of the country, underwent change. In the Welsh areas, where blood relationships and shared responsibilities had formed the basis of tribal organisation, the increasing power of the native princes caused disruption to society, which was no longer required to perform its self-regulating functions. In addition, the dues that had largely been provided in kind were converted into money payments and came to be regarded as a rent or tax upon the holding of land. In the areas under the Norman system, services and dues were also being translated into cash payments, and in addition the distinction between free tenants and serfs diminished, while the increasing number of non-agricultural people in the towns deriving income from commerce, crafts and trade, and accumulating wealth far faster than their rural neighbours, disrupted the manorial organisation still further. But though both tribalism and feudalism experienced change, they formed the basis for the differentiated nature of Welsh rural society up until relatively recent times.

Rural economic growth

For there to be any marked progress in the economy of rural Wales, a number of important developments were necessary. First, farmers generally needed to be capable of self-sufficiency, but at a level above subsistence so that a surplus was available for sale. Secondly, they needed a period of political stability in which to accumulate wealth and improve their crops and stock. Thirdly, they needed urban markets, and since none of any importance lay within Wales, it meant in effect that they required access to the expanding urban areas of England. The outbreaks of plague in the second half of the fourteenth century appear to have been decisive in beginning the changes. The high death rate caused a land surplus and greatly encouraged the enclosure of open arable fields to create compact farms, and also led to the further renting of land. Following the Acts of Union and the shiring of the border country, not only did the markets for produce become available, and possible to reach with some measure of security, but the move to consolidate estates proceeded with greater urgency as Welshmen were able to participate in commerce and invest in land. They became active too in enclosing waste and the commons, an activity which the new political stability made worthwhile. The dissolution of the monasteries also presented the new Welsh gentry with a rare opportunity to expand their holdings. However, at the other end of the social scale, existed a substantial number of impoverished peasants and landless farm labourers.

Subsistence farming thus gradually gave way to a more commercial system in which agricultural produce was marketed both locally and in distant expanding cities, such as London. Trade in corn was certainly underway in the second half of the sixteenth century from the favoured parts of south-west and south-east Wales to England and to Ireland. The most frequently mentioned crops were wheat and oats, though barley was also widely grown. Liming enabled fairly intensive working, and productivity in these lowland areas appears to have been high, judged by the standards of the day. In addition to grain, butter and cheese were being marketed, some of the goods being carried overland and some by small coastal vessels to the English ports. By far the most important exports from Wales, however, were the products of the pastoral farming to which most of the country was devoted: store cattle, wool and cloth.

Welsh cattle had been sold in England as early as the thirteenth century, but from the sixteenth century onwards the cattle trade dominated all other agricultural enterprises. In rural areas unsuited to widespread arable working, cattle provided the major means of acquiring a cash income. The herds driven to England were described by a seventeenth-century Archbishop, John Williams, as 'the Spanish fleet . . . which brings hither the little gold and silver we have'. Generally, black cattle were brought together in the summer fairs and assembled into droves. Some were transported by sea, but the majority were moved overland, often having been shod for the journey, and conducted by drovers to the Midlands or frequently to south-east England. On arrival, the cattle were sold at the great fairs of Barnet, Brentwood, Smithfield and elsewhere, and then were usually fattened before slaughter. Herds followed established routes, avoiding settlements, agricultural areas and tollgates, where possible. In Wales this usually meant keeping to the uplands, where today many a ridgetop track or secondary road, seemingly unconnected to villages, and not a few disused taverns alongside such roads, testify to these long-distance cattle movements. The drovers, being the men responsible for transferring rural wealth to market and returning cash to the districts from which they came, became established as business men, often financing the droves. They also acquired status within rural communities because they acted as a means of communication with relatives, business associates, even landlords in London and the other cities. Some eventually came to be bankers who issued their own banknotes. The names of a few of the banks, such as *Banc yr Eidion Du* (Black Ox Bank) which was established in Llandovery, and *Banc y Ddafad Ddu* (Black Sheep Bank) of Aberystwyth and Tregaron, which used notes bearing the imprint of an ox and a sheep respectively, plainly indicate their origins.

Sheep were also driven on the hoof to markets in England, but it was more usual for their wool to be sold. Sheep rearing had not been of great importance in medieval Wales, but during Tudor times the British woollen industry expanded considerably and Wales shared fully in this development, though Welsh woollen cloth was regarded as coarse and poorly made. Its coarseness derived from the fact that many kinds of wool were mixed for spinning into thread; the crudeness of its manufacture resulted from the scattered, domestic nature of the industry; the farmer himself, together perhaps with a few hands, was typically the producer in a small fulling mill driven by water power. The ubiquity of the term *pandy* (fulling mill) as an element in Welsh placenames confirms the widespread distribution of production. However, after manufacture, and quite unlike the cattle trade, subsequent commercial activity was mostly in the hands of English cloth merchants. They attended local fairs, purchased both wool and cloth, and removed it to Shrewsbury, Coventry, Bristol and London for further working. The powerful Drapers' Guild of Shrewsbury came to acquire a virtual monopoly over the trade. The monopoly was broken in principle by an act of 1624, but the Guild continued to dominate trade in Welsh cloth well into the eighteenth century. Some parts of Wales developed special products, for example, the county of Merioneth became celebrated for its stockings, with Bala as the main market. Exports overseas also developed to Europe, and later to the West Indies and America, where coarse Welsh cloth was widely used in the slave plantations of the south. The wealth that Welsh wool brought, not so much to the farmer producers, but to the merchants and dealers of the valley lowlands of the March, is represented among other ways by the many magnificent black-and-white, timber-framed houses of Shrewsbury and the border country, and by the fact that one of the few modern English words to be derived from Welsh is 'flannel' *(gwlanen)*, the cloth that was the speciality of Montgomeryshire.

Slowly, the income that came from these hesitant steps towards commercial agriculture filtered back into the rural areas of Wales. Dwellings were rebuilt or improved, they were given chimneys, window glass and often an upper storey, personal comfort was enhanced and domestic chattels increased in sophistication and number. It is true that the improvements were not constant through time or in all areas, but gradually, with a growing urban population creating an expanding demand for food and other agricultural products, a modest prosperity persisted through to the eighteenth century. Then came an important period of change.

Agricultural change

The need to feed a growing urbanised, industrial population had encouraged rapid and considerable changes in agricultural practice in England throughout the eighteenth century, changes which some writers have considered an Agrarian Revolution. Though commercial farming had brought many benefits to Welsh farmers, agricultural innovation generally lagged well behind that in most of England, especially behind the farming methods in the major arable areas such as East Anglia, and despite the foundation of one of the earliest agricultural societies in the British Isles, the Brecknockshire Agricultural Society in 1755. Wales was isolated by distance from the main markets of the lowlands; its roads were narrow and very badly surfaced; the emphasis of its farming was upon pastoralism, concentrating principally upon the production of store cattle and sheep on communal upland grazing; its farmers usually spoke Welsh and were unaccustomed to reading the new agricultural manuals written in English; the great landowners, the prime movers elsewhere, were mainly absent from Wales, while the smaller owners lacked the capital to institute widespread change; all were factors which provided barriers to the diffusion of improved techniques. But during the French wars of 1793–1815 some dramatic changes in economic, political and social conditions occurred which were soon to introduce new methods to Wales, and particularly to those parts directly accessible to England.

To begin with, the period was one of massive inflation in the price of agricultural products, and especially of grain, which doubled or even trebled in price within two or three years. The wars in themselves were the major immediate cause. Over 10 per cent of the population of military age was drawn into the army and navy, and not only had these men to be equipped, clothed and fed, but also the productive workers of the country who supplied these commodities were reduced in number. Goods of all sorts were much in demand but in short supply, and inflation was triggered. The war also involved the government in great additional expenditure which had to be met by taxation. Pitt was forced to introduce income tax in 1799, but direct taxation never formed a major source of government revenue. Most of the wartime revenue, perhaps the equivalent of one-sixth of the national income, was derived from customs and excise duties, which automatically increased the prices of many products. Grains were affected more than most other agricultural goods because the war interfered both with the areas of production on the Continent and with trade. It was part of Napoleon's policy to prevent grain reaching Britain, though this policy was not pursued consistently throughout the wars. The Corn Laws, which were intended to regulate the market price of grain by imposing heavy duties on imported grain when prices at home were low, and a nominal duty when prices at home were high, were suspended completely in each year from 1793 to 1801.

With a rapidly growing industrial population in the eighteenth century, Britain had become a net importer of grain, and consequently more susceptible than hitherto to economic influences from outside. The loss of national agricultural self-sufficiency, combined with war shortages, led to a balance of payments crisis during which large quantities of gold passed to other countries to settle outstanding accounts. While gold reserves were low, a small French landing at Carreg Wastad, near Fishguard in February 1797, though a military fiasco, caused a run on the banks which they were unable to meet. The Bank of England was forced to suspend the redemption of its notes in gold. An inconvertible paper currency in its turn led to a great increase in the number of notes in circulation, allowed a rise in the price of gold bullion and aggravated inflation still further.

While the government was concerned with the wartime scarcity, with inflation and with the distressed state of the poor, it felt little moral obligation to interfere more than was politically expedient with the free market. To have done otherwise would have contradicted the teachings of the new political economy so recently pioneered in the works of Hume and Adam Smith. High prices themselves, it was held, solved the conflicting claims upon the economy by excluding the weakest customers from the market. Resources which had once satisfied civilian needs were thus freed for war use. Of course, the landlords who formed the major group at Westminster had everything to gain from rising prices unmatched by rises in agricultural wages.

The results of the wartime inflation in Wales were as varied and pronounced as its causes. As the price of agricultural produce rocketed, and especially that of grain, every incentive existed for farmers to increase their output of foodstuffs. This they achieved in two ways. First, they brought as much land as possible under the plough, both land that was suitable, but also many areas that would normally have been considered quite unsuitable. Grassland was converted, crops were raised on marginal land and cultivation crept up the hillsides to elevations higher than any in the historic period. Much land on the moorland fringes of Wales, once cropped but now reverted to rough grazing, is a product of this period. Enclosure of the common land and waste is an important theme at this time, and is discussed more fully below.

The second way in which Welsh farmers sought to increase output was by improving their methods in order to generate greater efficiency. The Agrarian Revolution in eastern England was underway in the first half of the eighteenth century. Now, under the stimulus of inflated prices and as a result of the energies of such men as Arthur Young, Sir John Sinclair and William Marshall, the new techniques began to be adopted more widely in Wales. Prosperity came to many Welsh farmers, more to those in the lowlands than to those working at higher elevations, more to those who farmed large units than to those with smaller holdings, more to those who were freeholders or held land on long leases than to those farming on short leases. At one extreme there were great riches to be gained, but at the other, the tenant farmer of the uplands acquired little and sometimes actually suffered. He lost grazing rights, his rent often rose and, if unable to grow corn, he was obliged to withstand the higher prices and scarcity, particularly acute during the series of wet, poor harvests between 1795 and 1800 and between 1808 and 1812.

The changes that took place in Welsh agriculture during the

French wars were greatly facilitated by the improvements in communications which occurred during the second half of the eighteenth century. The development of the transport network is closely associated with industrial growth (see Chapter 5), but it had important effects also in farming. Coastal and river traffic had for centuries provided the means for the carriage of agricultural produce. South and west Wales were linked with Bristol, for example, while Liverpool, though less important as a port at this time, served north Wales. Mid Wales was fortunate to lie astride one of the most important of Britain's river arteries, the Severn, and Welshpool, near the head of navigation, had emerged as a focus of packhorse and wagon routes. The construction of canals greatly improved the transport of goods by water and by the end of the eighteenth century efficient, if limited, waterway links existed between some of the lowland agricultural areas and either the manufacturing centres or the major ports. But water transport was slow and inflexible and it was upon the roads that most agricultural produce was carried.

There were three traditional means of access: the south Wales coast road, the Usk–Tywi route and the north Wales coast road. These had always been used for the through traffic to Ireland, but had little served the countryside through which they passed. It was not until after 1750 that the turnpike trusts became active in Wales. Road trusts were groups of local people, usually landowners, who obtained authority under a private act of Parliament to take over or construct a specified length of road, keep it under repair and recover the cost by levying tolls upon the users at specially constructed tollgates or turnpikes. They produced a road network which for the first time compared favourably with that which had existed under the Romans. The surfacing of these roads would not have satisfied modern or Roman standards, for the influence of Telford and Macadam had not yet been felt, but most writers compare them favourably with the wretched parochial by-roads. Turnpike roads never formed more than a small proportion of the total road system, but they did provide quicker links within Wales and with England than had ever existed before and they were vital to agricultural development.

By the first decade of the nineteenth century the turnpike system was nearing completion (Fig 13). The through routes to Ireland in the north and south had been greatly improved, and gained in importance following the union with Ireland in 1800. Elsewhere

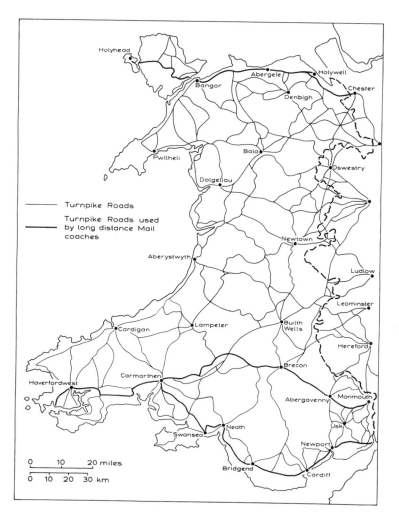

Fig 13 Turnpike roads, 1806

there was quite a good network and efficient links had been established with the major market towns on the English side of the border. The roads served not only to promote trade, but also as channels along which economic, political and social forces could penetrate and influence the countryside. Proximity to a good road meant much more than accessibility to a market; it meant a real link with conditions in lowland England. The more distant from an improved road and the more westerly the location, the more likely that a farmer would be isolated from the spirit of reform that was sweeping through Wales.

Enclosure

One of the ways in which foodstuffs could be produced in greater quantity to meet the demands of the market during the French wars was by enclosing the open fields and waste. By the eighteenth century the manorial system that had been established in the lowland areas of Norman domination had long broken down. The majority of the open fields had been enclosed and compact farms had emerged. Where open-field systems still survived, the opportunity was now taken to consolidate the strips of each individual into conventional holdings either by act of Parliament or by private agreement. But the process was relatively limited when compared either with the contemporaneous enclosure of arable fields in the English Midlands, where for example in the county of Northampton common fields covering over 50 per cent of the area were enclosed by act, and in the counties of Bedfordshire, Huntingdonshire, Oxfordshire and Rutland where over 45 per cent of the area was affected, or indeed with the enclosure of moorland and waste that was underway elsewhere in Wales.

In those parts of Wales where native society had prevailed, namely, in the uplands and over most of the western areas of the country where pastoral farming was pursued, the enclosure movement was much more pronounced, and took a somewhat different form. While the wartime inflation had not caused the price of meat and wool to rise as sharply as that of grain, prices still rose well above pre-war levels, and there was also great pressure of population upon the land. Through the eighteenth century population growth in many rural parts of Wales was as great as that in the embryonic industrial regions of the coalfields. The old system of transhumance was already in decline and consequently there had been a considerable amount of encroachment upon the upland common land. The *hafod, lluest* or summer residence, was increasingly occupied the whole year round, often by a branch of the family in the valley that previously depastured its stock in that area; the larger proprietors had extended their estates by pushing their upper boundary fences further into the moorland; and squatters had carved illegal small holdings for themselves in isolated patches away from the other enclosed land. The squatter settlement was often the result of the *ty-unnos* (one night house) tradition, common in Celtic countries, in which it was popularly believed, quite mistakenly, that if a cottage could be erected on the common in one night, so that smoke issued from the chimney by sunrise, then the builder had a legal right to the dwelling and to the land within one axe-throw in every direction. The size of some of the illegal intakes might suggest that there were more than a few prodigiously athletic axe-throwers in Wales at this period! None the less, the practice seems to have been fairly widely tolerated; other farmers and landowners were also benefiting from encroachment on the common, and to allow small patches of land to the poor at least reduced the burden upon the parish.

It had been possible since the beginning of the eighteenth century to bring about the enclosure of waste by private act of Parliament. The first act relating to Wales dates from 1733. Very few more had been passed before the outbreak of war in 1793, and those mostly related to areas in the border country. But during the wartime period there was a massive transfer of land from common to private ownership. Between 1793 and 1815, 76 acts were introduced covering some 200,000 acres (80,950 ha), and accounting for roughly one-eighth of the land then lying in common or waste (Fig 14). Parliamentary enclosure brought about not only a major redistribution of land in Wales, but also wrought important changes in the rural landscape of the areas it affected, and led to a reorganisation of the farming system.

Before an enclosure bill could be placed before Parliament the consent of the owners of roughly three-quarters of the parish acreage was necessary. Where an estate owned much of the land, as was often the case by this date, the approval of an enclosure act was a formality in a Parliament composed largely of landowners. Once agreed, commissioners named in the act began the work of apportioning the common among those who could prove rights. Survey skills as well as some legal knowledge were necessary and consequently the commissioners were often the stewards of the larger estates. There is no substantial evidence that in Wales the commissioners made unjust awards, but they did tend to favour the larger landowners, and especially the lord of the manor, where claims were unproved, and to be somewhat harsh on submissions to them that were based upon customary rights rather than legal title. Squatters

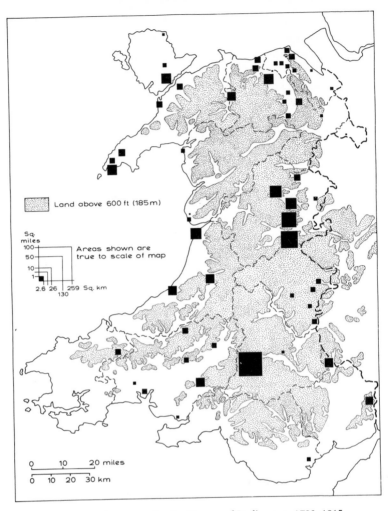

Land above 600 ft (185m)

Sq. miles
100
50
10
1
2.6 26 259 Sq. km
130

Areas shown are true to scale of map

0   10   20 miles
0 10 20 30 km

Fig 14 Enclosures authorised by act of Parliament, 1793–1815

were acknowledged to have rights of ownership only if they had been in occupation of their holdings for twenty-one years, otherwise their land was apportioned as if it were common. An appeal to Quarter Sessions against the terms of an award was possible, but carried little hope of success. The moorlands had been the centres of ownership disputes for many years and local opposition was sometimes intense. Feelings ran so high in Llanddeiniolen, Caernarfonshire in 1809, and on Mynydd Bach, Cardiganshire in 1812 that riot-

96

ing occurred, but such extreme reactions were rare.

In the areas of traditional native agriculture, land of three kinds was liable to enclosure: the upland moors, coastal waste and low-lying marsh and valley land. The first category appears to have dominated (Fig 14). Easily the most spectacular of the awards in the uplands led to the enclosure of 40,000 acres (16,200 ha) on Fforest Fawr, Breconshire in 1808, but eleven years earlier enclosure of a comparable area of Montgomeryshire had been sanctioned by two acts. Whatever the scale of the enclosure, the commissioners tended to create road, field and farm boundaries that were as straight as possible, consistent with the land surface, though it is true that new fields and farms were not made as rectangular as they were in less rugged and dissected country. Nevertheless, the newly enclosed areas of large rectilinear fields and farms, and straight enclosure roads (later often mistakenly attributed to the Romans) at the highest elevations provided a sharp contrast with the irregular patchwork of small fields and farms, and twisting lanes of the areas of older enclosure on slightly lower land. Before parliamentary enclosure the moorland edge lay at an elevation of approximately 1000ft (300m). This line, dividing two very distinct landscapes of quite different dates and modes of origin, still persists as a sharp and discernible boundary in most parts of upland Wales today. While consolidation of holdings was always the aim of both landowners and commissioners, the obstacles to achieving this were often considerable. Some fragmented holdings were inevitable, where a landowner's farm or farms did not abut the common, but in other instances where the creation of compact ownership blocks was theoretically possible, the problems presented by the irregular moorland edge, combined with the difficulties of apportioning fairly a rugged and exposed common, seem to have proved too much for the appointed commission.

Next in importance, in terms of area involved, to the acts of Parliament which enclosed the upland moors during the French wars were those which led to the enclosure and reclamation of coastal common and waste. For example, a very considerable area of coastal dune, marsh and mud flats on Morfa Dyffryn, between Barmouth and Harlech, Merioneth, was enclosed by an act of 1810, while a few miles to the north, coastal reclamation of another kind is illustrated by the enclosure of Traeth Mawr, the tidal sands of the estuary of Afon Glaslyn, near Portmadoc. Following an act of 1807, an embankment was built across the estuary which allowed the land behind it to be enclosed and improved. Again, a certain fragmentation of holdings was inevitable and, as in the uplands, many of these detached portions eventually emerged as separate farm units. Where farming was possible, a new rectilinear agricultural landscape appeared; elsewhere on dunes or saltmarsh, land was transferred from common into private ownership, but apart from fencing little may have happened.

The number of acts which authorised the enclosure of low-lying marsh and valley land were few in number and related to very small areas, when compared with the two types already discussed. Not much lowland of any kind remained unenclosed in Wales by the turn of the eighteenth century. But one example for the wartime period may be found in an award dated 1799, following an act of eleven years earlier, for some patches of common land situated between the rivers Severn and Vyrnwy, a few miles upstream of their confluence near Llandrinio. The land was nowhere more than a few feet above normal river level — indeed, some of the area was below — and the act provided for the embanking of the two streams to prevent flooding. The areas of common were so small, and the boundaries so irregular, that while the new hedge lines were straight, the fields were generally so tiny that today it is almost impossible to distinguish these fields from the adjacent fields in the longer-enclosed areas.

Parliamentary enclosure in Wales resulted in large parts of the countryside being modified: new hedges, fences and access roads were created and new farmsteads constructed, but changes in farming practice were much more subdued than in lowland England. For example, the newly enclosed upland moors were divided by a network of fences, earth balks or dry stone walls, but often stock was depastured on the rough grassland in precisely the same way as it had been before enclosure, except that instead of being able to range freely the animals were contained within the new, large fields. Little was done to improve the quality of the grass; indeed, it was not until the present century that serious efforts were made to reclaim upland pasture. However, preventing animals from roaming unhindered did have the effect of allowing the introduction here and there of scientific breeding. The agricultural improvements which did take place at this time were concentrated mainly in the lowlands.

While enclosure was permissive of agricultural reform rather than enjoining it, it is difficult to think of examples of other events, operating over a comparable length of time, which produced such marked changes and lasting effects in the countryside as the statutory enclosure awards. Not only did they have important implications for landscape and technical change, they also had far-reaching social consequences. The enclosure movement had been given official encouragement in the sincere belief that the whole rural population would benefit, but, in fact, many suffered. Though markets in agricultural produce were buoyant, small-scale farmers and tenants often could not afford the considerable costs of enclosure or could not compete with the large-scale landowners, and so enclosure, though not a direct cause, had the effect of accelerating the drift away from the land to the growing urban–industrial regions. It also diminished the prospects of the small farmers who remained. What opportunities there had been for additional income at minimal cost were removed with the apportionment of the common land. The larger estates grew and the smallholders tended to become labourers, either in industry or in agriculture. And at the very time when increasing numbers of agricultural workers were becoming dependent upon their wages alone, essential foods were more expensive than they had ever been before. Such were the difficulties that in 1795 the justices at Speenhamland, Berkshire, devised a sliding scale of poor relief to supplement wages, based upon the price of bread and the size of the family, a scheme that quickly became used throughout southern Britain. But these difficulties were minor compared with the acute agricultural depression that followed the wars in 1815 and persisted to mid century, when agricultural markets virtually collapsed. Gaols filled with debtors, many farmers were forced to sell up their holdings and more than a few rural banks failed.

Agricultural reform

The second aspect of note in the period of rapid change which coincided with the French wars was the introduction to Wales of the agricultural improvements already well-established in the English lowlands. The agents of change were the 'spirited proprietors', great landowners who by example and encouragement, and often by the means of agricultural societies in which progressive owners and tenants could exchange information on new farming methods, gave

99

the lead within their districts. The Brecknockshire Agricultural Society had been founded in 1755. It was followed by that of Glamorgan in 1772, Cardiganshire in 1784, and by the end of the wars there were local or county societies in all parts of Wales. They especially encouraged the improvement of grassland, vital if the output of cattle and sheep were to be improved to any degree. Traditionally there had been a widespread slaughter of cattle in the autumn at *Calan Gaeaf*, because of the lack of winter feed, and the population had spent winter eating salted meat. Now it was possible to keep cattle alive all year and market fresh meat. Crucial to this was not only an improvement in pasture quality and breeding stock, but also a revision of the crop rotations of the arable areas. Norfolk husbandry had shown that by growing wheat, turnips, barley and clover in succession, fallow years could be eliminated from the rotations and the productivity of land maintained, quite unlike the Welsh system in which grain was produced year after year until the soil was impoverished. The societies also offered prizes for the best crops, gave awards for the planting of woodland and for superior animals, sponsored new farm machinery and explained new fertilisers and methods of drainage. All these new techniques increased output and lowered production costs, and therefore allowed farmers to maximise their profits in the wartime sellers' market.

The emphasis was upon innovation and experimentation, and the changes for the better that took place during the period became a theme for those authors who commented upon Wales at this time. Arthur Young, a prolific writer on farming matters who produced many books and pamphlets, who was an assiduous correspondent and for over thirty years edited as well as contributed copiously to the forty-six volumes of *Annals of Agriculture*, had undertaken several tours of Wales in 1767 and 1776–8. He noted with astonishment the primitive state of most of Welsh agriculture at that time. In Glamorgan in 1767, for instance, he reported that in the northwestern parts of the Vale agriculture was 'totally contrary to the most common ideas in more informed countries'. He was particularly severe on the area around Bridgend and Merthyr Mawr, where there was much suitable light land, but no turnips grown, apart from those of an English farmer who, despite his success, had no imitators. By the wartime period, Arthur Young was printing in his *Annals* many articles and replies from correspondents in Wales, large landowners and others, reporting on the changes which were

Ruined buildings and spoil associated with lead workings near Cwmystwyth, Dyfed

Port Dinorwic, Gwynedd: once a prosperous slate-exporting port, now an equally prosperous harbour for pleasure boats

taking place. For example, Thomas Johnes of Hafod, Cardigan-shire, a well-known improver and prolific correspondent, gave information among many other things on the reclamation of waste in Wales and on the rules and premiums of the recently established agricultural society for the county of Cardigan; Lord Robert Seymour described irrigation and the reaping of corn in Carmar-thenshire; and Paul Panton, of Plasgwyn, Anglesey reported on cropping practices in his county.

But as with all changes in rural Wales during the French wars, the benefits of agricultural improvements fell disproportionately to the landed gentry and to those who farmed the better land. Smaller-scale farmers with lower profit margins had less capital available for in-novation and so improved their land and stock less swiftly. It is all too easy when reading accounts such as those quoted above, or those contained in the famous Board of Agriculture reports of 1794–6 and 1810–14, which partially had as their purpose the lauding of progres-sive farmers as an encouragement to the remainder, to overstate the speed, degree and spread of the new methods. There is one detailed source of cropping that throws some light on this matter, namely, the Acreage Returns of 1801, completed by the incumbents of each parish and sent to the Home Office. Though incomplete and to some extent inaccurate, these returns reveal quite clearly that eight years after the beginning of the wars, oats was still the dominant crop in Wales. In upland regions the crop was everywhere in first place, but it achieved this position frequently in the lowlands too in the western half of Wales. In south Pembrokeshire, Gower and in the Vale of Clwyd, barley attained first rank and only in the Vale of Glamorgan, in eastern Monmouthshire and where the rivers Severn, Wye and Usk extended lowland conditions westwards, did wheat appear as the most favoured crop. The progress of turnip husbandry on a parish basis may be inferred from the ranking of turnips among the crops grown. In only one parish in south-east Monmouthshire did turnips achieve second place; in five other parishes in the same area of Monmouthshire, in three parishes in the Vale of Glamorgan (one of them near where Arthur Young had been so critical in 1767) and in one parish in the Vale of Clwyd turnips were third crop; while as a fourth crop turnips appear fairly commonly in the three areas

Lewis Merthyr colliery near Pontypridd, Mid Glamorgan: in the background are terrace houses stretching up the valley side already mentioned, but also sporadically in Gower and south Pembrokeshire, and two parishes on the north Wales coast. Interestingly, one of the few returns from the uplands to place turnips as high as fourth rank was from the parochial chapel of Ysbyty Cynfyn, a few miles from the house of Thomas Johnes, and possibly including at least part of his estate. The strong supposition must be that those parishes with relatively high acreages of turnips among

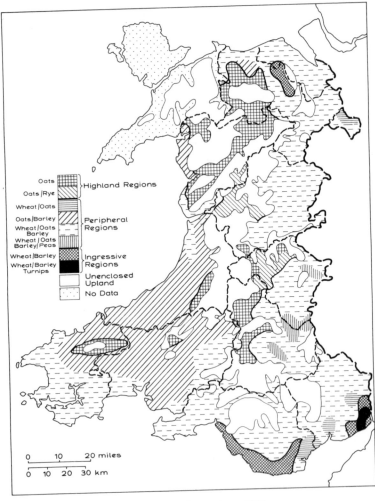

Fig 15 Cropping regions, 1801

their crops would include some turnip husbandry and therefore, given the thinking of the time, be in the van of agrarian reform.

Fig 15 is an attempt to summarise the distribution of crops in Wales in 1801 by identifying, with the aid of a statistical procedure, those associations of crops for every parish which might be considered typical or dominant. Crop combinations will clearly provide grounds for speculation about contemporary rotational practices throughout the country, except in Anglesey and Caernarfonshire for which the returns are not extant. As might be expected, parishes which concentrated on oats alone or oats and rye in combination (both hardy crops suited to a cool, wet environment) fringed the upland moors and were particularly prominent in the west. In a previous study these areas have been termed the Highland Regions. While cropland in these areas was small in acreage, compared with land under pasture, it is fairly clear that little had happened to change traditional cropping practices. Surrounding these regions in Fig 15 are parishes which are typified by combinations of crops characteristic of neither completely upland nor lowland areas, containing both crops like oats, usually found in the uplands, as well as dominantly lowland crops like wheat or peas. They have been termed Peripheral Regions. It is notable that while various crop combinations, including wheat and oats, occupy the areas to the east of the Welsh massif, it is oats and barley that are typical of the land to the west; the use of wheat as the major bread corn was a fashion that had spread extremely slowly from lowland England. Finally, there are two crop combinations which are composed of crops wholly typical of lowland areas: wheat, barley and turnips. These cover the Vales of Glamorgan and Clwyd and south-east Monmouthshire. The complete absence of the poorer grains and the frequent third and fourth ranking of turnips suggest strongly that an ingressive element existed, hence the term Ingressive Regions. But the four parishes in Monmouthshire and one in Glamorgan which are classified with a wheat–barley–turnips combination provide more than mere suggestion of the progress, however limited, of the favoured cropping patterns of lowland England.

Rural discontent

It has been suggested that for all but the rich, rural Wales was a land of social misery in the first half of the nineteenth century. Certainly the period from the end of the French wars to 1850 was one of acute agricultural depression for lowlands and uplands alike, relieved only infrequently by short interludes when markets showed signs of recovery. Rents continued to be high though agricultural commodities commanded far lower prices; there was widespread unemployment in the industrial areas with the removal of wartime demands which both reduced the sales of food and encouraged many industrial workers to return to the countryside from whence they had so recently come; new machinery was displacing agricultural workers; taxes remained high in order to pay for wartime debts; all factors led to a prevailing sense of insecurity and resentment. The gentry was by now largely anglicised and Anglican, while the remainder of the rural population was poor, increasingly nonconformist and Welsh-speaking. It was an almost classic recipe for class conflict between squire and peasant based upon deeply felt differences in wealth, language, culture, religion and politics. The longer the depression lasted, the worse matters became. In order to make ends meet, lowland farmers transferred from arable to pastoral activities and almost all neglected their hedging, ditching and liming in order that they might reduce their labour force. More and more of the landless needed aid from the parish.

Then came two critical decisions of the Westminster government. The first was a Poor Law Act of 1834, which imposed a much harsher code upon the able-bodied pauper. Outdoor relief to the poor ceased, parishes were grouped into unions with Boards of Guardians whose task it was to supervise the building and operation of workhouses, and the conditions of those who sought relief in the workhouses were deliberately made worse than those of the poorest employed labourers outside. Wales as a whole was outraged and its new nonconformist conscience pricked. Following quickly upon what were widely regarded as unjust measures, came the second government decision. In 1836 it was resolved to enforce a compulsory commutation of tithes, originally paid to the established church but by this time often in lay hands. The strength of nonconformity made tithes a vexed question; at a period of depression and cash shortage, to remove the option of payment in kind and insist upon money settlement caused a furious reaction.

While payments to the poor were reduced by roughly one-half, the tithe charge increased by 7 per cent. Almost anything that seemed to be an unjustifiable levy or tax upon rural activities was deeply resented as discontent smouldered. When serious civil unrest finally occurred in the period 1839–43, it was not surprising that it should have been directed mainly against the tollgates of the turnpike roads, the most visible and irritating of the sources of dissatisfaction though, as has been made clear above, certainly not its only cause. Imagine the annoyance of the farmer in a period of bad harvests and low yields, taking goods to a market in which he knew prices would be low, to find that on the way he had to stop several times to pay excessive tolls. Charges upon the movement of lime were particularly resented in the uplands. Some towns, such as Carmarthen, were ringed with tollgates, and almost like besieged cities. In January of 1839 the new workhouse in Narberth had been burned and this was followed in May by the destruction of a tollgate on the Carmarthenshire–Pembrokeshire border. Within a few weeks the same gate was destroyed again, despite the specially sworn constables who were driven off by a crowd of up to four hundred people dressed in women's clothes. The leader was addressed as 'Becca', and the Rebecca Riots were underway — for was it not written in the book of Genesis, 'And they blessed Rebecca and said unto her, let thy seed possess the gates of those which hate them'? One more gate was destroyed and then the riots ended as suddenly as they had begun.

No further disturbances of this kind occurred for three and a half years, then without warning they broke out again, this time with greater violence and of greater duration, beginning in the winter of 1842 and lasting through the following year. Each group, large or small, had its Rebecca who, with her daughters, underwent the ritual of deciding whether the gate was necessary, and if not, what should be done with it. The conclusions were always the same. The rioting spread through Carmarthenshire and Pembrokeshire, into south Cardiganshire and west Glamorgan, and towards the end even into parts of Radnorshire. Special constables, London policemen and large detachments of troops failed to stem the destruction. Indeed there was widespread sympathy for the rough justice and redress of grievances administered by Rebecca: she even received a good press in the London *Times*. But by the late summer of 1843 matters were getting out of hand; sympathy was lost as a result of the death of an aged female gatekeeper, two active Rebeccas were at last captured and convicted, and the work of Rebecca seemed naturally to come to an end.

The Rebecca Riots have now passed into Welsh mythology, and the many Rebeccas have jointly achieved in south-west Wales the notoriety of Robin Hood. Largely as a result of the fear of recurring violence, but also because of the publicity afforded by *The Times*, a commission was established in 1843 to explore the causes of the riots. This certainly drew attention to the plight of the rural poor and also led to the removal of the worst features of the turnpike trusts. Many of the smaller trusts were amalgamated, debts of the older trusts were liquidated by new county road boards, tolls were simplified with payments applying to longer stretches of road, and the hated tolls on lime were reduced by half. While Rebecca had not won a total victory, she had engineered a substantial advance for the smaller farmers and the landless poor. Further remission was to come in the 1850s and 1860s, with improving economic conditions and with the penetration of the railway system into rural areas, which allowed Welsh farmers for the first time direct and swift access to the markets. It meant that those involved in pastoral farming need no longer market beef, cheese and mutton alone, but could now send to market more profitable fresh milk, a product which experienced little competition from the growing imports of meat and cheese originating in the Americas and the Empire. However, such were the problems of geographical isolation and small-scale working in an unfriendly environment, that it took two world wars and substantial levels of financial support from central government and the European Economic Community before real and wide-ranging economic prosperity came to the hills and rural valleys of Wales.

CHAPTER 5

Industrialisation

In the popular view, the industrial development of Wales is the story of coal and iron, and there is much substance in this view. Certainly industrial Wales of the two coalfields, as defined in Chapter 1, was a product of the Industrial Revolution, largely during the nineteenth century, and owed its growth to the spread of mining for coal and to the rapid expansion of metal manufacture. The marks upon the landscape in the form of the urban–industrial agglomerations of north and south Wales are there for all to see, and it is plain that this industrialisation has contributed substantially to the present character of the Welsh population and society. However, in order to gain a complete picture of Welsh industry, a longer time perspective and a broader approach is needed.

Early industry

As already seen in Chapter 4, one important industry developed at an early time and in a rural setting. Though woollen manufacture had originally been located in the small industrial towns of south Wales, the industry reached its peak in the late eighteenth century near the sources of its raw material in the counties of mid and north Wales. In Montgomeryshire particularly, in Llanidloes, Machynlleth, Newtown and elsewhere, it became a factory industry, though manufacturing never approached the production of some English districts. Ironically, the industry went into decline during the period of coalfield industrialisation, for it could not compete with the greater mechanisation and scale of its competitors in Lancashire and Yorkshire. Other industries, stemming directly from the land of Wales, emerged even earlier.

Through the Middle Ages the mining of important minerals had begun in a small way. Shallow pits and drifts were used, for example, on both the northern and southern outcrops of the south Wales coalfield to recover coal for domestic and other purposes. Generally, the workings were little more than surface scratchings; the problems of flooding were formidable in the absence of a steam pump. There is, however, one record of a sizeable mine at Llansamlet, Glamorgan before 1400, where miners worked underground by candlelight and with primitive tools, the coal being hoisted to the surface by hand. Iron smelters were also at work in the coalfield at an early date. Their ironstone was derived from the coal measures and from the Carboniferous limestone fringing the coalfields, while their furnaces and forges were fuelled by charcoal obtained from the ample forest cover, especially of the south Wales coalfield. The limestone was also used for agricultural lime. In other parts of Wales there are early records of lead mining, particularly for the north-east of the country and also for Cardiganshire and north Carmarthenshire. Usually the extractive industries were small scale and widely scattered. Their location was more often than not the result of chance discovery.

After the Acts of Union (1536–43), with a unified legal system and more settled conditions, there was greater incentive for local industrial development and for investment by English prospectors and metal manufacturers. One of the attractions for English industrialists was the abundant timber which provided charcoal for smelting, and after restrictions were placed upon the use of Wealden forests, a number of Sussex ironmasters moved to Wales. The sixteenth century therefore witnessed a swift expansion in the mining of all available minerals.

The mining of coal increased sharply at this period as its usefulness as a fuel became more widely recognised. It was used now not only for domestic heating and cooking, but increasingly for the smelting of non-ferrous metals. Shafts of over 100ft (30m) in depth were common, and it became the practice to use timber roof supports. Techniques were limited, however, and working was confined to areas where the coal seams were near the surface. It was not until very much later that extraction could spread to the southeastern part of the north Wales field and to the centre of the south Wales field where deep mining was necessary.

Coastal trade in coal grew quickly; Neath and Swansea seem to have been the most important export ports, while Bristol, other westcountry ports and Ireland were the main destinations, though coal vessels from the south Wales ports in 1600 ranged as far as the Channel Islands and western France. It has been estimated that by the end of the seventeenth century coal comprised 90 per cent of the Welsh exports, but at the time it had few competitors. Trade in coal, principally from those areas where productive coal measures lay close to the coast as at Swansea and Neath, in turn led to early industrialisation.

Iron working also expanded swiftly after the union of England and Wales. Local enterprise was augmented by English ironmasters and also by a number of German and Dutch metallurgists who were introduced by the crown in an attempt to improve methods of metal production; high-quality iron and brass were always in demand for ordnance. Mining and furnaces were widely dispersed through Wales, but with time came to be concentrated on or near the coal-fields, where the major iron ore reserves were located. There was also a tendency in the eighteenth century, as the size of forges increased, for Welsh-owned undertakings to be acquired or managed by English ironmasters from Sussex, the Forest of Dean or Shropshire (where Abraham Darby had used coke rather than char-coal to smelt iron in 1709). By the year 1800, the beginnings of the major iron-working regions in south Wales were already in existence at Llanelli, in the Swansea–Neath area and in a narrow belt stretch-ing across the heads of the coalfield valleys from Hirwaun in the west to Blaenafon in the east and including the most important area of all, that of Cyfarthfa-Dowlais (Merthyr Tydfil), which the Homfrays and Crawshays among others were later to transform.

Copper was the most important metal to be produced in Wales until it was overtaken by iron during the eighteenth century. Copper mining had been pursued in scattered locations in the west and north-west of the country, sometimes in conjunction with lead in north Cardiganshire, but always on a very restricted scale. Then in 1761 the old Roman workings of Parys Mountain near Amlwch in northern Anglesey were rediscovered, and a few years later major new finds of high-quality ore were made close by. Within a very short period Wales came to rival Cornwall as a producer of copper ore. The mines at Parys Mountain at one stage in the late eighteenth century employed well over a thousand men and were the most pro-ductive in Europe. Copper smelting, on the other hand, was never very important in Anglesey, which was far from a coalfield, though small smelters in the port of Amlwch were sustained by coal imported on returning ore ships. At first, most of the ore was smelted in Cornwall, but after the mid 1780s and the break up of the

111

Cornish domination of the industry, Neath and Swansea became the centres of copper smelting.

The output of lead, though available in workable quantities in all counties of Wales, increased mainly in the two areas in which it had been traditionally worked, Flintshire and north Cardiganshire. In north-east Wales the ore occurs in Carboniferous limestone in a narrow belt from Diserth to Wrexham, with particularly rich deposits in Halkyn Mountain from which there was easy access to the Dee ports. Silver was also produced from some of the mines. In Cardiganshire both lead and silver were found in the valleys draining westwards from the Pumlumon range, and an extensive mining region developed with many mines and ancillary buildings, some owned and operated by Flintshire companies. The size of the industry can still be gauged from the many ruins and the considerable spread of spoil heaps which still today reflect the peak of lead-mining activities in Cardiganshire in the eighteenth century. The area is rugged, and even now remote, so the problems of transport of a heavy commodity were formidable. At first, Cardiganshire ore was sent to Neath and Swansea, later to Flintshire for smelting and marketing.

The slate industry of north-west Wales also responded to the more favourable economic conditions which prevailed after the Acts of Union. Like the copper industry, and in broadly the same area, slate working had been pursued by individuals or small groups up to the 1780s. Even so it had important domestic markets in England and Ireland. As early as 1688 over one million slates had been exported. Then in 1782, Richard Pennant, who had earlier succeeded to the Penrhyn estates at Bethesda, decided to reorganise the industry by buying out the leases of the small undertakings, injecting capital and working the quarries on a much more extensive scale. His example was followed at the Dinorwic quarry at Llanberis, and later at Nantlle and in Blaenau Ffestiniog, Merionethshire, where mining was common. Within ten years Caernarfonshire alone was producing 60 per cent of Britain's slate, over half of it at that time from Bethesda. At other, less important, areas of production, around Corris in southern Merionethshire, Corwen on the Merionethshire–Denbighshire border and in the district of Maenclochog in northern Pembrokeshire, development was later and less intense. The weight and bulk of the product led quickly to improvements in the transport links between extractive site and port. Initially new roads were constructed or old roads resurfaced, then among the first tramways to be built in Wales linked Bethesda with Port Penrhyn, Llanberis with Port Dinorwic, Nantlle with Caernarfon and Blaenau Ffestiniog with Portmadoc.

On the eve of the Industrial Revolution, therefore, there was a general spread of small manufacturing and extractive establishments through Wales, and also the beginnings of industrial concentrations of larger and more productive industry. Most parts of the country had experienced industrialisation of one kind or another; perhaps only the counties of Brecknockshire, Radnorshire and Pembroke-shire were plainly short of an industrial base. Yet at Parys Mountain, in Snowdonia, in Cardiganshire and Montgomeryshire, and cer-tainly upon and near the two coalfields, especially in the Neath–Swansea and Merthyr Tydfil areas, industrial nodes of various kinds existed, awaiting exploitation or rejection by those who, in the late eighteenth and nineteenth centuries, possessed the capital for invest-ment and also the new technologies of the industrial age.

The Industrial Revolution

It was to be the coalfields that experienced the major developments of the Industrial Revolution, principally in the metallurgical indus-tries and in coal mining. This is not to suggest that the other indus-tries, elsewhere in Wales, declined immediately; indeed for a while some of them flourished as a result of the demands for materials and goods generated by the growing coalfield industries. But eventually, and largely as a consequence of the competitive pressures of other producers, the non-coalfield industries withered. Lead, copper and silver extraction, though approaching exhaustion, ceased produc-tion because new, larger and more economic deposits became avail-able overseas in the nineteenth century. The smelters in the Swansea area continued to produce using this cheaper imported ore. Though woollen mills prospered for a while — flannel was particularly favoured by the coal miners of south Wales — they could not with-stand the greater scale and the cheaper cotton materials of the north of England, but a few woollen mills, some still water-powered, have survived in rural Wales until today. Slate mining and quarrying is also still pursued, though the bulk of the industry closed about the date of World War I, when cheaper substitutes for almost all slate's uses were evolved.

The expansion of economic activity upon the coalfields was the result of two main factors, both of which rewarded coalfield locations by reducing the production costs, and consequently increasing the profits, of those enterprises sited close to coal supplies. The first was a benefit which stemmed from the work of Abraham Darby, in 1709, in Coalbrookdale, Shropshire, where he developed a process in which coking coal was used to smelt iron in place of charcoal. About forty years later his son improved the technique and made good pig iron in quantity, again using coal and coke. Soon after 1750, these ideas spread to south Wales. John Guest, an ironmaster of Broseley, set up a coke-burning furnace at Dowlais, while in 1789 John Wilkinson of Stafford was using coke for the same purpose at Bersham, near Wrexham, in north Wales. Within a few decades the charcoal-burning furnaces had become uneconomic and obsolete. The iron works which lay off the coalfields were closed, and new furnaces were concentrated near the coal measures, particularly on the north-east outcrop of the south Wales field. No longer did the iron industry need supplies of timber; now it sought as a priority easily won coal from shallow levels suitable for coking, together with the iron ore supplies which were present in the blackband and clayband deposits of the coal measures. Both these requirements were amply satisfied in the narrow east–west coal measure depression at the heads of the south Wales coalfield valleys running from Hirwaun through Merthyr Tydfil to Blaenafon (Fig 16). In addition, this slender belt of development was fringed to the north by an outcrop of Carboniferous limestone which provided the flux needed in the furnaces.

The second factor which encouraged a concentration of heavy industry upon the coalfields was the development and use of steam power. Boulton and Watt produced a steam engine which Watt began to supply commercially in 1775. Though by 1800 it is thought that there were only six steam engines in south Wales and two in the north, they came into general use very quickly thereafter. They were widely employed in pumping water out of coal and iron mines, thus allowing deposits at greater depth to be worked; they were a means of crushing iron ore before it was introduced into the smelter; but most important, steam engines could be used to create the blast needed to raise the temperature in the furnaces. After 1828 a hot blast was introduced which reduced the need for coking. In all these ways the steam engines quickly improved output and efficiency and,

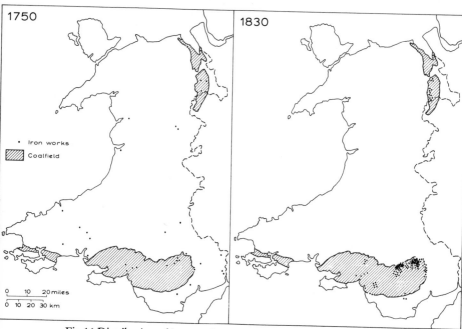

Fig 16 Distribution of iron works, 1750 and 1830 *(after Carter)*

since they were fuelled by coal, tied industry even more closely to its coalfield locations.

At first, the Welsh coalfields were receivers of technology and expertise. In the Merthyr Tydfil area, for example, in the wake of John Guest at Dowlais, came Bacon and Brownrigg from the north-west of England to found the Cyfarthfa Works, later bought by Richard Crawshay, a Yorkshireman. They also established the Plymouth Works. The Homfrays, like Guest from Broseley in Shropshire, built the Penydarren Works. Thus the four world-famous iron works at Merthyr were either established by, or expanded as a consequence of the efforts of, English ironmasters. But once these coalfield regions became established, and the demands of the French wars did much to achieve this, a momentum was created and they in turn became centres of innovation.

The Cort process greatly stimulated the iron industry of south Wales. In the 1780s Henry Cort, at his iron works in Hampshire, perfected a method in which pig iron could be refined and bars produced by use of a reverberatory furnace and rollers. It may be that Peter Onions at Merthyr Tydfil had developed the same system at about the same time — there was certainly controversy and litigation over the patent. However, the process was so widely adopted in south Wales by 1790 that it became known as 'the Welsh method'. Its advantage was that it improved the quantity, economy and the speed of pig iron production and led south Wales to the point where during the French wars it was producing roughly one-third of British pig iron. The success generated further research and experimentation. For example, Homfray in south Wales devised an iron floor for his furnace and improved methods of producing a blast; John Wilkinson at Bersham developed a new means of cylinder boring, and so was not only able to manufacture cannon with greater accuracy, but also able to contribute to the improvement of the Boulton and Watt steam engine. But perhaps the most far reaching of the early discoveries was a method of using anthracite coal in smelting iron ore. In south Wales, little industrial development had taken place west of the Vale of Neath, other than at Swansea and Llanelli, because along roughly that line the steam and bituminous coals of the eastern coalfield give way to anthracite and semi-anthracite types, coals which burn to an ash and therefore do not produce good metallurgical coke. After 1837, as a result of experimentation at the Ynyscedwyn iron works near Ystalyfera by George Crane, the owner, and David Thomas, his manager, the iron industry could spread into the western section of the coalfield, where the Amman and Gwendraeth valleys were industrialised. Two years after the discovery of the smelting process, Thomas was persuaded to emigrate to the anthracite fields of Pennsylvania to build and supervise furnaces there. He was followed by a very large number of Welsh iron workers, coal miners and rural folk. By the end of the nineteenth century, roughly half the Welsh-born population of the United States was in Pennsylvania.

By mid century, the coalfields had become important and prosperous industrial regions. A short period of depression and readjustment had followed the end of the wars in 1815, but recovery had been swift. In the north Wales coalfield industrialisation was on a smaller scale than in the south, but there was also greater diversification as a result of the smelting of lead, copper and zinc, and the development of a chemicals industry. In south Wales, particularly in the north-eastern part of the coalfield, the concentration was upon iron production, but further west in the Swansea area the traditional working of copper and other metals, including tin, yielded a

116

more varied industrial base: a number of different metal industries, galvanised- and tinned-iron production and also some chemical plants arose as a byproduct of metal manufacture.

The days of uninterrupted boom were to be strictly limited, however, and industrial patterns which might have seemed immutable gradually changed. The iron industry, and especially that on the north-east outcrop of the south Wales field, soon began to suffer from the exhaustion of local ironstone and certainly from the increasing cost of its extraction. After 1856, when the Bessemer process was introduced, the difficulties increased. The Bessemer converter reduced the time taken in production and greatly improved the quality of steel, which henceforth could be manufactured sufficiently easily and cheaply to come into general use for constructional purposes. But this and other new processes required ore free from impurities, and especially from the phosphoric impurities of the south Wales ironstone. Not only had the iron works of the northern outcrop to withstand the costs of remodelling the plant, they also had to bear the additional costs of imported ore, transported from the coast to an inland location and up a considerable gradient. Economics dictated that, when newer and larger steel plants were being established in the second half of the century, they should be located on the seaboard, at Newport, Cardiff, Port Talbot, Swansea and Llanelli. In north Wales a similar migration was to take place towards the ports. Of the non-ferrous metal industries, tin continued to prosper with the expansion of the tinplate section of the iron industry, but the remainder suffered badly after mid century from the exhaustion of British ores and also from overseas competition.

The full industrialisation of north and south Wales could not have occurred without, first, the development of the transport network and, secondly, considerable technical advances in the coal mining industry. Both transport and coal began to develop as servants of the Industrial Revolution; both acquired roles in the course of time which allow them to be regarded as separate industries.

Communication systems

Even after the advent of the turnpikes, the condition of the roads in rural Wales was quite unsuitable for the needs of growing industrial regions (see Chapter 4). Road surfaces were inadequate for the transport of heavy goods and the network was often totally insufficient especially in the south Wales coalfield which before industrialisation had been a poor and remote rural upland (Fig 13, see page 93). Packhorses and horse-drawn wagons had made heavy work of the roads in the earliest phases of industrial development. It was natural as industrial output increased that attention should turn to the use of navigable waterways, and to the construction of canals and tramways. These tended to focus upon the ports because the movement of bulky commodities by sea, whether raw materials or finished goods, was far easier and cheaper than by land, and to some degree the facilities and the tradition of coastal trade already existed (Fig 17).

River navigation from the sea inland increased considerably in the eighteenth and nineteenth centuries, for example, from Conwy to Trefriw along the river Conwy, and as far as Derwenlas along the river Dyfi from its estuary. But few of the navigable rivers served industrial areas or regions rich in minerals, and important extensions to port hinterlands were usually made by the building of canals and tramways. Canals at first were designed to bypass difficult stretches in otherwise navigable rivers, such as in the lower reaches of the rivers Dee and Nedd. Later major port-feeder canals were built direct to, or as near as practicable to, the industrial areas. In north Wales, most of the schemes came to nothing, though Llangollen was linked to the English canal network by the Ellesmere canal, for which Telford designed two spectacular aqueducts at Froncysylltau and Chirk to carry the canal over major river valleys. In south Wales, however, several important canals were driven into the coalfield between 1790 and 1800. In the east, the Monmouthshire canal ran from Newport to Crumlin and Pontypool. The Pontypool branch was eventually extended to Brecon. From Cardiff the Glamorganshire canal ran inland to Merthyr Tydfil, with a branch to Aberdare. The Neath canal penetrated to the northern rim of the coalfield, little short of the Hirwaun iron works, while the Swansea canal served the iron manufacturers at the head of the Tawe valley.

The canal system was supplemented by the tramways, in which horse-drawn trucks travelled on wooden or iron rails. Many of the early metal works in Wales were at high altitude in order to be close

Treforest Industrial Estate, Mid Glamorgan: a government-sponsored development of the 1930s

Old but sound terrace housing, originally built for coal and iron workers at Dowlais, Mid Glamorgan: note the coal and ironstone workings at the end of the street

Llanwern Steelworks, Gwent: one of a number of new steelworks on the coast of south Wales

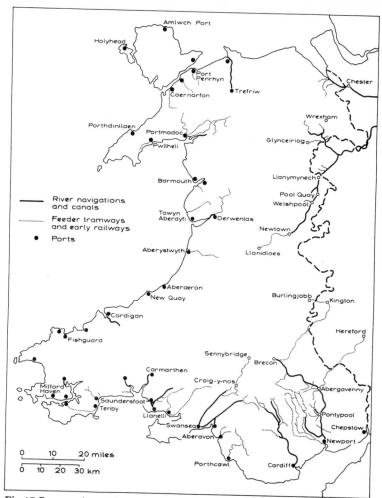

Fig 17 Ports and port-feeders of the pre-railway and early railway age *(after Moyes)*

to their supplies of raw materials. Tramways were built connecting these with their nearest canal. The system was efficient because heavy loads were drawn downhill to the canal while the horses were left with the empty trucks for the return uphill journey. None of the major canals of south Wales was without its feeder tramways (Fig 17). Elsewhere, tramways or mineral lines ran direct to the ports. A number of these tramways were the precursors of the narrow-gauge tourist railways of today. It was a natural progression that the power of the steam engine should be applied to the tramway. A taste of things to come was given in 1804 when, on a tramway constructed by Samuel Homfray to connect his iron works at Penydarren with the Glamorganshire canal at Quakers' Yard, Richard Trevithick successfully ran his steam locomotive drawing ten tons of iron and seventy people, possibly the first steam engine to run on rails. Trevithick demonstrated that the railways were more flexible, had a greater capacity and were certainly swifter as transporters of goods and passengers than the canals. The event heralded the end of the canal as an important mode of communication and the dawn of the railway age.

It is difficult to ascribe a precise date to the start of the railway age, because the improvements in track, steam locomotion, speed and payload though swift, did not happen overnight, but by the 1830s the mineral lines were being actively extended and new track was being laid, often to duplicate the less efficient canal system which continued in operation for some time. The lines were frequently associated with new dock schemes. For example, an early line which spawned a host of imitators was the Taff Vale Railway, which was incorporated in 1833 and connected Merthyr Tydfil with the Marquis of Bute's new docks in Cardiff. The formerly unconnected mineral railways soon linked together to form regional systems as the ambitions of the rail promoters expanded. It was but one step further to open up through routes as part of a national strategic network. While the hub of the national rail system was London, the importance of traffic with Ireland ensured that major strategic lines would pass through Wales. Though Telford had greatly improved the London–Holyhead road, it still took over 28 hours for mail coaches to travel the 270 miles (435 km). The Chester–Holyhead rail link therefore assumed great importance. It was opened throughout its length in 1850. It hugged the north Wales coastline through Prestatyn and Conwy to Bangor, overcoming some considerable engineering difficulties, then crossed the Menai Strait by the Britannia Tubular Bridge constructed by Robert Stephenson a little to the south-west of the suspension bridge which carried Telford's road into Anglesey. There was less incentive to complete a rail link with Ireland along the south Wales lowlands, since the destination could only be a largely rural southern section of Ireland. However, Brunel had engineered a broad-gauge line from Chepstow to Cardiff, Swansea and Carmarthen, which was linked to the Great Western

Railway and thence to London in 1852 by the construction of a bridge at Chepstow. A westward extension to Haverfordwest came two years later where the line was diverted to Neyland, on Milford Haven, which Brunel had, under financial pressure, chosen as a steamship terminus for connections to Waterford and Cork. A third line reached the west coast of Wales in 1864 when the mid Wales railway connected Shrewsbury with Aberystwyth. While the earlier mineral lines had radiated from interior resources and industrial bases outwards to the coast, the new main lines were orientated east–west, a fact which was later to have some very important consequences.

A number of other through routes were planned, but for technical or financial reasons never completed. Perhaps the best known, certainly the most dramatic, was the Manchester–Milford railway through central Wales. Its intention was to provide the industries of Lancashire with an alternative port that would rival Liverpool and Southampton. The scheme had been outlined as early as 1845 and sections of the line were built or engineered connecting Llangurig with Llanidloes and Newtown, and then by existing lines to south Lancashire, and southwards from Strata Florida to Carmarthen. But the Manchester & Milford Company failed to span the very difficult Llangurig–Strata Florida section and by an act of 1865 the southern limb was diverted through Ystrad Meurig north-westwards to Aberystwyth.

A third phase of railway development saw the completion of the Welsh network. From 1860 onwards sinuous railways, often single track and following the river valleys where possible into the upland areas, sought to interconnect the major east–west through routes and to compete with rival companies. For example, the London & North Western Railway built its line from Craven Arms, south of Shrewsbury, through Radnorshire to join a line already in existence from Llanelli to Llandovery. Such rail links served, though only incidentally, the rural settlements through which they passed and their very existence was to a large extent fortuitous, a result of the varying success, technical and financial, with which individual competing companies pursued the expansion of their existing systems. The junctions between feeder lines, and between feeders and main lines, were often made in very sparsely populated areas. This is why so many rail junctions in Wales until relatively recently were located not in settlements, but in the deepest countryside, as for instance at

Dovey Junction near Machynlleth. At the same time, and on firmer financial grounds, the coalfield railways were interconnected and sometimes duplicated. One of the earliest, and in the view of many the least typical, was the breathtaking line from Pontypool through Aberdare to Neath, planned in 1846 as an attempt to intercept the trade of the valleys of the south Wales coalfield for distribution over the inland rail system, rather than allowing it to reach the ports. Somewhat similar, though later and less spectacular, was the Abergavenny–Merthyr Tydfil branch line which employed the trackbeds of some earlier tramways. The expansion of coal mining for export in the second half of the nineteenth century greatly encouraged rail developments on the coalfields, particularly in south Wales where intense competition grew up between the various ports for the trade.

While the railways grew to serve the industrial areas of north and south Wales, which could not have expanded fully without them, the completion of the network elsewhere, and the development of the long-distance main lines had important effects. First, because the main lines terminated at Paddington and Euston stations in London, the railways became the means of denuding Wales of both materials and population. Secondly, and the mountain core of Wales is itself partly responsible for this, the Welsh railway system developed no focus within the country. Until Cardiff became the capital city in 1955, and to some degree afterwards, many appointments to major posts in Wales were made in the Great Western Hotel at Paddington, the building that some irreverent wags have claimed to be its only natural capital. Thirdly, the rail system eventually allowed the urbanised industrial population of the coalfield to seek recreation at the seaside, once the playground exclusively of the rich. Barry and Porthcawl in the south, for example, both coal export ports, could be reached easily by passenger train and from the 1880s began to develop as resorts for day trips and longer visits. Soon Tenby and Aberystwyth came within range. In north Wales, Rhyl, Colwyn Bay and Llandudno served the industrial population of the northern coalfield, but they also, because of their proximity to Merseyside and south Lancashire, drew visitors from across the border.

It was not until the period between the wars, by which time county councils had assumed responsibility for, and had begun to improve, the road system, that motorised transport began slowly at first, but later with increasing speed, to displace railways as the major carriers of goods and passengers in Wales.

The mining of coal

Like the canals and railways, coal mining had been essential to the industrialisation of the Welsh coalfields and was equally susceptible to technical change. While the output of the metal industries was relatively low and the demands for steam engines still small, coal mining remained in those parts of the coalfield where coal measures were exposed at or near the surface, in the western part of the north Wales field and on the north and south outcrops in the south Wales field. Here coal was mined from levels driven into the hillsides or from shallow pits. Once the steam engine had been adapted for pumping water and for hauling coal, it became possible to sink deeper mines, and the introduction of the safety lamp to Wales in 1816 made it safer to work in them. Through the first half of the nineteenth century metal manufacture expanded, the steam engine was applied to more and more purposes, and at the same time the sale of Welsh coal for domestic use began to become important. In order to increase output, coal mining moved onto the concealed fields, to the east in north Wales and to the centre of the field in the south.

It was the south Wales field that dominated as the coal industry emerged as a separate and largely independent enterprise. By 1860, output of coal in south Wales exceeded ten million tons; that figure doubled within twenty years and the coalfield reached a peak production in 1913, when fifty-seven million tons were raised, over half of it for export. Part of this expansion of output was due to the popularity of Welsh bituminous coal for home sales. In 1830, George Insole, a Cardiff coal factor, had shipped four hundred tons of coal to London, where its superiority over the smokier Newcastle coal was swiftly appreciated. It led to further sales in London and other English cities, but also to new domestic markets overseas, particularly in the early days in France. In the decade after 1840 it was the lower sections of the valleys that were favoured. There was easy access to ports and it was here, in an arc from Llantrisant to Pontypool, that the bituminous types of coal were available (Fig 18). But as the industrial uses expanded — for manufacturing machinery, for the railways and for the new steamships — demands for steam coal increased and mining moved into the centre of the coalfield. By 1860 the production of steam coal overtook that of the bituminous types and the serious exploitation of the resources of the Rhondda and

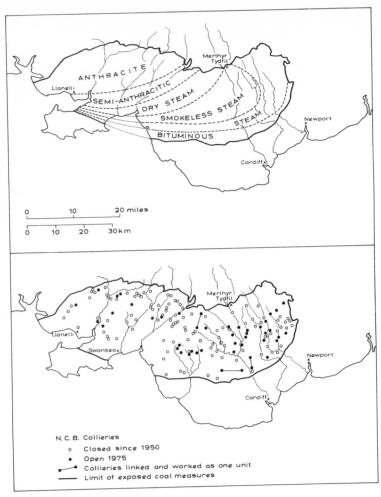

Fig 18 Coal types and National Coal Board collieries in south Wales, 1950 and 1975 *(after Humphrys)*

adjacent valleys had begun, to meet what up to World War I became an almost insatiable demand.

The development of the east-central part of the south Wales coal-field had two important and related implications. First, since the coalfield has a basin structure, it follows that the further working proceeded into the coalfield, the deeper the coal lay. Deep mining presented formidable technical problems of drilling, draining, ventilating and haulage, but these problems were not such that at the height of the Industrial Revolution, they could not be fairly readily overcome in pits of up to 2500ft (750m) in depth. In order to ease matters, shafts were sunk as close to the coal seams as possible, namely, from the valley bottoms, and also great use was made of the major east–west anticline feature (usually known as the Pontypridd anticline) which brought coal seams nearer the surface and divided the coalfield, in effect, into a northern and southern trough. Thus it is that the narrow zone running from Pontypridd to Maesteg, and crossing a number of north–south valleys, marks an important belt of production within the coalfield. The second implication of working the middle of the coalfield follows closely from the first and relates to the nature of urban–industrial expansion. Before the early part of the nineteenth century, the centre of the coalfield had been largely unoccupied. When coal mining began, it created virtually a single industry region, quite unlike the more diversified area on the north outcrop. Further, since economy dictated that not only the pitheads, but also the various modes of transport, housing and mining spoil heaps should be located on the valley floor, or as near to it as possible, mixed urban areas emerged often composed of closely juxtaposed but incompatible land uses elongated along the narrow, deeply entrenched river valleys. Further growth of housing, particularly, frequently took the form of terrace building along the valley sides; many a house in the coalfield has an additional storey on the downslope side. By this means the population of the Rhondda valley increased more than fourfold in the twenty years between the censuses of 1871 and 1891.

To the west of the Vale of Neath, where the anthracite and semi-anthracite coals were to be found, development was much slower. There had been early industrialisation and coal mining in the area around Swansea, and after 1837 some further industrial growth elsewhere using the Thomas anthracite technique, but markets for these harder and less volatile coals were limited. It was not until after 1880 that mining and export became important. Anthracite cannot effectively be burned in open fireplaces, but is very suitable for closed stoves and central heating systems. In the last two decades of the nineteenth century markets of this kind opened up in the countries fringing the Baltic and in north-west Europe.

Since World War I the coal industry of Wales has been in almost continual decline. There was a brief recovery in the middle 1920s, but by 1931 the signs were clear for all to see. Coal-fired ships were actively being replaced by oil-burning vessels; road transport was replacing that by rail; there was an industrial depression which speeded the introduction of electricity as an important source of industrial power; the coalfield itself lacked investment; and, as an early exploited field, it suffered because the richest and most accessible seams were already worked out. During World War II, almost all the export markets were lost, few to be recovered afterwards, so that by today a shrunken industry produces less than one-fifth of its peak production in 1913, with roughly one-tenth of the labour force. The largest consumers of Welsh coal today are the coke ovens of south Wales, electricity generating stations, again mostly in south Wales and a very much reduced domestic market.

Modern industrial development

It has already been shown that there was a drift of heavy industry away from the north outcrop of the south Wales coalfield towards the coast during the second half of the nineteenth century. Newport, Cardiff, Port Talbot, Swansea (of course, with a much older metallurgical tradition) and Llanelli became the new centres of iron, steel and tinplate production, port–cities into which high-quality overseas ores were imported and from which exported commodities were shipped. In north Wales, a more varied picture emerged. In addition to the metal industries, there was paper manufacture and several textile and chemical plants. While all may have seemed well for half a century, it was a dangerously undiversified industrial pattern, particularly in south Wales where there were only two major industries, metals and coal, and indeed, in the centre of the coalfield and on the north outcrop, where there was only one of consequence.

When the industrial depression occurred between the wars, Welsh industrial areas were ill prepared to meet it. The coal trade, already losing markets for technical reasons, now had to suffer also the general fall in economic activity. The metal industries were similarly, though not universally, hard hit; contraction in capital investment, and with it the need for metal goods, is the harbinger of manufacturing recession. Unemployment rates rose sharply and there was widespread distress. Population erosion from rural areas had been a feature of Welsh life for a century or more; now people began to leave the urban–industrial areas too. Between 1921 and 1931 alone, the counties of Glamorgan, Monmouth and Brecknock lost nearly a quarter of a million people. Since there were few employment opportunities in Wales, most of them moved to still expanding light industrial regions of the English Midlands and the south-east. The number of distinctly Welsh names, such as Morgan and Thomas, to be found in the telephone directories of these areas is testimony to the strength of population migration at this period (see also Appendix I). Plainly there was a need to diversify industry to broaden the economic base in order to retain workers in or near the existing industrial regions.

The Welsh industrial regions were not the only manufacturing areas in Britain to suffer. Other regions, chiefly old-established and in the north of the country, were over-reliant upon particular industries, which went into decline in the period between the wars: the cotton industry was almost exclusively based in Lancashire, the wool industry in the West Riding of Yorkshire, knitwear goods came especially from Nottingham, fine steel and cutlery from Sheffield, shipbuilding characterised Tyneside, the pottery industry dominated the small region around Stoke-on-Trent, many parts of the coalfields were solely dependent upon the extraction of coal or some other mineral, and so on. This lack of diversification meant that all were susceptible to shifts in demand as a result of general economic circumstances, to changes in technology or fashion, to cheaper sources of material in new locations and to changes in power requirements. The widespread regional imbalances in prosperity, economic potential and population migration was such that when solutions were sought to these problems, they were advanced at a country-wide scale. South Wales, of course, was one of the beneficiaries of the activities centred in Westminster.

In 1934 the Special Areas Act was passed. It designated four special areas, one in central Scotland, two in the north of England and the fourth in south Wales, covering much of the coalfield and the Vale of Glamorgan. Commissioners were appointed to promote the rehabilitation of the depressed regions, though at first the powers and financial backing given to them were quite inadequate to deal with the enormous problems faced. But so great were the needs of the older industrial areas that the initial modest provisions were boosted to create a battery of physical and fiscal controls the like of which were not to reappear in Britain until the 1960s. One means by which the commissioners were able to attract new, usually light, industry into south Wales was the establishment of an industrial trading estate at Treforest, north-west of Cardiff, operated on a non-profit-making basis (others were located in the north of England and central Scotland). More generally, the commissioners encouraged the siting of new industries in the south Wales special area by giving relief to firms prepared to locate there in respect of rent, rates or income tax; they could also waive other taxes, such as the new National Defence Tax. Finally, the commissioners were given facilities for easing the transfer of those workers who moved out of the special area to take jobs elsewhere. They instituted retraining schemes to convert labour to skills needed in the growth industries and gave grants and loans to assist in migratory moves. Undoubtedly the work of the commissioners ameliorated conditions in south Wales, and employment rates fell in the late 1930s. They were assisted also by an upturn in trade which began to revitalise the old basic industries in the years before World War II. Even so, it took the war itself to remove the worst pockets of unemployment from south Wales, while sufficient concern was still felt for the future for the government to set up a Royal Commission under the chairmanship of Sir Montague Barlow (the Barlow Commission) to explore the whole problem of the distribution of the British workforce.

South Wales underwent a transformation during World War II. The metal industries now had markets again and were worked to capacity. In addition, munition and other factories were built on or near the coalfields, partly to have them located in a relatively safe area away from mainland Europe, partly to utilise the underemployed resources of the region. London and the Midlands were regarded as vulnerable and without sufficient spare skilled labour. The small arms, explosives and aircraft component industries were largely light in nature and automated. For the first time in south Wales as a whole there were industries with considerable capacity which could absorb men disabled in the basic heavy iron and steel, tinplate and coal industries, but which could also employ female labour. Unlike Lancashire, for example, south Wales had previously few manufacturing industries in which women could be employed. These new industries not only broadened the industrial base, they also initiated important social changes, reducing considerably the outward movement of young female labour to England in search of jobs and in the long term modifying the role and status of women in Welsh society.

In industrial terms, the influence of the wartime government-directed location of strategic economic activity was far-reaching. As soon as the war was over the output of munitions and weapons ceased, but in so doing, provided manufacturing floorspace for light industry at a time when factory buildings in many other parts of Britain were in very short supply. A second consequence of the war-time period was an industrial workforce, male and female, skilled in factory operation. A third benefit was that the achievements of the war industries demonstrated without doubt that light factory industry could flourish in Wales. The fear that the unemployment levels experienced between the wars would be re-established gave point and urgency to government action to take advantage of the fresh industrial climate. All major political parties were committed to Keynesian economics at the end of the war, and though there may have been disagreement over the means by which it should be achieved, the end, full employment, was generally accepted. An important element in regional economic policy, to which the Distribution of Industry Act of 1945 gave effect, was to utilise existing factory space in Wales, and to add to it by the provision of advance factories, the creation of additional industrial estates at Bridgend, Hirwaun and Fforestfach (near Swansea), and the awarding of grants and low-interest loans to incoming industries. A new, and generously drawn, development area was designated in south Wales, covering the entire coalfield, the Vale of Glamorgan and Gower, and another development area was outlined in north Wales to assist the southern part of the coalfield which was overdependent on coal mining.

For a while the system worked well. New industries flooded into the development areas: components of the vehicle industry, electrical goods, mechanical engineering, timber and furniture, chemicals, clothing, paper and printing, and textiles among others. The years 1945–51 and 1964–75 are regarded as ones in which particular success was achieved in attracting new firms. A reorganised steel industry continued to prosper and even the coal mining industry experienced a minor resurgence following nationalisation. Government investment in new roads and motorways, and in the building of new towns first at Cwmbran in Gwent, and later at Newtown in Powys, contributed towards economic expansion. But changes in

131

political control at Westminster led to fluctuation in industrial policy. A period of economic freewheeling in the mid 1950s culminated in a minor recession in which the steel and coal industries were forced to contract. New legislation in 1958 added to the development areas, for the first time including the largely rural area of north-west Wales. This was followed in the 1960s by yet more legislation which, in a number of steps, eventually brought the whole of Wales into one or another assisted area category. The expansion of government support into rural areas has encouraged the spread of small-scale light manufacturing into the market towns of mid and west Wales, where it has provided jobs in areas in which the traditional farming activities now require less labour than hitherto. More recently, assisted area status has been removed from central Wales.

Reviewing both the minor and major fluctuations in trade cycles since 1945, the conclusion is inescapable that though now greatly more diversified than in the period between the wars, Welsh industry has still not the resilience to sustain reasonable levels of employment in the industrial regions. Over a quarter of Welsh industrial employment is in the old basic industries. A high proportion of the new industries are branch plants of multinational or English companies which have the understandable tendency to concentrate production in their major or home factories in time of recession. Accessibility to the markets of the English lowlands and of Europe is another problem. While not as important as in the heavier industries, the ease of marketing of consumer goods is an important element in factory location and much of Wales, as it has been throughout history, is not only distant, but also often perceived to be more distant than it actually is.

Ironically, perhaps still the most prosperous of the industrial regions of Wales is located in or near one of its national parks. In the late 1950s and 1960s, Milford Haven, the deep water of which had attracted once-important fishing and small ship-repair industries, and also the Royal Navy, caught the eye of international oil companies which located oil refining and terminal facilities there. It has grown to become a major oil port, to have one-quarter of Britain's oil refining capacity and to be an important source of raw materials for the petro-chemical industry. The irony lies not only in its location within an area of exceptional natural beauty, but also in the fact that for such a large series of enterprises, it employs fewer than three thousand workers in its capital-intensive plants.

The legacy of the Industrial Revolution is a set of problems which has as yet been only partially resolved. Ingenuity and technical skill, in the same measure but perhaps of a different kind from those in evidence during the period of rapid industrialisation, are still required if industrial Wales is to survive in prosperity. They are attributes that may soon be put to the test.

CHAPTER 6

The Radical Tradition

Wales before radicalism

Perhaps the most striking feature of Welsh life for the past hundred years is the radical tradition, the way the great majority of the people have been loyal to left-wing politics: the radical wing of the Liberal Party from 1868 to 1922, the Labour Party from 1922 to 1970. Yet little in the previous history of the Welsh could have led one to foresee this development. From the sixteenth to the early nineteenth centuries, Wales was a backward province of Britain playing little or no part in politics, obediently royalist in the great upheavals of the seventeenth century, passively controlled in the eighteenth by great landowners such as the Williams-Wynn baronets of Wynnstay who, because of their vast properties in mid and north Wales, were sometimes called 'Kings of Wales'. The Acts of Union had provided Wales with MPs, but they were few in number and lacked cohesion or influence. Ludlow, which might have provided a focus for the Welsh gentry, ceased to be a provincial capital when the Council of Wales and the Marches was abolished in 1689. Welsh Jacobitism there certainly was, but it lacked force or organisation and could in no way be compared with Jacobitism in Scotland. The great forces which transformed Welsh life in the eighteenth century — the Methodist Revival, the Agrarian and Industrial Revolutions, the cultural changes which might be called a Welsh Renaissance — had few immediate political repercussions during the century; they were more like slow-burning fuses leading to powder kegs hidden around the corner.

Those forces, and many others, prepared the way for an age of political awareness. A small significant middle class appeared, the standard of living of the common folk rose and contacts with English cities greatly improved during the eighteenth century. By the early years of the century a considerable book-reading public had emerged and a great programme of popular education (largely in the Welsh language) ensued in the middle of the century. The framework of a modern cultural life appeared, with new religious, educational and cultural organisations. By the last quarter of the century the middle class and some of the common people began to take an interest in politics; for example, we have some evidence of reformist views being adopted by independent Welsh craftsmen, masons, carpenters, dyers and the like, although they were all virtually excluded from the electoral struggles between the Whig and Tory gentry families.

The first clear sign of popular political discussion emerged over the American wars in the 1770s, although Welsh debate was probably prompted by discussion among London Welshmen. War taxation was unpopular; Welsh religious dissenters were inspired by the religious freedom of the American states; many Welshmen had emigrated to America during the century; and there were close commercial contacts between Welsh and American ports in this period. Even though Welshmen took considerable interest in the opening stages of the French Revolution after 1789, America still remained the more powerful influence. This was partly because at this time the Welsh imagination was stirred by the tale that America had been discovered in about 1170 by a Welsh prince Madoc, and that his companions' descendants might still be found somewhere in the mid west. The Madoc myth, and the prospect of a freer life for Welsh communities in America, persuaded a number of Welsh leaders to found communities of Welsh settlers at the end of the eighteenth century, and also helped to shape a specifically Welsh climate of political opinion in the same period.

However important that may have been, it was, like the interest in radical reform of government or society, a minority concern. The excesses of the French Revolution, especially the attacks upon Christianity in the 1790s, killed the fresh young growth of radical politics in Wales. Methodism was the most powerful religious movement which appeared during the century, and by the 1790s the Methodists had coloured the beliefs of older dissenting groups, and this meant that thinking Welshmen were persuaded to concern themselves with theology and leave politics alone (see Chapter 7). Early industrialism and the hardships of war and war taxation caused strikes and riots, but these, together with clubs and societies for political discussion, were suppressed by the British government in the 1790s. The few daring Welsh-language journals edited by radical pioneers such as Morgan John Rhys ceased publication. At the beginning of the nineteenth century, there seemed to be little political life, let alone radicalism, in Wales.

The emergence of radicalism

In the opening decades of the nineteenth century the old régime continued, with a small group of powerful nobles and squires controlling the parliamentary elections and the meetings of the Quarter Sessions, and in Wales these families were mostly strongly Tory. Reaction and hostility to reforms probably represented the political viewpoint of the majority. However, the repressive controls of the government had been relaxed even before the coming of peace in 1815 and by then there were signs of a rebirth of interest in political discussion, as for example in the new Welsh newspaper *Seren Gomer* founded in Swansea in 1814. The return of peace in itself brought great problems to Welsh industries and to Welsh farmers, and there ensued violent industrial strikes and riots (for example, in 1815 and 1819), and unprecedented poverty and distress throughout the countryside. The rapid growth in the number of religious dissenters in Wales in this period made their leaders question the privileges of the established church, and made them concerned with moral and even social questions of the day. The emergence of a vigorous Welsh-language periodical press from 1814 to 1850 was a sure sign of the growing social and political awareness of the leaders of the common people.

In the first quarter of the century, much of the debate in the press concerned theological and cultural matters, but gradually the Welsh began to discuss public questions such as temperance, sabbatarianism, the abolition of slavery, the disestablishment of the Church of England and the emancipation of the Roman Catholics. This last topic was a most delicate question since the Welsh dissenters were in favour of religious liberty but hostile to 'Papists'. The old dissenters were pioneers of political discussion, but the Methodists were opposed even to moderate electoral reforms such as those of the Great Reform Bill of 1832; the reactionary Methodist leader John Elias told Lewis Edwards that Lords Grey and Brougham were leading the country to disaster.

The overhaul of the machinery of government which was begun by the Reform Bill of 1832 was of great concern to the upper and

136

middle classes; of equal importance for the common folk were social, industrial and religious reforms. There was only a muffled cry of protest from Welsh people, for example, when in 1830 the Courts of Great Sessions, the autonomous law courts set up for Wales by the Tudor Acts of Union, were abolished. The significant changes of this period which fostered the growth of radicalism were found in the growing political awareness of the common people, caused by poverty and distress in the countryside and the increasing militancy of the workers in the rapidly growing industrial areas of Wales. Many lesser strikes and riots occurred in the 1820s but the most important came in 1830 and 1831. The Coalminers Union in the north of England influenced the outbreak of strikes in the coalfields of north-east Wales in 1830-1, but these were put in the shade by the exceptional ferocity of the widespread rioting at the great industrial centre of Merthyr Tydfil in 1831.

Industrial development was spread fairly evenly in the north, middle and south of Wales at this period, but Wales had a peculiarly lop-sided Industrial Revolution, with the rapid expansion of heavy (iron, steel) and extractive (coal mining, slate quarrying) industries, with huge labour forces brought together in raw frontier settlements in the wilds, yet with only a feeble development of the financial or commercial revolutions which might in other circumstances or countries have caused the appearance of a large middle class of resident capitalists. By the 1820s and 1830s the distribution of industry became far more uneven, with an unprecedented rush of population to the hills and valleys of Glamorgan and Monmouthshire, most of it at this point still coming from the poverty-stricken cottages of the Welsh countryside, though it later came from Ireland and England. A highly self-aware working class emerged in these industrial settlements, with little counter-balancing influence by the middle class, so that master and man seemed in Wales to be placed in exposed positions of inevitable antagonism.

The industrial population was in close contact with English working-class agitators, and it is not surprising to find that south-east Wales was one of the main centres of the attempted revolution of the Chartists in 1839, though the attack upon Newport was a fiasco. The crisis of the countryside, which stemmed from the agrarian troubles which began about 1815, came to a head from 1839 to 1843, and much of the south and west of Wales was torn in those years by the Rebecca riots (see Chapter 4). The Rebecca Riots arose and subsided mysteriously, and the ideological element in them was probably small. But, taken together with the great industrial riots, they made British governments fear the potentially seditious or revolutionary state of the Welsh.

Side by side with growing industrial and rural unrest, was the growth of semi-political debate over religion and education in the 1830s and 1840s. The Anglican church began to make strenuous efforts to fight back the rapid growth of the popular evangelical sects, Methodists in the west and north, older dissenters such as Baptists and Independents in the south and east of Wales. In the late 1830s the Anglicans were enlivened by the ritualist Oxford Movement, and from 1837 onwards they embarked on an aggressive programme of school building in Wales: this in turn caused a great reaction against them by Methodists and dissenters. The great debate over Welsh education was extremely heated and left its mark on Welsh politics for the remainder of the nineteenth century. Another legacy from this crucial period in emergent Welsh politics resulted from the fact that the centres of the Methodists and dissenters and of their extremely vociferous journals were chiefly in the countryside, not the industrial areas, so that the sufferings of the rural peasantry long remained an abiding concern of Welsh politics, often at the expense of the concerns of industrial workers.

The Treason of the Blue Books

Two great forces in Welsh life came together in the later 1840s to change the political climate: one was the concern of the British government at the rapidly deteriorating character of industrial and agrarian life in Wales; the other was the growing debate on Welsh education. In 1846 the government instituted a searching inquiry into Welsh education, morals and language teaching and, as was usual, it appeared in the form of Blue Books, in 1847, but they caused a storm of controversy and were said by their detractors to have blackened the character of the Welsh nation to such a degree that the episode has been known as 'The Treason of the Blue Books' after a Welsh political satire which compared them to the 'Treason of the Long Knives' in early Welsh history. According to the old Welsh fable, the chieftains of the ancient Britons together with their leader Vortigern, were invited to a banquet by the Anglo-Saxon leaders Hengist and Horsa. Each Briton was seated at this banquet alternately with an Anglo-Saxon warrior. At a prearranged signal the Anglo-Saxons drew their long knives, which had been concealed in their boots, and slew the Britons. As a result of this treachery the remaining Britons were forced to cede large areas of Britain to the Anglo-Saxon invaders. Hence the myth of the 'Treason of the Long Knives'. The commissioners, who were three young English Anglicans, were said to have described the nation as backward, barbaric, dirty and unchaste, and mostly blamed this situation on nonconformity and the Welsh language.

The great controversy had major political effects. The Methodists abandoned their passive and reactionary stance and joined forces with the dissenters, thereby creating a united nonconformist front and marrying the political liveliness of dissent to the genius of the Methodists for discipline and organisation. Another effect was to make the nonconformists aware of their exclusion from the political system and power structure, and hence to launch renewed campaigns to take over the electoral system. From 1847 to 1868 the nonconformists, with their powerful journals and influential popular leaders, such as William Rees 'Gwilym Hiraethog' or Thomas Gee, made a large section of the common people politically aware and gave them a coherent philosophy. However, it was a time of comparative peace and prosperity in Britain (following the 'Hungry Forties') and so in its formative years radical agitation concentrated on electoral reform, educational advance and moral improvement.

From 1844 onwards the Liberation Society (with its centre in England) urged nonconformists to campaign to abolish the established church and to remove many other disabilities. Great efforts were made to open schools and colleges and to lay the foundation of a non-sectarian Welsh university. Meanwhile, the radicals toiled tirelessly to widen the franchise and to put nonconformists into the House of Commons. In the 1850s and 1860s some Welsh radical leaders, such as Michael Daniel Jones of Bala, became so disheartened at the slow progress of radicalism and the continued harassment of the peasantry by alien landlords, that he and others organised emigration to form Welsh communities overseas in America and Canada, the most unusual of these radical emigration ventures being the establishment in 1865 of a Welsh colony in Patagonia, then in the southern frontier zone of Argentina. The vindictiveness of landowners indirectly helped the radical cause as popular orators made heroes and martyrs of those tenants who were evicted for voting for radicals in the election of 1859. The great progress that Welsh radical agitation had made by the 1860s only became clear after the Reform Act of 1867, which extended the franchise in Wales significantly, in the famous general election of 1868.

The triumph of radicalism after 1868

The Reform Act of 1867 vastly increased the number of voters in industrial towns like Merthyr Tydfil. In 1868 Merthyr elected as one of its MPs the radical leader, Henry Richard, also a nonconformist spokesman. Only a few nonconformist MPs were elected, but the real significance of 1868 was the considerable number of radicals, most of them at this time being Anglican landowners, elected in Wales after centuries of rule by Tory aristocrats. The Welsh radicals were Liberals, but are usually called radicals because they were allied to the radical wing of the party and because, in all probability, the words *radical* and *radicaliaeth* (radicalism) sounded less awkward in the Welsh-language journals than the more clumsy *rhyddfrydiaeth* (Liberalism).

The election of 1868 was considered to be the dawn of a new era in Welsh politics for it inaugurated a period lasting till 1922 when radicals sat for the great bulk (sometimes all) of the Welsh parliamentary seats. It was partly because of public revulsion against the eviction threats of Welsh Tory landlords in 1868 that the government soon afterwards brought in elections by secret ballot to stop the victimisation of tenants. In 1884 further Acts were passed to extend the franchise and to redistribute constituencies more equitably, and the radical trend of 1868 was confirmed and extended. In 1888 county councils and other local councils were set up to replace the ancient Quarter Sessions and parish vestries, and radicals came to power here again, thus signalling the end of centuries of political control by the aristocracy.

In what sense did Welsh radicalism differ from British Liberalism? In many things it did not, but a number of factors gave it a cohesion and a definite Welsh character. Its programme was distinctly nonconformist. Many bills to lift the disabilities of nonconformists, and to disestablish and disendow the Anglican church in Wales were presented in the late nineteenth century, and the bill to disestablish the church eventually became law, after years of debate, in 1914. The first piece of legislation treating Wales as a distinct country was the Act of 1881 by which public houses were closed on Sundays, a tribute to the Welsh radicals' enthusiasm for temperance and sabbatarianism. The nonconformists' zeal for education also coloured the radical programme: in 1889 the Welsh Intermediate Education Act introduced by the radicals, and forwarded by sympathetic conservatives was passed which gave Wales its own network of public secondary (or 'county') schools, and in 1893 the three university colleges which the radicals had done so much to found were joined in a national federal University of Wales.

From 1879 onwards Welsh farmers (in common with others in western Europe) suffered an acute economic crisis lasting many years, largely arising from the new competition from more economic farmers in countries such as the United States and Canada. So much of Wales consisted of marginal land that the crisis was particularly bad in these areas and embittered relationships between landlords and tenants. The radicals for many years were concerned with *Pwnc y Tir* (the Land Question), that is, the more equitable sharing of the profits of land in Wales. A typical example of radical agitation of the 1880s was the so-called Tithe War in west and north Wales, an organised refusal by tenant farmers to pay the tithes to the 'alien' Church of England.

Radicalism was also given a special tone by its sense of Welsh patriotism, its Welshness. Before the 'Treason of the Blue Books' radicals had thought little about Welshness, the most self-conscious Welsh patriots before then being Anglicans, often Anglican parsons. After 1850 Anglicans distanced themselves more from Welsh movements, and nonconformists began to claim that they represented the whole of the Welsh nation. This sense of mission came to colour the radical movement more and more in the late nineteenth century, by which time a 'radical tradition' had been created. Welsh radicalism thus did not represent a particular class, such as the bourgeoisie or working class, but virtually all the people, all Welshmen of good will being supposed to be united against the 'alien rule' of a small group of squires and clergy. The people of good will were the *Gwerin* of Wales (literally the 'folk' or 'mass of people'), and these were steadfast chapel folk whether masters or men, with all the virtues of nonconformity, added to which they had the cultivated virtues of love of education, poetry and music. Tory squires and clergy were thus excluded from the Welsh nation, although it was a Conservative

141

government which passed the 1889 Welsh Intermediate Education Act. The sense of national mission of the Welsh radicals grew to such an extent that by the 1880s and 1890s they pressed for limited forms of administrative devolution and for Home Rule.

The high point of the radical Home Rule movement was the *Cymru Fydd* (Young Wales) movement within Welsh radicalism. Already in 1886 and 1887 the radicals had formed the North and South Wales Liberal Federations, and in 1888 an English capitalist arms manufacturer Stuart Rendel, MP for Montgomeryshire, a man extremely sympathetic to Welsh aspirations, was elected chairman of the Welsh parliamentary party, that is, the radical MPs at Westminster. There was at this time a great revival of cultural nationalism which now influenced demands for Home Rule by some of the radicals led by T. E. Ellis, MP. Just as the Irish church disestablishment and Irish land laws influenced demands for similar legislation for Wales, so the Irish Home Rule bills of this period influenced Welsh radicals. But in Wales, unlike Ireland, nationalism was not popular save in the cultural field, and in 1895–6 the progress of *Cymru Fydd* was stopped in its tracks by the opposition of the great centres of power and wealth in south-eastern Wales, Newport and Cardiff. Home Rule, then, was a failure, yet it left a legacy of demands for devolution inside radicalism which caused the setting up of Welsh institutions in this period: the University (1893), the National Museum and Library (1907), and devolved government departments such as the Central Welsh Board and the Welsh National Insurance Commission.

Although there was scant interest in devolution or Home Rule after 1895 the radicals still thought of themselves as the Welsh parliamentary party up to 1914. For instance they organised the so-called Welsh Revolt from 1902 to 1906, a powerful resistance all over Wales to paying taxes to support schools, on the grounds that the 1902 Education Act of the Conservatives forced the taxpayers to support religious (mainly Catholic or Anglican) schools. The sweeping Liberal victories in Wales as elsewhere in the 1906 elections, the law disestablishing the church in Wales in 1914 and above all the meteoric rise of the Welsh radical leader David Lloyd George as Chancellor of the Exchequer and then Prime Minister, gave Welsh radicalism a brilliant glow of success in this period. As it turned out, however, this was to be a sunset glow (Fig 19).

142

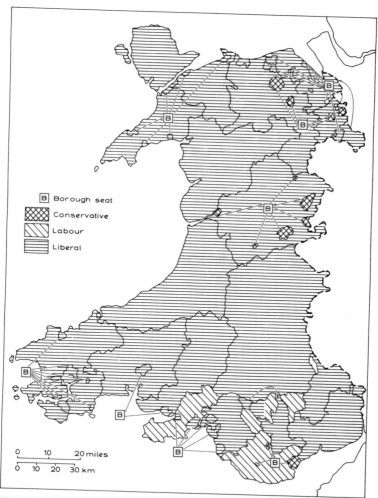

0   10   20 miles
0   10   20   30 km

Fig 19 General election result, December 1910 *(after Madgwick and Balsom, National Atlas of Wales 2.2a)*

Radicalism and the rise of Labour

Lloyd George remained Prime Minister until 1922, at the head of a coalition government, but by then the political climate in Wales as in England had greatly changed, the greatest change in Wales being the rise of the rival force of Labour. It is curious that although Wales was profoundly industrialised early in the nineteenth century, with great upheaval and violence in rural and industrial areas, the Labour movement was slow to emerge. It is true that a Welshman, Robert Owen of Newtown, invented the term 'socialism', but his great pioneering work was carried on largely outside Wales. From the 1840s to the 1890s the Welsh workers were somewhat isolated from the rest of the British working class, their interests being served vicariously by Welsh radical leaders whose tradition subsumed the middle class, workers, peasants and intellectuals under the heading of the *gwerin,* and who emphasised the harmony of economic interests of master and man in industrial enterprise. In the last decades of the nineteenth century one finds in the ranks of the Welsh radicals not only miners' leaders like William Abraham 'Mabon', but also men like D. A. Thomas (later Lord Rhondda) one of the most powerful Welsh coal owners.

The compromise of Liberals and Labour (sometimes called Lib-Labbism) broke down in the 1890s, and almost disappeared after the great stoppage in the south Wales coalfield in 1898. In the same period there was great unemployment in the steel and tinplate industries (connected with the tariffs of the American President McKinley) and, more unexpectedly, the slate quarries in north-west Wales became the centre of bitter conflict, which led to a disastrous lock-out lasting from 1900 to 1903. Social and industrial strife followed decades of harmony and compromise.

Keir Hardie was elected MP for Merthyr Tydfil in 1900, the first victory of the Independent Labour Party, and although Labour and Liberalism remained in alliance until 1914, they made uneasy bed-fellows. In 1908 the south Wales miners allied not with the Liberals but with Labour, despite the sweeping Liberal electoral successes in 1906 and the enormous prosperity of the coalfield. The Liberals (as they now called themselves more often than radicals) feared the rise of Labour and the spread of militancy and violence on the industrial scene, the most terrifying example of which were the Tonypandy Riots of 1910. From 1909 onwards the Central Labour College in London had an especially powerful effect in raising the class consciousness of Welsh miners, and Noah Ablett founded the Plebs League in the Rhondda Valley in 1909. Keir Hardie's paper the *Merthyr Pioneer* ridiculed the Welsh Liberals with their 'Little Bethel stage of Wales for the Welsh', which the new internationalist Labour movement was overtaking and rendering archaic. Yet it was not anything intrinsic to Wales or the Labour movement which really cleared the stage for the triumph of Labour, but rather the great changes wrought by World War I.

Welsh radicalism, only partially an electoral creed, had been more a way of life or a culture, and to this way of life the Great War dealt a body blow, destroying the optimism and harmony on which it rested. During and after the war the Welsh nonconformists became acutely aware of decay and loss of faith. For the first time the Welsh-speakers became aware of linguistic decline; the 1921 census was the first to show an absolute drop in the number of those able to speak Welsh. Welsh radicalism now had the air of quaint provincialism in contrast with the international concerns of the world after 1918, issues of class, economy and foreign relations. The radicals became deeply aware of their own divisions: during the war they had been divided over issues such as military conscription, then came the rift between Asquith and Lloyd George and their respective followers, and Lloyd George's downfall as Prime Minister in 1922 led to a severe crisis for the Welsh Liberals from which they never recovered.

The Labour ascendancy

The tattered mantle of Welsh radicalism now fell neatly on the pro-letarian shoulders of Labour. From 1920 onwards there was a rapid spread of militancy and syndicalism in the mines and factories of south Wales. The general elections of 1923 and 1929 showed a marked decline in Liberal representation and a corresponding rise of Labour, so that by 1929 almost half the Welsh voters were Labour, making Wales the largest and firmest Labour area in Britain. Even in the rural hinterland which, despite its falling population, had given the characteristic tone to older radicalism, there was rapid change after 1918. The Land Question had sorely exercised older radicals such as E. Pan Jones, but after about 1900 a period of relative agricultural prosperity drove the question into the background. After 1918 new economic circumstances made Welsh landowners sell their farms, mostly to their own tenants. In a survey of 1873 it had been found that 571 great landowners (about 1 per cent of the landowners of Wales) owned 60 per cent of all the land. In the period 1918 to 1922 some 25 per cent of Welsh land changed hands, more again from 1924 to 1925. The 'alien squires' now lost their economic hold on rural society. The privileges of the Anglican clergy had been taken away in 1914, and in 1920 the Anglicans formed the new

Church in Wales. The supposed enemies, the 'alien' clergy and squires, of generations of radicals had gone.

Labour advanced most quickly in the south, especially the south-east of Wales, and from 1919 onwards had in its thrall the most powerful Welsh county councils, those of Glamorgan and Monmouthshire. Industrial Wales swiftly became a stronghold of the far left, militant Labour MPs and councillors and, hard on their heels, a strong showing of Communists. In the rural areas, Liberals, many of them faithful to Lloyd George, held power until as late as 1945. Thus there appeared once again the rift in Wales between what the political scientist Alfred Zimmern in his memoirs in 1927 called 'Welsh Wales' (the north and west) and 'American Wales', the cultural melting-pot of the south-eastern coalfield and coastal belt, where earlier waves of internal Welsh migrations were flooded by far greater waves of immigrants from Ireland and England and further afield, and where the Welsh language and nonconformity were only minority concerns. Of course, there were a large number of Labour leaders in the 1920s or the 1930s to whom 'Methodism meant more than Marx' and whose culture was not very different from that of the older radicals. But the tone of the Labour ascendancy was set by the anglicised towns and factories of the south-east of Wales, and it aimed to be a contrast to the Welshness of the older radicals; it had little sympathy even with the Home Rule tendencies to be found in the earlier Independent Labour Party (the ILP). It emphasised the international character of the workers' struggle, and the role of the centralised state and centralised planning to bring about social justice.

The formative years of Welsh Labour were the 1920s and 1930s, years of terrible economic crisis from 1921 onwards, strikes culminating in the General Strike of 1926, followed by the world depression of 1929, all of which sharpened class conflict and led to the almost irreversible ruin of industries and communities, and emigration out of the south Wales industrial valleys on an unprecedented scale.

A considerable number of Welsh Labour MPs were trade unionists, many of them former miners. Although there was an awareness of the internationalist character of the movement and a belief in centralism, the special character of Welsh Labour was to be found in its deeply laid local roots and its sense of community solidarity in the face of industrial hardship and tragedy. It was

146

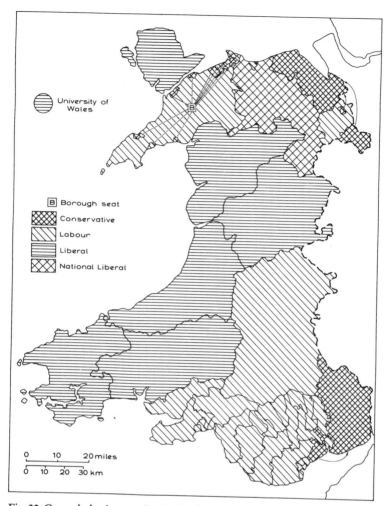

Fig 20 General election result, 1945 *(after Madgwick and Balsom,* National Atlas of Wales *2.2b)*

Labour which formed a social network of activity and resourcefulness which tried to hold communities together in the face of adversity and hopelessness. The depression of the 1930s strengthened the position of Labour in many parts of Wales until it resembled in its monolithic power the radicalism of the previous century. Although World War I had dealt a body blow to the radical culture of Wales, World War II did not have the same effect on Labour; quite the con-

147

trary, it helped to return prosperity of a sort to south Wales and confirm the importance and success of centralised economic planning. The 1945 general election saw Labour more firmly entrenched than ever in Wales (Fig 20).

After 1945 Labour spread into the rural areas as well, and so it could be said that Labour had become the party of the great mass of the Welsh people: workers, intellectuals, ministers of religion, the petty bourgeoisie and much of the bourgeoisie (Fig 21). What is remarkable is that the Welsh remained faithful to Labour for so long, without experiencing the revival of Conservatism occurring elsewhere in Britain in the 1950s, and without the Liberal revivals which have come from time to time. Labour even continued up to the election of 1970 to strengthen its hold upon Wales, drawing great cohesive power from its heroic period in the depression, and its record of improving social conditions, housing, health care in areas of poverty and deprivation, and depending heavily on its power base in the trade union movement, which was in turn dependent on Wales's heavy and extractive industries.

Did Labour develop any particularly Welsh characteristics? For many of the Welsh Labour leaders, such as the famous Aneurin Bevan, MP for Ebbw Vale and architect of the National Health Service, there was no room for Welshness in Labour politics. In the crucial decades of Labour's emergence Home Rule was a dead duck: the Liberals had briefly discussed Home Rule in 1920 after which the topic was dropped. The new nationalist party *Plaid Genedlaethol Cymru* (later simply *Plaid Cymru*), founded in 1925, had little popular support and was treated by Labour with derision. But such a large party as Labour always contained varied and shifting groups within it, and there was always a number of Labour MPs and councillors inside the party pressing for Welsh causes, and even moderate regional autonomy. In 1938, for example, a delegation of Labour MPs pressed the government (in vain) for a Secretary of State for Wales; in the 1930s and 1940s Wales came to be treated as a 'region' in several matters; in 1944 a day was set apart for discussing purely Welsh issues in the House of Commons; the Labour party itself became organised on Welsh regional lines in 1947; and in 1948 the government established an advisory council for Wales. Conservative governments also came to appreciate the special needs or aspirations of Wales, and appointed a Minister for Welsh Affairs in 1951; in 1955 they formally recognised Cardiff as the official capital.

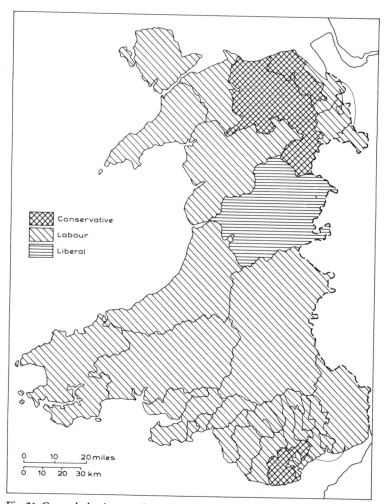

Fig 21 General election result, 1966 *(after Madgwick and Balsom,* National Atlas of Wales 2.2c)

Naturally, when Labour came to power in 1964 following thirteen years of Conservative government, pressure from one section of the Labour Party for measures for Wales was considerable, and resulted in the setting up of a Welsh Office and a Secretary of State for Wales, the first occupant of the post being the distinguished politician and MP for Llanelli, James Griffiths. Such moves appeared to win popular approval for in the 1966 general election

Labour held 32 of the 36 Welsh seats, an achievement comparable to the control the radicals had had over Wales in the period before 1914 (Fig 21).

Challenge from Nationalists and Conservatives

The Labour triumph of 1966 was, however, the prelude to a period of cross-currents and cross-winds, so that from 1966 to the 1980s Labour was in considerable difficulties in Wales. The Carmarthen by-election in the summer of 1966 was won by the leader of *Plaid Cymru*, Gwynfor Evans. The party, founded in 1925, had had some influence as a pressure group, but this was its first election victory (see Chapter 3). During the 1960s there were signs of growing political awareness among Welsh-speakers, such as the founding in 1962 of the Welsh Language Society (*Cymdeithas yr Iaith Gymraeg*), and a growing public debate over Welsh issues. In Scotland too there was a parallel growth of nationalism. In 1969 the Labour government set up a royal commission to discuss possible devolution, and this reported in 1973 in favour of a form of Home Rule for Wales and Scotland. The minority Labour government from 1974 to 1979 brought in measures of devolution for Wales and Scotland, but this was in the face of growing opposition to such measures at Westminster and the regions. The government's proposals were put to the vote in referenda held in Wales and Scotland on 1 March 1979, and the government's proposals were defeated, in Wales overwhelmingly so. The government fell, and in the ensuing elections Labour fared badly.

The growth of conservatism in Wales, which first appeared in 1970, was confirmed (Fig 22). Labour lost north and west Wales to a mixture of Conservative, Liberal and Nationalist MPs, the southern coastal belt returned to the Conservatives, the only Labour areas firmly held being the areas of heavy industry inland from the south coast, and in north-east Wales. Conservatives had done fairly well in Wales in one or two exceptional elections earlier in the twentieth century. The shift towards conservatism observed in 1979 was confirmed again in the election of 1983. In some cases, as in Anglesey, the shift may be related to the increase in the numbers of English residents moving to retirement homes on the island. In other areas, factors are more complex. Heavy industries, which had given Labour in Wales strength for decades, began to change in the 1960s

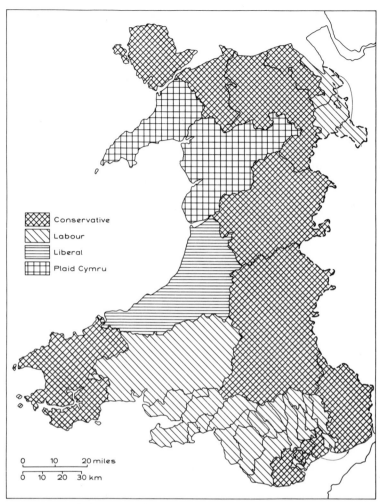

Fig 22 General election result, 1979 *(after Madgwick and Balsom,* National Atlas of Wales *2.2d)*

and 1970s, leaving a trail of serious unemployment, or giving way to a varied economy of light industries or industries of the new technology. Furthermore, many of them require workers to travel great distances from their old homes to their new workplaces. In the same period the farmers, who had in Wales been largely Liberals and then moderate Labour supporters, distanced themselves from Labour and often became Conservatives. Within the ranks of the Labour party there was a change in the nature of the Labour MPs in the 1960s and 1970s, away from the older locally based trade-unionist MP to a new type of MP more likely to be a middle-class intellectual from the professions. It seems that Labour had long counted on the loyalty of the small, cohesive local community centred on one or other of the heavy industries, and found it hard to adapt to a world of social mobility and varied industries.

The recent rise of Welsh conservatism has made the rise of nationalism in the 1960s appear more as a temporary phenomenon, rather than the deep and permanent shift which it appeared to such observers as Hechter (see the Bibliography). Hechter postulated that the British Empire had, besides overseas colonies, internal colonies as well and that English capitalism exploited Wales as an internal colony. That is, there was a capitalist core exploiting an ethnic periphery, the latter existing only to provide the core area with raw materials and heavy industrial products. This difference would produce a division of labour on cultural lines and, in time, would produce an uneven economic development. The theory claims that this is what has happened in late-twentieth-century Wales, which is relatively poor compared to the south of England. Linked with the failure of regional development plans in the 1960s, this uneven development has given rise to acute nationalism. This theory is rejected by other analysts, and indeed it is less convincing in the 1980s, with the comparative decline of nationalism and the rise of much more varied industrial patterns.

It is hard to predict whether the Welsh will return to their pattern of loyalty to left-wing politics which they maintained until the 1960s. What makes it so hard is that part of the time British influences are predominant, and on other occasions Welsh or localised issues come to the fore. The volatility of the Welsh electorate in the past twenty years is unprecedented. Having tramped along the progressive roads for a hundred years, the Welsh electors find themselves not so much at a crossroads as at a roundabout.

Park and Dare Hall, Treorci in the Rhondda Valley: a symbol of radicalism in the south Wales coalfield

The memorial to Aneurin Bevan, Tredegar Mountain, Gwent

CHAPTER 7

Church and Chapel

Over the past two hundred years one of the most pervasive features of Welsh life has been the chapel, that is religious dissent or non-conformity. In earlier times 'dissenters' were so called because they dissented from the Anglican church, and later on were called 'non-conformists' because they refused to conform to it. Although these words describe religious minorities, Welsh nonconformity has had an influence comparable to that of Catholicism in Ireland and Poland. At a time when political and economic developments seemed to draw the English and Welsh people closer together, religious change in Wales drew them apart. But it is salutary to remember that however all-pervasive the chapel influence became after 1800, nothing in Welsh life before 1750 would have led one to expect such a phenomenon.

Wales before 1750 appeared to be a passive, obedient set of four dioceses in the Anglican province of Canterbury. Although the British ancestors of the Welsh had been converted to Christianity during the Roman Empire, and although they subsequently formed part of so-called Celtic Christianity beyond Roman influence, Welsh churches became subject to Canterbury and Rome even before the final loss of Welsh independence in 1282. The Welsh were a part of Catholic Christendom up to the Tudor Reformation. This great religious change was accepted by the Welsh without revolt or rebellion, partly because they felt an overriding loyalty to the Welsh dynasty of Tudor, and partly because Elizabeth I's régime gave them the Reformation in their own language. Wherever Welsh was spoken the service was in Welsh. Catholic recusants there certainly were, tragic martyrs and distinguished writers among them, but they were exceptions proving the rule that the great majority of the

The Anglican parish church of Peterston-super-Ely, South Glamorgan: an area of early Anglo-Norman penetration

155

Welsh of the sixteenth and seventeenth centuries were loyal if unenthusiastic Anglicans. Puritan heroes and martyrs there also were: modern Welsh nonconformity made much of the young Puritan Welsh martyr, John Penry, executed by Elizabeth's government. But if one examines the early Puritan causes in Wales, the Independent church at Llanfaches (Gwent) founded in 1639 and the Baptist church at Ilston (Gower, Glamorgan) founded in 1649, it is clear that Puritanism was an imported influence barely touching the mass of the Welsh-speaking population.

Origins of the Great Awakening

Welsh Methodism owes its origin to the Great Revival or Great Awakening, dating from the sudden conversion of Howell Harris on Whit Sunday 1735. Methodist writers and preachers argued that the revival, an evangelical enthusiastic revival within the fold of the Anglican church, was caused by the fact that the Tudor Reformation did not touch the Welsh deeply, that the state of the church grew steadily worse after the ejection of Puritan ministers in 1662, and that the ignorance and immorality of the Welsh people was such by the 1730s that a sweeping religious revolution was necessary. With greater hindsight and objectivity, however, it can be seen that from the 1660s onwards the Welsh were deeply aware of the immorality of the people and the shortcomings of the clergy since the advent of Methodism was preceded by eighty years of a slow, complex, quiet revival. As a result of the efforts of the Commonwealth régime in the 1650s, a number of English Puritan sects were established in Wales, mostly in towns but sometimes in the countryside, and these sects survived the persecution of the government after 1662. By 1715 (if we take the contemporary statistics collected by Dr John Evans as a rough guide) Wales had sixty-nine dissenting causes, some to be found even in rural Carmarthenshire, but with only ten in north Wales. Evans estimated that Wales had about 20,000 dissenters, that is, about 6 per cent of the population, a figure only a little less than the proportion of dissenters in England. Although their origins were to be found in Roundhead missionary zeal, by 1715 these dissenters were thoughtful, introspective folk, people of some independent means, yeomen, the 'middle sorts', quiet in relation to the church or state, and tending to divide amongst themselves over theology or church government. For example, from 1729 onwards Welsh dissenters were riven with disputes over Arminian liberalising challenges to the older conventional high Calvinism. There were at least three elements in Welsh dissent: wild Pentecostal enthusiasm, the order and discipline of Calvin's Geneva and tolerant liberal rationalism, which took the form of Arminianism, Arianism and Unitarianism during the eighteenth century. These elements enlivened and disturbed Welsh popular religion at least until the mid nineteenth century. In some cases Welsh Puritan sects came to a sudden end. Welsh Quakers, for example, found the persecution of church and state unbearable, and organised a mass emigration to Pennsylvania to the 'Welsh Tract'.

Another sign of change and quiet revival before 1735 was the rise of an extensive printed-book culture between 1660 and the mid eighteenth century, consisting often of translations of pious English tracts, for the serious individual or for reading in a family circle. This great mass of serious yet popular literature was an indication of growing evangelism and mission in the Anglican church itself. A further sign was the foundation in 1699 of the Society for the Promotion of Christian Knowledge (SPCK) in which Welshmen played a prominent role, and which founded schools in Wales and a network of distribution points for religious literature.

More important by far than the SPCK schools were the circulating schools (so called from their peripatetic masters) organised by Griffith Jones of Llanddowror (Carmarthenshire) from 1737 until his death in 1761. Anglicans in England and Wales supported the charity-school movement with a special sense of urgency: they felt that the Welsh were primitive and unreformed, still close to paganism and Catholicism, poor and isolated from the enlightenment of English Protestant propaganda. Griffith Jones, an Anglican clergyman, used many of the methods, such as open-air preaching conventions, that were later to be used by the Methodists. Indeed, there are many signs that Methodism was the result of two or three generations of growing religious activity in Wales.

The Methodist Awakening

Howell Harris's conversion in 1735, the often-quoted beginning of Welsh Methodism, came as a result of the preaching of the vicar of Talgarth (Breconshire). Harris then became a great preacher, but was never allowed to take Anglican orders. He was joined by

William Williams of Pantycelyn (Carmarthenshire), Daniel Rowland of Llangeitho (Cardiganshire) and many others, and within a year or two this activity had become a self-conscious movement of Anglican evangelism, with self-appointed preachers criss-crossing Wales gathering vast crowds. In the wake of the preaching conventions came a network of small societies meeting in private houses to discuss religion, especially the spiritual progress of the individual member. Harris claimed that the older dissenters — called by the Methodists the Dry Dissenters — had only appealed to the head, not to the heart, and Methodism now seemed to appeal to the vast underprivileged masses, to the young, to women and to the very poor. The Methodists used enthusiastic methods: frenzied, emotional preaching — the listeners spontaneously dancing and leaping about — and simple lyrical songs, hymns often set to versions of popular folk songs or the latest hits of the English theatre. They were called Methodists because they closely resembled the slightly later English Methodist movement led by George Whitefield and John Wesley. In 1742 Whitefield and Wesley quarrelled over theology, and the Welsh Methodists felt themselves closer to the Calvinist Whitefield than to the more Arminian Wesley. The various leaders of Welsh Methodism came together in 1743, and by 1747 Whitefield and Wesley came to a gentlemen's agreement that while Whitefield and his Welsh friends would evangelise Welsh Wales, Wesley would keep out, merely visiting occasionally the English-speaking causes in areas such as Gower. Methodism in Wales in the main therefore became Calvinistic Methodism.

It spread with remarkable rapidity in the mid-eighteenth century especially in south Wales and in areas where there were old dissenting causes, areas used to theological debate and open to outside influences. In 1752 Harris quarrelled with the other Methodist leaders, and this led to a split, with a consequent weakening in the movement's progress, until it was patched up in 1763. By then the older dissenters had begun to copy Methodist techniques and moved into the field of popular mission, often winning converts from Methodism. In the 1760s the Methodists turned their attention to north Wales where they tilled virgin soil, and in the latter half of the eighteenth century it was in the north that they had their greatest success. The second wave of the revival came in 1762, and this was especially marked by the singing of Williams of Pantycelyn's hymns. The dissenting sects, such as the Independents and Baptists,

158

having copied the Methodist techniques, also expanded rapidly towards the end of the century. Methodism remained within the Anglican fold until 1811, despite the disapproval of the bishops, and in that year the Welsh Calvinistic connection or body was set up. In 1816 the Welsh religious historian, David Peter, calculated that while there were 267 Independent causes in Wales and 176 Baptist causes, there were as many as 343 Methodist causes, so that they were the largest non-Anglican body in Wales. Most of these causes were of fairly recent origin, and although their influence was far greater than their numbers, the non-Anglicans were still probably a minority in Wales in 1800. This does not disguise the fact that there had been a religious revolution.

The Welsh Methodists were aware that their Great Awakening had much in common with other evangelical movements — pietist evangelical and revivalist movements in England, Ireland, Scotland and Germany in the 1730s and 1740s — indeed, they read avidly translations of pamphlets about the similar Great Awakening in the American colonies. Why were the Welsh Methodists so much more successful than the older dissenters or the comparable Methodist movement in England? Some reasons are positive: the Methodists used new methods to reach parts of the population that other religions had failed to reach; they also appeared at a time when the individual's sense of his own personality had just developed, and at a time when there was something of a vacuum in Welsh popular culture, with the decay of ancient communities and ancient semi-pagan forms of popular culture. To those who wanted joy and thrills, they gave them; to those who wished for order in their own lives and a sense of belonging to a disciplined society, they gave something too. But in Wales they worked in a society still very different from England, and there were also negative reasons for their success, namely the lack of rivals. Dissent and Methodism in England (which also expanded in the same period) had to contend with the massive force of well-organised Anglicanism. The church in Wales by comparison, while doing its best using the medieval machinery of administration adapted to Tudor circumstances, was weak and poor with much of its wealth appropriated by laymen, barely able to provide suitable services or teaching to the common people. Other rival influences were also lacking: Wales did not have England's grandiose aristocratic life, its humming commercial and business activity, its banks and industries; it was not touched by its urban secularism, its theatres and coffee houses, its novels and bawdy plays; and it lacked England's lively political involvement. Without these rivals, Methodism, with a revived dissent in its train, rose to extraordinary heights of influence in Wales.

Dissenters and Methodists

By the end of the eighteenth century the Anglican church was deeply alarmed at the falling away of its membership. In 1803, for example, in the largest Welsh town, Merthyr Tydfil, non-Anglican worshippers outnumbered Anglicans by eight to one. In 1817 it was stated that only about forty Anglican communicants could be mustered in the whole town. The rate of growth of dissenting causes was phenomenal in the late eighteenth and early nineteenth centuries: the Independents, for example, had about 87 congregations in Wales in 1742, 100 in 1775, 120 in 1785, 500 in 1839 and 684 at the religious census of 1851. From 1800 to 1850 an Independent chapel was opened in Wales on average every five weeks. The Baptists and Methodists expanded rapidly in the same period, and one should not forget lesser denominations such as the Unitarians and Wesleyans. Sir Thomas Phillips estimated in 1849 that chapel members were about one in eight of the population and regular attenders at chapel (many of whom were called 'hearers') were one in four. By 1851 it was clear that Wales was covered with chapels. It was discovered that 34 per cent of the Welsh attended places of worship (compared with a mere 24 per cent in England), that in Wales the sittings for attending worship were divided thus: 20 per cent for the Anglicans, 71 per cent for other denominations. On Census Sunday 1851 only 9 per cent of worshippers went to Anglican churches, while 87 per cent went to chapels. Anglicanism only remained strong in border areas and where English was regularly spoken. Large numbers of people were not committed to any religion, but by 1851 it was clear that Welsh Wales had become a nonconformist nation.

During the later eighteenth century, Methodism aided the growth of other sects, and they had all made evangelical religion popular, through great emphasis on preaching, frequent enthusiastic revivals and the Sunday school. The first half of the nineteenth century was the golden age of the preacher, men such as John Elias of Anglesey (Methodist), Christmas Evans (Baptist) or Williams of the Wern (Independent), who wielded tremendous moral authority: John

160

Elias was known as the 'Methodist Pope' and his pronouncements on current affairs called 'The Bulls of Bala'. When he died in 1841 all work on the island of Anglesey ceased and ten thousand people went to his funeral. Such men transformed people's lives and destroyed the last vestiges of the merry customary life of the communities which had survived since the Middle Ages. Revivalism was originally only a tenet of Methodism, but the other sects were increasingly drawn to it, to some extent because of the growing contact between Welsh sects and America, especially with the communities of Welsh emigrants in America, for example the Welsh were greatly impressed by the revivalist philosophy of the American, C. G. Finney. Methodist historians have counted at least sixteen important religious revivals in Wales between 1785 and 1905: some local, others widespread, some connected with the onset of the cholera epidemic, some enthusiastic, others so sober and dignified that many might not call them 'revivals', some were connected with great preachers, others with social causes such as temperance or teetotalism.

The Sunday school was not a Welsh invention, but it had a unique significance in Wales. Thomas Charles of Bala was an Anglican cleric converted to Methodism in 1784 and it was he who adapted the methods of the circulating schools to the use of Methodism, building up an excellent network of teachers and classes for adults as well as children, until the Sunday school became an extremely popular institution and a remarkable instrument of popular literacy in the Welsh language. The nonconformists were divided and halting in their efforts to build day schools, while by contrast the Anglicans had a good record of building a large number of day schools all over Wales in the first half of the nineteenth century. In the same period while the nonconformists concentrated on Bible reading and theology, the Anglicans were concerned with general culture, and although their day schools generally taught in English, they themselves were the main supporters of Welsh culture, history, music and literature.

It was the Anglicans who dominated the *eisteddfod* as an institution (see Chapter 9) and much of the press, but it was the nonconformists who came more and more to control the popular press, the teeming world of often short-lived periodicals forwarding sectarian aims; they too produced a vast mass of books and pamphlets on the bitter theological wrangles of the early nineteenth century. After 1800 there were signs of fresh life in Welsh Anglicanism: there were bishops and priests of higher calibre, and the attempt by Anglicans to influence Welsh opinion through the press, the *eisteddfod* and educational programmes, is an example of this new vigour. In the eighteenth century the nonconformists had had their academies and training schools: in 1827 the Anglicans opened a Welsh college, St David's College, Lampeter (Cardiganshire). The beginnings of an Anglican revival, however, served also to embitter the debates and wranglings over religion which so marked nineteenth-century Wales.

There was a considerable difference between the Methodists who advocated Toryism and non-involvement in politics and the dissenters who were often involved in social reform movements, such as the Peace Society or the Anti-Slavery Movement. During the French Revolution, Welsh political radicals were almost always drawn from the ranks of the sectarians, such as the Baptist Morgan John Rhys. Methodists, however, had to contend with the public accusation that their private societies were revolutionary cells. Under the influence of John Elias, from about 1815 to his death in 1841, Methodists became distinctly reactionary, and in this they showed their kinship with Anglicanism, *Yr Hen Fam* (The Old Mother). Yet there were many social and moral questions drawing Methodism and Anglicanism apart, and attracting Methodism towards the dissenters. After the removal of political disabilities from dissenters and Catholics in 1828–9, they felt less need to identify themselves with the Anglicans, and by the mid 1830s they were deeply alarmed at the rise of the Tractarian or Oxford Movement inside the church. The turning point in the relationship between the church and the Welsh Methodists was in the furore over the government Blue Books on Welsh morals and education in 1847 (see Chapter 6).

The nonconformist triumph

In the 1830s and 1840s the government was much concerned with Wales because Welsh life was disrupted by strikes and riots, not only in the rapidly expanding industrial districts, but from 1839 to 1843 in the rural south-west as well. At the same time the Welsh became deeply concerned to improve their position in the world by means of a thorough overhaul of the educational system, and in this period also there was great alarm amongst the nonconformists at the revival in the Anglican church. From 1832 onwards the ecclesiastical reforms, such as the setting up of ecclesiastical commissioners, enabled the church to put a stop to ecclesiastical abuses, to form new parishes, to endow parishes in poor areas, to rebuild old churches and to build new churches and provide them with ministers. A large number of new Anglican schools were built in Wales. The Oxford or Tractarian Movement brought new zeal into the church. There was therefore great public interest in Wales in the government inquiry into the state of education, morals and the opportunity the working classes had in Wales to learn English. The Blue Books reported in 1847 that the lamentable state of Welsh education, society and morals was to be blamed on two factors: the survival of the Welsh language and the spread of nonconformity. In this analysis, Methodists had been lumped together with the dissenters, and little of the vast amount of evidence collected had been taken from nonconformist witnesses. When the Blue Books were published they caused a furore (see Chapter 6). The controversy and debate had the effect of producing a united front for the first time among the nonconformists; it caused the Methodists to become politically aware and made all the nonconformists eager to make their voice heard in the corridors of power. The Anglicans were now identified with Toryism and Englishness, the nonconformists with Liberal radicals and Welshness.

The 1840s and 1850s, then, saw a change in the nature of nonconformity, from being a collection of sects or groups to being a 'nonconformist nation'. Nonconformity came to influence Welsh politics, so that radical policies had to become subservient to the needs of nonconformity. Likewise with Welsh higher culture: music and literature became subservient to the needs of nonconformity, with few exceptions. The power of the denomination as a whole became greater within each sect than the power or initiative of the local congregation: even among the Independents, the principle of decentralised congregationalism had to yield to the growing power of the centralised Union after 1872. Instead of being minorities hostile to the way of the world, the nonconformists came to embrace the world and dominate it. The nonconformist way of life became 'the Welsh way of life'. Chapels continued to spring up everywhere, were expanded or rebuilt as the congregations grew larger and more prosperous, still retaining, however, the classical styles of the eighteenth-century square preaching boxes up to the end of the nineteenth century. Anglicans had adopted pointed Gothic architecture in the 1830s, and English-language chapels in Wales gradually adopted Gothic styles, but Welsh-language chapels rarely did so, and this was a sign of their stubborn loyalty to their Puritan and eighteenth-century origins. The same stubbornness was reflected in their loyalty to Puritan virtues and theology, almost unchanged until the late nineteenth century, with few divisions or heresies. As Professor I. G. Jones has observed: 'There was no demand for Primitive Methodism: Welsh Methodism was primitive enough.'

Despite the renewed vigour and reorganisation of the Anglican church in Wales from the 1830s onwards, the chapels continued to expand their influence. Canon E. T. Davies has called the chapels 'ecclesiastical republics' because of the great power and importance of the laity in each chapel. The system of founding causes was simple, unencumbered and very flexible; the semi-independent congregation gave importance, status and power to poor underprivileged folk, and the decentralised administration of the sects was at that time suited to the dispersed neighbourhoods of rural Wales (and of much of early industrial Wales as well). Puritanism and abnegation helped a poor society to gain independence economically and raised funds for the ministry and for building chapels and vestries, custodians' houses and manses.

It was in many ways the triumph of the chapels which made Wales the 'Land of Song' (see Chapter 9). Just as the second wave of the Methodist Revival in 1762 had made extensive use of music, so the nineteenth century made extensive use of choral singing. The Anglicans in Wales developed a system of choral unions and festivals in the dioceses in the middle decades of the century at much the same time as the chapels developed their choirs and hymn-singing assemblies, the institution of the *cymanfa ganu* (singing assembly). The first was held at Aberystwyth in 1830, but the one which made them fashionable was held by Ieuan Gwyllt in Aberdare Temperance Hall in 1859, a year of great religious revival. By the 1870s they had become a universal fashion, aided by the tremendous popularity in Wales of Curwen's sol-fa music notation which made musical scores simple for the multitudes. M. O. Jones, the musical historian, calculated that in 1895 there were at least 280 *cymanfa ganu* assemblies in Wales, with at least 134,000 people taking part, that is almost one in ten of the population.

The growing involvement of the chapels in political life was a sign of growing confidence and power. The 1859 general election saw for the first time Tories and Liberals evenly balanced. The extension of the franchise in 1867 meant that in the general election of 1868 the nonconformist vote counted and a majority of Liberals (or radicals) was returned from Wales. The extension of the franchise and redistribution of constituency acts in the 1880s redoubled the force of the chapels, and by 1890 Wales had a considerable number of nonconformist MPs coupled with large numbers of nonconformists on the new county and parish councils.

One sign of the arrival of chapel power was the first piece of parliamentary legislation to treat Wales as a special national unit, the 1881 Welsh Sunday Closing Act, which neatly combined three concerns of the Welsh nonconformists, a sense of Welshness, teetotalism and sabbatarianism. Another sign of increasing chapel power was the growth of the movement to disestablish and disendow the Anglican church in Wales. This had been suggested in 1793 in the paper of the radical dissenters *Y Cylchgrawn Cymmraeg*, and was raised from time to time by dissenting leaders, but it was under the aegis of the Liberation Society (which of course advocated the disestablishment of the Anglican church in England as well) that the isolated voices became a chorus during the 1860s. Disestablishment was introduced into the House of Commons in 1870, but it made little or no progress until 1894 when it became part of the Welsh Liberal programme, and now the church was attacked from a more sharply nationalistic standpoint as the 'alien' church. When the Liberals swept to power in 1906 it was only a matter of time before disestablishment became law, though it was delayed by a Royal Commission on the church in Wales which met from 1906 to 1910, and the bill only became law after the outbreak of war in 1914.

This was in many ways the greatest political triumph of the Welsh nonconformists. Just as there was a sunset glow of Welsh Liberalism in the period 1906 to 1914, so also there was the most astounding spiritual conflagration of nonconformity in this period, the Welsh revival of 1904-5.

The revival of 1904-5

Welsh churches, especially the nonconformist chapels, were convulsed by a great enthusiastic spiritual revival during the years 1904 and 1905, and much attention was given to the work of an electrifying young lay preacher, a former miner from Loughor

(Glamorgan) called Evan Roberts. By 1912 church membership in Wales was 10 per cent higher than it had been in 1903, and it has been calculated that the year 1907 probably saw the highest church membership that there has ever been in Wales. This sudden dramatic increase caught the attention of the world's press. A less cursory examination, however, shows that the revival was the result of two decades of growing concern among the chapels over diminished spirituality and increasing materialism, and was also the result of a decade of increasing zeal on the part of the evangelical wing of church and chapel.

In 1891 the Methodists under Dr John Pugh began their popular missions, the Forward Movement; in 1893 came the mission of John Evans of Eglwys-bach, and there were many evangelical or pentecostal conventions around 1900 such as the Llandrindod 'Keswick in Wales' Conference of 1903, all raising the zeal of church and chapel. Church and chapel in Wales were on their mettle in this period because of the relaunching of the disestablishment campaign in 1894, and because of the so-called Welsh Revolt from 1902 to 1906 against Balfour's Education Act. The political involvement of christians in those affairs, together with the Social Gospel movements, as that of R. J. Campbell, caused a certain reaction towards individualistic salvationism. Church and chapel were also worried by the growing uncertainties and academic criticism in Welsh theology, the growth of agnosticism, the equating of religion with morality or social conscience and with aesthetic values, all of which had begun to undermine the Welsh Puritan Calvinist front since 1880. Church and chapel were both anxious over the challenge of secularism, modern sports and entertainments, the spread of organised games, athletics, theatres, music halls, spa and seaside holidays, fashion in dress and hairstyle, all of which deeply affected the Welsh after 1880. These forces, some positive, others negative, came together in the evangelical convention at Blaenannerch (Cardiganshire) in 1904, at which the young Evan Roberts was shaken to the core, and from which experience he began to travel the length and breadth of Wales with tremendous effect. He and his friends, often young untried laymen and women, began two years of great preaching conventions night after night, bringing church members to a new-found sense of salvation and bringing in thousands from the world outside.

The revival was interdenominational, although it affected chapel more than it did church; it brought to the fore laymen more than ministers, women more than men and young people more than old. It caught the imagination of the press, and its dramatic qualities sparked off many evangelical revivals in other countries: Holland, Germany, Denmark and America among others. The revival was little concerned with theology or church government, but it gave rise to two sects, directly or indirectly: the Apostolic Church with its headquarters at Penygroes (Carmarthenshire), set up in 1906, and less directly, the Elim Four Square Gospel movement, founded by two Welshmen George and Stephen Jeffreys from Maesteg (Glamorgan).

Two contemporary observers from France, Rogues de Fursac and Henri Bois, felt at the time that the revival was connected with an upsurge of Welsh national feeling from the 1880s onwards, and with a crisis of Welsh identity, a crisis of adaptation to the new forces of the twentieth-century world, and among Welsh nonconformists in particular, this crisis arose from a realisation of the decline of the chapel in society since its triumph in the middle of the nineteenth century. The vigour of the Radical nonconformist establishment, the general optimism of the British Empire, the numerical successes of revivalism in the 1890s and 1904–5, all masked an inner weakness. There were rival forces at work undermining the power of the chapel, and they had been at work for some fifty years before 1904.

Rivals to nonconformity

One obvious feature of the later nineteenth century was the revival of the Anglican church in Wales. Evidence collected in 1905 showed that some 40 per cent of the Welsh people went to some place of worship: of these, 25 per cent were Anglicans, 23 per cent Independents (or Congregationalists as they now were called), 23 per cent Calvinistic Methodists, 19 per cent Baptists, with other lesser sects such as Unitarians and Wesleyans trailing behind. In the nineteenth century the church : chapel ratio had been 1 : 4; now in 1905 it was 1 : 3. In 1850 there had been in Wales only about 700 Anglican clergymen: by 1910 there were 1543 clergymen serving 1527 churches, so manpower and church buildings had vastly increased. Church restorations had begun in the rural parishes in the 1840s, but in the last decades of the century a vast amount of capital was expended on churches in towns and industrial areas. The Royal

Commission on Religion in Wales in 1906 found that there were about 530,000 nonconformists, and 193,000 Anglicans in Wales. This proportionate increase of Anglicans lent urgency to the nonconformists' disestablishment campaign.

Church and chapel were one, however, in their sense of inadequacy in facing the rapid changes in Welsh society towards the end of the nineteenth century. It was not unexpected that the Methodist *Sasiwn* (Association) at Tredegar (Monmouthshire) in 1840 should condemn trade unions (John Elias was still alive); more surprising that the hostility should have been sustained late in the century. William Abraham 'Mabon' in the south and W. J. Parry in the north, and union leaders like them, effected a rapprochement between religious bodies and trade unions in the 1870s and 1880s, but a further breach was opened between them when in 1898 the new militant unionism appeared and swept away the old 'Lib-Labbism' compromise between masters and men. It is also surprising that the deepest concern of Welsh religious bodies, even those such as Independents who had long been progressive in politics, should have been rural. Even Henry Richard and Dr Thomas Rees, based as they were in urban and industrial areas, retained a rural outlook. Just as the church found it hard to shake off its image as the organ of the manorial communities of the remote past, so by 1900 nonconformity found itself stuck in the mould of rural Wales of the early 1800s.

The church found it much easier than the chapel, for example, to welcome into its fold the English-speaking immigrants into Wales or the Welsh who had turned to speak English. By 1900 only 50 per cent of the population spoke Welsh. Some denominations, such as the Independents and Baptists, decided that their new English-language causes should be affiliated to sister organisations based in England. It is thus that English-language Independents joined the Congregational Union of England and Wales, and are by now for the most part in the United Reformed Church. The Welsh-language causes have retained their separate identity in the Union of Welsh Independents. The Anglicans did their best to provide services in both languages where necessary, or used a separate parish church for each language. The only uniquely Welsh religious body, the Welsh Calvinistic Methodists, could not effectively hive off English-speakers to a sister organisation in England, and so developed English-language causes, even hiving off Welsh-speakers to form the nuclei of such English causes, mocked and satirised by the nationalistic Methodist Emrys ap Iwan as the 'Inglis Côs'.

Another challenge to nonconformity came with industrialisation and the opening up of old localised communities to secular influences. It was with shock that it was learned in 1905 that 60 per cent of the Welsh people had no connection with any religious body. Such a situation had been observed among the English working classes as early as 1851, but the common folk or *gwerin* of Wales had been the backbone of the chapels. Now self-conscious secularism was added to the older indifference: Aberdare had a Secular Society in 1905–6 meeting in the Temperance Hall, and larger towns and cities were more secular than Aberdare. Since the 1870s there had been a spread of sports and entertainments of all kinds, affecting all classes of society. The chapels found it more and more difficult to compete in a more open society. As the sects had grown larger during the nineteenth century so their sense of separateness from the world had weakened, and their sense of concern for the world's affairs, politics and morals increased. There was a corresponding decline throughout the latter half of the nineteenth century in purely theological debate, for example, on that favourite question of public discussion in the early nineteenth century, the Atonement.

Another aspect of the growing secular concerns of the chapels, as they became large all-embracing denominations, was their growing cultural role. In the eighteenth and early nineteenth centuries, Welsh writers and antiquaries had seen the chapels as the enemies of Welshness. But after 1850 the chapels came to see themselves as the guardians of all that was best in Welsh life, and Welsh higher culture was reshaped in their mould. Between 1850 and 1900 the chapels developed their choirs, orchestras and even opera and drama groups, their literary and debating societies, their mutual improvement societies, their groups for temperance and social work, their weeknight children's temperance meetings, The Band of Hope, and by Edwardian times they held innumerable *eisteddfodau,* all of which gave Welsh chapel life in this period a sense of humming activity, but it was all very remote from the aims of the founding fathers in the seventeenth and eighteenth centuries.

The enormous growth in the cultural role of the chapel caused a confusion of aims and purposes. Recent writers have suggested that from the late 1870s onwards there was a growing crisis of confidence in Welsh nonconformity, despite all the superficial success: growing doubts and confusions over the theology, growing mistrust of the old Puritan values, growing public dislike of the prestige of the ministers and the *Sêt Fawr* (the 'Big Pew', where the deacons or elders sat immediately below the centrally placed pulpit). In 1888 the Methodist leader Principal Thomas Charles Edwards criticised Welsh chapel theology for its narrowness, aridity and irrelevance; the different sectarian chapels, he said, were 'tombstones to dead controversies'. The chapels seemed less and less able to deal with the problems of the end of the century: rapid social mobility, rapid changes in economic circumstances, moral confusion, the new conditions of industrialism, secularism, state education and familiarity with the English language and English ways. In some sense, then, the Great Revival of 1904–5 was an attempt to return the Welsh people to the Puritan certainties of an earlier age, and to the emotional sincerity and simplicity of eighteenth-century enthusiasm. The short-term effects of the revival were remarkably successful, but World War I showed that in the longer term, the rivals to chapel (and to a great extent the rivals to church) were too powerful to be put off by the revival of 1904–5.

World War I and its challenge to Welsh religion

The 1914–18 war had a dramatic impact upon Welsh life and religion. Before the war, Wales expressed Liberal optimism; it experienced great economic prosperity; the absolute total of Welsh-speakers continued to rise near to the million mark just before 1914 (and there were uncounted thousands of Welsh-speakers abroad, in England, the Empire and in America); Welsh radicalism led by David Lloyd George appeared to be in its hey-day; Welsh chapels were being rebuilt and expanded; and chapel membership had never been so high. The period after 1918 was a stark contrast. Liberal Edwardian optimism had evaporated; the depression and slump hit Welsh industries such as coal especially hard; the total number of Welsh-speakers was now seen to be seriously on the wane in the 1921 census; there was widespread emigration out of Wales, especially of young people; and Welsh Liberalism was compromised and confused by the war and by the career of Lloyd George, indeed the

An early Baptist chapel at Dolau, near Rhayader, Powys (built in 1767)

Statue of Daniel Rowland, one of the leaders of Welsh Methodism, Llangeitho, Dyfed: to the right lies the Methodist chapel

The impressive façade of a Victorian chapel in Aberystwyth, Dyfed

war seemed to mock the very values the chapels had professed to admire, for example, Lloyd George's Conscription Act was in stark contrast to the chapel principle of the individual's rights of conscience. The Labour movement was not as closely identified with the chapels as Liberalism had been, indeed Keir Hardie's paper had mocked the 'Little Bethel' Liberal Welsh mentality. Disestablishment of the church had become law in 1914 amid a good deal of public boredom. By 1920 the church was reorganised in Wales as a separate province under its own archbishop, Archbishop A. G. Edwards, who as Bishop of St Asaph had been the doughtiest defender of the church's rights in the most bitter stages of the battle over disestablishment. By 1920, however, there was little open hostility between church and chapel, and the quarrel over disestablishment seemed to belong to a remote past.

The growing secularism of life, leisure and politics was of course a general European phenomenon in the twentieth century, but it struck particularly hard at the kind of religion of the Welsh chapels, which had depended heavily upon enthusiasm, personal conversion and revivalism, with little emphasis upon authority, structure, historical tradition or institutional forms. Since 1918 the chapels have experienced a slow decline in membership, aggravated greatly in some areas by rural depopulation, in others by industrial slump (as in many south Wales valleys), and in the urban and English border areas by the advance of the English language (Figs 23 and 24). The church in Wales (as the Anglican church is correctly termed after 1920) has been more effective in retaining its communicants and attracting the English immigrants into Wales that have appeared in large numbers since 1945, drawing great strength from its sense of historical tradition, organisation and structure (Fig 25). By contrast, the chapels which had for several generations served small, localised communities sometimes consisting of extended groupings of large families, with several generations living in close proximity, and with a high degree of intermarriage within the same chapel or same sect, found it hard to cope with modern social trends, with open communities, mobile populations and small, scattered families. The spread of mass media entertainments, such as the cinema, billiard hall and dance hall after 1920, greatly weakened the position of the chapel as the centre of cultural life. The spread of the secular educational system, for example, the Workers' Educational Association or University Extra-Mural classes, weakened the chapel's role as a

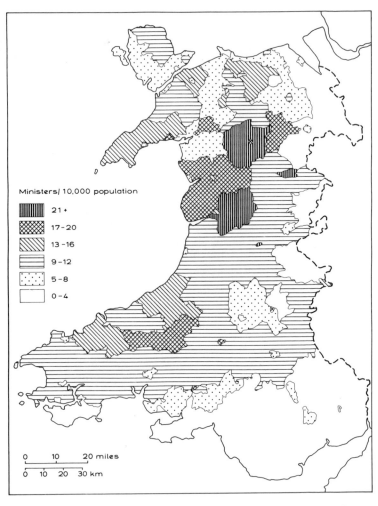

Fig 23 Religious affiliation: nonconformist strength, 1971 *(after Williams, National Atlas of Wales 3.3b)*

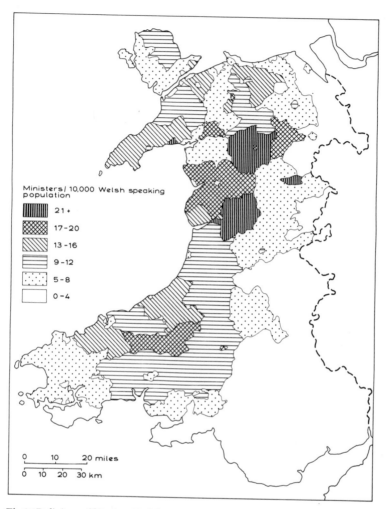

Fig 24 Religious affiliation: Welsh-medium nonconformist strength, 1971 *(after Williams, National Atlas of Wales 3.3c)*

175

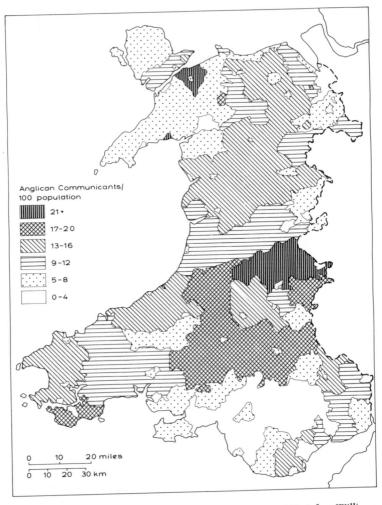

Fig 25 Religious affiliation: Anglican communicants, 1969 *(after Williams, National Atlas of Wales 3.3d)*

popular educator. The strength of the chapel's discipline in Victorian times had depended to some degree on its reflecting the work patterns of the local people, the 'Big Pew' being the preserve of the richer farmers in rural areas and the foremen or leading figures of the mines or quarries in industrial regions. After 1920, and even more so after 1945, new work patterns, new factory hierarchies and systems of discipline made the old patterns irrelevant. New shift systems required men to work on Sundays, and in making women work in the week, forced them to do their housework on Sunday mornings and so abandon chapel. Since 1945 the schools and academies for training men for the ministry have become fewer, the number of men entering the ministry has dropped and more and more chapels have been forced to join together under the pastorate of one minister. Large numbers of chapels, many built as recently as the Edwardian period, have been converted to secular uses as clubs or garages, and a vast number have simply been demolished.

This chapter has not dealt with all aspects of religion in Wales (eg the revival of Roman Catholicism in the recent past), but has isolated one important distinctive element: the rise and gradual fall of the power of nonconformity. Different nonconformist influences, often from outside Wales — Puritanism from England, revivalism from North America — converged in Wales when Welsh society was ready for them and were then transformed into a distinctively Welsh way of life for close on two hundred years. Religion has deeply coloured most aspects of Welsh life since the mid nineteenth century, for example, conditioning the politics of radicalism, and, if the late Morgan Phillips was correct in saying that the British left owed more to Methodism than to Marx, Welsh nonconformity also influenced the rise of Labour in Wales. Even in decline since 1920, church and chapel have had a considerable effect on Welsh life, and from time to time there have been movements of renewal, for example the vigorous force of Neo-Calvinist evangelism has led to the setting up of new nonconformist causes in recent years. But it would need more than the power of the revival of 1904–5 to return for Wales to see again a renaissance of the chapels.

CHAPTER 8

The Dragon's Two Tongues:
Life and Letters

The Welsh have a passion for words, written, spoken or sung; it is not surprising, therefore, that Wales has a rich literary tradition. For most of the present century the language of the majority of the people has been English, and so has been their literature, but for the long centuries up to 1900 the most important literary tradition was Welsh.

The origins of Welsh literature

The tradition goes back to the sixth century AD. For many centuries Welsh poetry, folklore, history and law were handed down by word of mouth, so that the manuscripts containing the earliest literature date from no earlier than the twelfth century. The early Welsh poems preserved in these manuscripts appear to date from the late sixth century. They were composed somewhere in what is now the south of Scotland or far north of England, during the first attempted Anglo-Saxon conquest of those areas. The earliest poet of the tradition, Taliesin, was the household bard of Urien, prince of Rheged, who reigned about 570–90 AD. But the most famous of these early poets was Aneirin (Aneurin is a later misspelling) who composed, around 600 AD, a series of linked elegies for a band of warriors sent from what is now Edinburgh to fight against the Anglo-Saxons at present-day Catterick Bridge in Yorkshire. The warriors, who were almost all killed, were the companions of the poet himself, and since they lived in the kingdom of Manaw Gododdin, the poem is simply called *Gododdin*.

The Welsh literary tradition did not have much of a future in what the Welsh soon came to call the Old North, but it was transferred within a few years to present-day Wales, and formed the basis of

178

what it is right to call a tradition because subsequent poets learned those poems and even memorised long word lists of obsolete vocabulary throughout the Middle Ages in order to understand them. For example, Owain Cyfeiliog, prince of Powys from 1149 to 1195 wrote a famous poem called 'Hirlas Owain' (Owain's Horn) about his warrior band as they passed the mead horn from mouth to mouth around the royal banqueting table. The poem not only echoed the style of Aneirin, over five centuries before, but even lifted the odd line complete from the *Gododdin.*

The tradition was that of heroic poetry, as in all early societies; the poet's concern was to praise his leaders, often by reference to past heroes, and so there is a sense of archaism, a 'backward look', a sense of conservatism and continuity. The poet was probably feared and admired as a seer or prophet, and so just as the poet constantly referred back to past heroes, so also he referred to prophetic events in the future, when past heroes such as King Arthur would return to make the Welsh once again great. This is understandable in the society of the small Welsh medieval kingdoms which were always on the defensive and often in retreat.

The courts of the princes

The most prolific period for Welsh prose and poetry occurred at a time of considerable political recovery for the Welsh, dating from Gruffydd ap Cynan's rise to power after the battle of Mynydd Carn in 1081 until the fall of Llywelyn ap Gruffydd in 1282, and much of it has been preserved. To the copyists of this period we owe the survival of the texts of the Welsh laws attributed to Hywel Dda (about 900 AD), a great deal of political, gnomic and nature poetry and a series of dramatic lyrics dating perhaps from the ninth century, but referring back to the life of the sixth-century hero, Llywarch the Old. These poems refer to various tragic incidents in the Anglo-Saxon conquest of Shrewsbury, and are amongst the simplest and easiest medieval Welsh poems which a modern Welsh-speaker can understand. Several Welsh scholars have suggested that these poems and others like them were the dramatic verse highlights of long prose sagas related by the court storyteller. The tales themselves have disappeared.

The courts of the medieval princes therefore had a strong sense of Welsh history and tradition. The literature composed by the court poets in this period is extremely elaborate and difficult for modern taste to appreciate. The robust qualities of early heroic society by now had been overlaid with Christian morality and by feudal and chivalric influences from England and France. To the princes and their courtiers the sense of poetry was no more important than the sound, and the foundations were laid for the extremely complex system of consonantal alliteration and rhyming called *cynghanedd* (harmony) and equally complex metrical forms, which were finally perfected in the fifteenth century.

One unusual feature of this society was its use of prose for artistic purposes. It is from this period that the surviving Welsh prose tales and romances come which are known (from the title chosen by the translator Lady Charlotte Guest) as *The Mabinogion*. The central core of the tales are the 'Four Branches of the Mabinogi', four tales put together probably by one author in the middle of the eleventh century, and since they are highly dramatic and conversational in style, they were probably meant for recitation at court. The stories are set in some ancient heroic age, before the coming of the English, and seem to be based on much earlier sagas of Celtic gods and goddesses, their unifying theme being the life and death of the hero Pryderi. Besides the 'Four Branches of the Mabinogi', there are other prose tales: the strangest is that of 'Culhwch and Olwen', in which the young hero Culhwch wins the daughter of the giant by accomplishing impossible tasks and killing the giant. It contains many elements of extremely primitive lore and religion as well as more recent references to Arthur. Also in *The Mabinogion* are native historical tales such as 'The Dream of Maxen', referring to the imperial pretender Magnus Maximus in 383 AD and his connection with Wales. A third type of tale surviving is the Welsh romance, such as 'The Lady of the Fountain', which is not so primitive in feeling and shows the influence of French medieval romances.

Such literature was for the consumption of the Welsh princes and their courts, but much of the same heroic and historical material was made known to Europe in this period by the Welsh medieval author, Geoffrey of Monmouth, who published in 1136 his Latin *Historia Regum Britanniae* (History of the Kings of Britain), the book purporting to be a history of the early Welsh. Giraldus Cambrensis (Gerald the Welshman) probably expressed the views of many fellow-countrymen at the time in saying that it was mere fiction, but it nevertheless helped to launch the international fame of Arthur and his knights. This period was one of cultural interchange, and in addition to the rich and elaborate court poetry, the law texts, and prose tales such as *The Mabinogion,* the Welsh also had a rich Catholic Christian devotional literature.

Bards and gentlemen

When the native princes of Powys and Gwynedd disappeared at the end of the thirteenth century, it might have been expected that the whole of this brilliant literary culture would have disappeared with them. It was however taken over, after the loss of independence, by the native gentry, the *uchelwyr,* their bards and monastic copyists. The *uchelwyr* were great survivalists and came to terms with the Marcher lords and with royal officials in the royal principality. The bards formed something akin to a medieval trade guild, with rules, regulations, examinations, degrees, schools with masters and grades of disciples. The bards were musicians, heralds, genealogists, chroniclers, secretaries and clerks for the Welsh gentry, and they travelled all over Wales to work for the gentlemen and entertain them at high days and holidays.

Despite the difficulties of the first decades after the conquest, the gentry came to dominate Welsh society in the fifteenth and sixteenth centuries, and their bards produced a vast amount of native literature. The most original and brilliant of the late medieval bards was Dafydd ap Gwilym (who flourished from 1320 to 1380). Like other bards, he sang the praises of his masters, but he was also an innovator in that he composed lyric verse describing his exploits as a lover and, most unusually, sang of his love of the natural world, in poetry of wit and humour, in language of great zest, colour and panache. The poetic form he perfected was the *cywydd,* a long lyric of rhymed couplets written in strict metre and alliteration. This became the dominant metrical form of the Welsh bards even into the late seventeenth century, and many thousands of these *cywydd* poems, almost all in praise of the Welsh gentry, were composed. Like that of the earlier heroic or princely ages, this poetry was intensely conservative, with cross-references to figures or events in earlier Welsh history, such as 'The Treason of the Long Knives' (see Chapter 6), or to chivalric heroes like Roland and Oliver, to saints such as Catherine or Anne, and even to Celtic prehistory. The frequency of such allusions shows that the gentry audience was intensely aware of its cultural heritage. The bards in turn memorised all kinds of lore about the Welsh past: for example, the 'Triads of the Isle of Britain', facts about early Welsh history grouped mnemonically into threes, were probably meant to educate the bards.

The culture of the bards and the *uchelwyr* was to a large extent Catholic Christian and feudal or chivalric. Dafydd ap Gwilym's family were servants of English kings in west Wales, and his vocabulary, speckled as it was with borrowings from French and English, is a mirror of the variety and openness of late medieval Welsh society, but it was also isolated enough not to be overwhelmed, and to retain its uniqueness, which it maintained by its archaism and sense of continuity with its distant past.

Humanism, the Reformation and Welsh literature

The Welsh gentry welcomed the rule of the Tudors, and their new legislation, such as the Acts of Union (1536–43); indeed the Welsh bards had seen the most famous Welsh gentleman of all, Henry Tudor, later Henry VII, as the fulfilment of the ancient Welsh prophecies that a Welshman would once again rule the island of Britain. The Tudor legislation had harmful long-term effects on Welsh native culture, however, for English became the language of opportunity and advancement, and the official language of administration and the law. The gentry and professional classes, who had for over two centuries been the mainstay of Welsh higher culture, were drawn into a world of grammar schools, inns of court and English towns and cities. The political changes took place at a time of great change in European culture in general, towards a secular, gentlemanly culture of printed books and the ideals of Renaissance humanism. Not so general, but just as profound, was the other great change which deeply affected the Tudor state, the coming of the Protestant Reformation. Political, cultural and religious changes came into Wales in the sixteenth century through the medium of English and caused a cultural and literary crisis. In comparison with new forces in society, Welsh literary culture seemed narrow, exclusive, reactionary and even barbaric — certainly irrelevant. The official Tudor historian, an Italian humanist called Polydore Vergil, dismissed Welsh history as myth and fancy. Welsh bards and scholars were goaded by such taunts to defend their heritage by trying to modernise their culture. Sir John Price of Brecon, for example, was incensed by humanist attacks, and produced in 1546 the first Welsh printed book. An example of the clash of cultures is the debate in the form of an exchange of poems over a number of years between the Protestant Archdeacon, Edmund Prys, and his friendly rival the old reactionary bard, William Cynwal, in the later sixteenth century. Prys urged the Welsh to modernise their culture and to bridge the gap between the old bardic world and the new world of humanism, and Cynwal defended the old. The bardic tradition, however, lasted until the mid seventeenth century, though in a rather enfeebled form, and it is said that the very last 'household bard' was Siôn Dafydd Las retained at Nannau (near Dolgellau) who died as late as 1694. The tradition lasted long enough for much bardic lore and learning to be handed on to Tudor scholars, humanists, antiquaries and prelates.

Although Welsh was excluded from the state administration, in the reign of Elizabeth Welsh returned as the language of the Anglican liturgy in the churches of Wales. The Prayer Book and New Testament were translated in 1567 and the whole Bible appeared in 1588. The translator, Bishop William Morgan, used as his standard that approved by the bards, and this was then heard throughout Wales, the common people soon becoming accustomed to hearing one standard Welsh language. This was of incalculable importance in the survival of the language.

There were a few Renaissance humanist scholars prepared to bridge the gap between the old and new learning. One such was a gentleman and scholar from north Wales, William Salesbury, who was familiar with bardic lore, was an educated humanist and a zealous Protestant. He published a Welsh dictionary and a book of ancient proverbs, and helped to translate the Prayer Book and New Testament. Other scholars such as Dr Siôn Dafydd Rhys tried to publish Welsh grammar and bardistry in Latin so as to open the secret world of the Welsh to the whole world. Men of this sort, however, were few and far between, and the humanist scholarly movement petered out in the early seventeenth century, its last monument being the Latin–Welsh Dictionary of Dr John Davies of Mallwyd in 1632. The bards had been gathered into a successful *eisteddfod* in 1567 held under Elizabeth I's patronage, but by 1600 the order was in decay. The seventeenth century, however, saw a remarkable salvage operation performed at the eleventh hour by a line of Welsh antiquaries to save at least some of the culture of the Middle Ages.

A Welsh printed-book literature did in fact appear: not, as the humanists would have liked, a literature of learning and civility, but one of Protestant piety and devotion. From the reign of Elizabeth to 1660 a steady number of mainly Anglican tracts were translated into Welsh, a few original works, and then from 1660 to the mid eighteenth century the stream became a flood. Some of the authors rose above the merely didactic and devotional and wrote original works which became classics; such were the prose works of two Puritan authors of the mid seventeenth century, Morgan Llwyd and Charles Edwards. In the sixteenth and seventeenth centuries a vast repertoire of lyrics, folk verses, epigrams, carols and ballads, often composed to be sung in free metre verse though with a good deal of bardic ornamentation using *cynghanedd* (alliteration), was composed. Religious teachers saw their chance with these verses and composed pious versions in the same style. Thousands knew by heart the verses of 'The Old Vicar', the Anglican Vicar Prichard of Llandovery who wrote his *Cannwyll y Cymru* (Welshman's Candle) in the early seventeenth century.

Revivals and Romanticism

Welsh writers of the eighteenth century were aware that they were part of a cultural re-awakening; they felt they were restoring Welsh literature after its decline during the reign of Elizabeth. The origins of the change lay in the later seventeenth century, but there was a vigour, purposefulness and resourcefulness, even a swagger, about many Welsh writers of this period which had long been missing. Many of them sneered at Puritans and Methodists, but the work of the SPCK, the circulating schools of Griffith Jones and the Methodist revival, all contributed to a huge increase in the reading public. There was a corresponding increase in the number of books published in Welsh. Printing presses appeared in Wales after 1718, and there was a network of book pedlars, bookshops and libraries for the first time inside Wales. Seventeenth-century authors were lucky to get one book printed in a lifetime: Williams of Pantycelyn, who died in 1791, had by then published over ninety books, most of them in Welsh. It was the rise of a serious, pious, book-reading public from 1660 onwards, and a decline in the vigour, even amongst the commonest folk, of the ancient traditions in music, history and literature, which spurred Welsh writers into action and made them reorganise Welsh literary culture for a contemporary, middle-class world. The *eisteddfod* as an institution was revived in 1701, and then throughout the century Welsh authors organised subscription lists, arranged publications and new editions of ancient texts, published dictionaries and grammars, books preaching the virtues of Welsh and its literature. The result was akin to a miniature Renaissance, but some two hundred years late. Instead of reaching back to Greek and Roman classical literature, however, Welsh authors revived their own medieval literature. The rules of *cynghanedd* now had to be taught to amateur bards through handbooks, and early in the century poets such as Lewis Morris, an official of the royal mines in Cardiganshire, produced excellent pastiches of the *cywydd* poems of the fourteenth century. The result of all this activity was not really a revival of medieval culture, for it was all mixed with the latest literary fashions from London, so that revived Welsh eighteenth-century poetry might easily contain three disparate elements: Welsh medieval forms, Augustan classicism and the sublime epic grandeur of John Milton. Such were the characteristics of the poetry of the celebrated eighteenth-century Welsh bard, Goronwy Owen, who emigrated from Britain to work in William and Mary College, Williamsburg, and died in 1769 in America.

Artistic poetry accounted, however, for only a small part of the poems written in Welsh during the century; by far the greatest number were in fact hymns. The hymn was the vehicle of the Methodist revival, and Williams of Pantycelyn wrote vast quantities of hymns, unashamedly using homely Carmarthenshire dialect for this purpose. He had innumerable imitators and followers. Williams also wrote good prose works, usually books of moral and spiritual advice, though sometimes moral tales that in some ways resemble short novels. A number of prose works of the eighteenth century became classics, for example the biting satire by Ellis Wynne, *Gweledigaetheu y Bardd Cwsc* (Visions of the Sleeping Bard), written in 1703 and *Drych y Prif Oesoedd* (Mirror of Early Ages), a religious history of the Welsh, by Theophilus Evans. One of the paradoxes of the revival of the eighteenth century is that on the one hand the medieval Welsh language was studied, revived and reused, and the rules of *cynghanedd* recovered and re-employed; on the other hand, the hymns relied on very racy dialect, and the prose works too used modern colloquial Welsh. The dictionaries of this period made sure that there were Welsh words for all possible needs.

Welsh and Anglo-Welsh

Many of the Welsh authors of the eighteenth century translated devotional works from English, such as Ellis Wynne and Theophilus Evans, and indeed Evans himself was the author of an English attack on the Methodists, *The History of Modern Enthusiasm* (1752). Many, if not all, Welsh authors were deeply influenced by English literary fashions, and a fair number were authors of English works. There was a great deal of writing about Wales and things Welsh during the eighteenth century, the authors writing in English, such as Edward Lhuyd, Henry Rowland and, later on, Thomas Pennant. Pennant wrote on the history of north Wales, but he was also a world famous scientist. Another Welshman, equally famous outside Wales as within, was the philosopher, Richard Price, who caused a great furore by writing in favour of the American Revolutionaries at the time of the War of Independence. In fact, there were so many writers writing about Wales in English by the late eighteenth century that it could be argued that 'Anglo-Welsh' appeared at this time.

Wales, its history, its landscape and its people became a matter of interest to the English in this period, and it was through this cultural interchange of Welsh and English that many of the ideas of the Romantics influenced Wales. This can be seen most clearly in the life and work of a Glamorgan stonemason Edward Williams 'Iolo Morganwg', whose literary career spanned the years 1770 to 1826. Iolo Morganwg absorbed all the varied ideas of European and English Romanticism, and adapted them for the Welsh people, giving them romantic lyric poetry, romantic history and, in 1789, reviving the order of bards. He combined this with pacifism and druidism, and eventually in 1819 latched his order, with all its ceremonial and mythology, onto the revived National Eisteddfod. Iolo had an incredible facility at imitating Welsh medieval poetry, and during a long life produced so many pastiches, imitations and downright forgeries that generations of readers and scholars were misled by his brilliant inventions. As if to underline what we have said about 'Anglo-Welsh', Iolo also published works in English.

Workers, peasants and preachers

Iolo Morganwg was in many ways a portent of the age to come, not only in his romanticism, but also in the fact that he was a

186

stonemason, a radical in politics and a Unitarian dissenter in religion, and spent much of his later life visiting the greatest Welsh industrial settlement, Merthyr Tydfil. In some ways this new society had emerged as early as the 1790s: Welsh writers were in that period much exercised by the myth of Madoc's having sailed out from Wales to discover America in about 1170, and Iolo Morganwg and others were involved in ventures to liberate the common people of Wales from oppression at home by establishing Welsh settlements in America. The great reaction, however, which set in after the initial impact of the French Revolution, a reaction which in Wales lasted many decades, disguised the emergence of a new Welsh industrial society. For the first thirty or forty years of the nineteenth century Welsh culture was dominated by reactionary Methodist leaders and by equally reactionary romantic Anglican parsons, and it was the latter who wrote most of the poetry and history of the time.

However, the forces of nonconformity, radicalism and industrialism eventually came to the fore, and Welsh culture came into the hands of workers, peasants and preachers, so that while the Welsh in the nineteenth century greatly admired England and things English, the literary culture produced in Welsh in that century could hardly have been more different.

In some ways the nineteenth century was the most prolific century for Welsh literature: the population rose by leaps and bounds and the number of Welsh-speakers and readers rose steadily, the common people became more literate and rich enough to afford books, pens and paper. The *eisteddfod,* which had been revived as an institution during the eighteenth century, rose to greater heights of influence and popularity in the nineteenth, and continued to be the main spur of artistic activity. A vast quantity of *eisteddfod* literature was produced still in the mould set by the previous century, a mixture of revived medieval forms and *cynghanedd,* Goronwy Owen's taste for the ideal, the epic and the sublime, to which were added the moral and religious concerns of the nineteenth century. The Welsh language itself, revitalised and extended in its modes and vocabulary during the eighteenth century, came under the baneful influence of romantic scholars after 1800 such as the imaginative but wrong-headed grammarian William Owen-Pughe. Pughe produced a logical but unreal Welsh grammar and orthography, remote from everyday Welsh, which gave rise to a most artificial Welsh literary style.

The greatest part of nineteenth-century literature was not artistic, however, but religious and political. Floods of hymn books, devotional primers, tracts and expository studies appeared in Welsh. There were dozens of journals and periodicals. It was not a middle-class world, and so the novel was slow to take root. However, a vast number of biographies, secular and saintly, appeared in Wales in this period and these were a substitute for the novel. The first Anglo-Welsh novel, *The Adventures and Vagaries of Twm Shon Catti* by T. J. Ll. Pritchard appeared in 1828, and very soon after that attempts were made to introduce English novels into Welsh in translation. Religious literature was much more in demand, and so great was the appetite for religious literature that it was profitable for publishers in London, Edinburgh and elsewhere outside Wales to print Welsh books. Welsh communities had grown up in America, and Welsh books were printed in America from the early eighteenth century, the Welsh-Americans helping greatly to extend the market for Welsh books in the nineteenth.

As the century advanced, so the Welsh cultural world changed. After 1870 Welshmen became literate in English, society became more secular and industrialised and Welsh literature became more varied and less uniform. For example, there was a great advance in poetry written not in *cynghanedd* but in the 'free metres', for example, the work of John Hughes 'Ceiriog' (who wrote innumerable short lyrics, many of them for singing) or William Thomas 'Islwyn' (who composed philosophical, questioning, long poems in blank verse), both men born in 1832. A further sign of change is the growth in the popularity of articles, essays and novels, though the only novelist who achieved a prose classic was Daniel Owen, a tailor from Mold (Flintshire) whose short stories and novels were published between 1876 and 1895. Daniel Owen depicted, often with wit and humorous characterisation, the life of the small town of the industrialised north-eastern borderland. He could also be critical of the hypocrisy of Victorian capitalism and respectable Calvinism.

The popularity of Daniel Owen's work shows that in the last decades of the century the Welsh reading public had grown tired of an exclusive diet of radical journalism and Puritan piety, and Welsh literature began to change rapidly: its standards grew more critical, secular and scholarly, while its tone became more aesthetic and even romantic. Sometimes the influences were semi-political, from the *Cymru Fydd* (Young Wales) movement, whose cultural effects were more powerful than its political ones, and at other times they were personal. Sir John Rhys, philologist and anthropologist, principal of Jesus College, Oxford, around the turn of the century, greatly influenced a brilliant generation of Welsh undergraduates who brought this new tone and atmosphere to Welsh literature. Two examples will suffice here: Sir Owen M. Edwards, Fellow of Lincoln College, became a tireless essayist and publisher, accustoming the Welsh public to a light, easy, humorous prose style far removed from the earnest pomposity of the prose of the older generations; secondly, Sir John Morris-Jones by his writings and adjudications at the National Eisteddfod, refined and cleansed grammar and style of Victorian infelicities, taught the Welsh poets the glories of *cynghanedd* and encouraged a more purely aesthetic or artistic attitude to poetry. Once again, a revitalisation of Welsh literature had come hand in hand with a revival of ancient art forms.

Twentieth-century Welsh writing

Writers such as Owen Edwards and Morris-Jones laid the foundations of the 'Welsh Renaissance of the Twentieth Century'. Despite the insistence of this school on down-to-earth and concrete language and critical standards of scholarship, it was also a neo-Romantic movement, tending to romanticise Welsh society, its Victorian radicalism, its nonconformity and its rural peasantry, the *gwerin*. This we find in the work of such writers as Crwys Williams 'Crwys' and Eliseus Williams 'Eifion Wyn'. A certain wistful romanticism also affected the early work of Robert Williams Parry and W. J. Gruffydd. The most original and distinguished figure of the early twentieth-century school was Thomas Gwynn Jones, a man who produced an immense and varied output in poetry and prose over many years. Gwynn Jones was the greatest master of traditional *cynghanedd* since the poets of the later fifteenth century, and for much of his subject matter drew upon ancient legends and myths. He was a radical and a nationalist, and could also be an extremely biting satirist of his contemporaries, but his sense of history and mythology enable him to be classed with the neo-Romantic movement of Edwardian Wales.

World War I had a chastening and depressing effect on Welsh society, and the amount of literature arising from the experience of the war was small compared with the corresponding literature in

English. The long-term effect of the war, however, was profound, and many have felt that the Welsh literature of the twentieth century's second quarter has been the greatest achievement of the century.

The 1920s saw the emergence of a school of writers, mainly scholars and prose writers, of energy and resourcefulness: the literary criticism of Saunders Lewis, the urbane and witty essays of R. T. Jenkins, the criticism of W. J. Gruffydd, the short stories of Kate Roberts and D. J. Williams, the analytical essays of T. H. Parry-Williams (also the writer of epoch-making verse using slang and doggerel). All these authors seemed more mature and combined to bring the Welsh out of the cultural nursery or chapel vestry. They were grown-up, self-aware, liberated, critical, urbane — all at the same time. The period is marked by the critical essay, the short essay of self-analysis and by the short story. The short stories of D. J. Williams are cast in a fairly traditional mould, the tales of a story-teller. Kate Roberts, whose career has stretched from the 1920s to the 1980s, brought the artistic short story to its greatest perfection. Her stories are terse, spare, severe, they appear to be 'plotless', and they deal with a narrow slice of life, often the hard times of poor Caernarfonshire quarryfolk, analysing each aspect of that life in microscopic detail.

It is difficult to explain why, as with World War I, World War II also failed to produce much war literature. Two reasons which have been suggested are that the war, as an experience lived entirely through the English language, was hard to assimilate into Welsh literature, and that the war was not an experience with which Welsh authors could identify as Welshmen. One feature emerging after 1945 was a growing sense of Welsh patriotism, even nationalism, among Welsh authors. It has been claimed that this goes back to 1936, the time when a British government bombing school in Llŷn was burned down by three Welsh patriots, two of the three being Welsh authors, Saunders Lewis and D. J. Williams. It has been argued that this created a crisis of conscience in Welsh writing; it deeply affected the poetry of Robert Williams Parry from 1937 onwards and shaped the vigorous astringent poetry of D. Gwenallt Jones 'Gwenallt'. Many, if not all, Welsh-language writers after 1945 have been affected by this mood of 'engagement'.

As far as literary form is concerned, the most important post-war change is the rise of the novel. This in itself shows a greater sense of confidence in the resources of Welsh society and in those of the language itself, but it is also a sign that the *gwerin* of Wales had become far more bourgeois and middle-class. Kate Roberts, although still writing short stories even in extreme old age, has become better known since 1950 as a novelist. It was T. Rowland Hughes with his series of popular novels such as *O Law i Law* (From Hand to Hand) in the late 1940s who tipped the balance in favour of the novel, but it was Islwyn Ffowc Elis with his novel *Cysgod y Cryman* (Shadow of the Sickle) in 1953, a young man's novel about young people, who really launched the fashion for novels by young Welsh writers which has continued unabated from the 1950s to the 1980s. Islwyn Ffowc Elis and his followers, such as Jane Edwards, Eigra Lewis Roberts, John Rowlands and many others, have evolved a racy, idiomatic, colloquial language that is a fair compromise between the beautifully turned elegant and pure diction of the authors of the 1920s and 1930s and the excessively slangy broken Welsh of the contemporary common man. One way of avoiding this problem of language is to write historical novels, and it is no surprise that there is a great vogue in current Welsh literature for them. Before 1945 the problem could clearly be seen in the field of Welsh drama: there were hundreds of small amateur dramatic companies, catered for by popular dramatists like John Ellis Williams, often performing comedies written in local dialect. Saunders Lewis's plays for many years were written in a remote and elevated diction and placed in the distant past, in prehistory or in foreign countries. After about 1950, however, playwrights like Saunders Lewis have felt able to produce work in a more contemporary non-dialect idiom which enables the dramatist to write about current Welsh life. This change has been forwarded by the rise of radio, and more recently television drama.

In the field of poetry the most striking change since 1945 has been the rise of the poetry of the international modern movement, *vers-libre*, liberated in form, rhyme and subject matter. This movement came surprisingly late into Welsh, but it can be seen in the later work of D. Gwenallt Jones 'Gwenallt', and in the work of younger poets such as Bobi Jones in the 1950s and Gwyn Thomas in the 1960s. For a tradition as intensely conservative as the Welsh, this was a literary revolution indeed, and it set up a serious reaction against modernism.

Since 1920 a large amount of Welsh writing has been produced for a local public by amateurs who regard literature as an enterprising hobby. Such writers became increasingly impatient with college-bred authors with 'highbrow' tastes, metropolitan in standards if not in residence. The reaction began in the field of prose first in the late 1950s and 1960s, with a tremendous vogue for rural reminiscences by the last survivors of the monoglot Welsh world of the 1880s, and then after 1970 the reaction invaded the field of poetry, with the fresh attention paid to the work of the *bardd-gwlad* (country poet) and to a revival of *cynghanedd*. One of the most unexpected features of current Welsh literature is the widespread enthusiasm for learning, writing and reading *cynghanedd*. It is only fair to say that the leading light of this movement is the young poet, Alan Llwyd, a college graduate and a civil servant living in the city.

Anglo-Welsh literature in the twentieth century

Although there have been English books written by the Welsh down the centuries, the distinctive Anglo-Welsh School only emerged after 1900, when English had become the language of a majority of the common people for the first time. The father of the Anglo-Welsh was Caradoc Evans (1878–1945), short-story writer and playwright, who described the life of Cardiganshire peasants and preachers. Gwyn Jones said of the effect of Caradoc's work: '*My People* in 1915, a book which for Welshmen added a final horror to war as surely as *My Neighbours* in 1919 and *Taffy* in 1923, robbed them of the peace that should have followed'. Radical nonconformist Wales was shown in the most unflattering light possible. The Anglo-Welsh school, then, was a reaction against the values of radical and rural nonconformity. The writers who emerged in the 1920s and 1930s such as Gwyn Jones, Glyn Jones, Gwyn Thomas (not the Welsh-language poet) and many others, were mostly from the industrial valleys of the south. Dylan Thomas was from the town of Swansea and Geraint Goodwin was from the English-speaking eastern borderland. Glyn Jones has observed that their distinctiveness as a school of writers came from the fact that they were the first generation to exploit a certain virgin territory in English (the Welsh valleys) and yet they were all very close to Welsh-language life, often the children of Welsh-speakers. In fact Glyn Jones sees Anglo-Welsh literature arising at the point when the children of the leaders of Welsh radical and chapel society begin to speak and think in English.

The English public became aware of the distinctiveness of the school in Keidrych Rhys's magazine *Wales* in 1937. Many of the

Anglo-Welsh authors were short-story writers, but the most famous of them was the poet, Dylan Thomas. They were eloquent, verbose, rebellious virtuosi, defiant in their belief that they were breaking out of an old Welsh strait-jacket. There was a good deal of mutual suspicion between them and Welsh-language authors, although Gwyn Jones's *Welsh Review* from 1939 onwards tried to be a platform in English for writers in the two languages. One writer who remained all his life true to his original vision in the 1930s was the novelist Gwyn Thomas, his constant and unchanging inspiration being the downtrodden exploited poor of the Rhondda valleys in the depression. Dylan Thomas remained free from political involvement, but other writers were left-wing, engaged, goaded into writing by the tragedy of industrial Wales.

From 1937 to about 1950 that brilliant generation had astounding success in Wales, England and America. Richard Llewellyn's novel *How Green was my Valley* gave people all over the world a highly romanticised picture of the family life of a very old-fashioned Welsh mining community. Dylan Thomas's radio play (later adapted as a great stage success) *Under Milk Wood,* portraying a day in the life of a small Welsh port, again in a highly romantic idiom, also became world famous. Many of that generation continued to write even up to the 1980s with great success, but already after 1945 a new kind of Anglo-Welsh writing began to make an impact. One early sign of the change was the work of the outsider David Jones, whose *In Parenthesis* (1937) compared the experience of Welshmen in World War I with the experience of Welsh soldiers in the poetry of Taliesin and Aneirin. After 1945 a change occurred towards writing which was less comic, less verbose and closer in spirit to contemporary Welsh-language authors. In 1946 there appeared the first book of R. S. Thomas, *Stones of the Field,* the first of many volumes of poetry and a great influence on later Anglo-Welsh authors, although he himself rejects the label Anglo-Welsh. In the same period we find the first novels of Emyr Humphreys, a novelist self-consciously Welsh who always takes Welsh problems seriously and never exploits Welsh territory for local colour or for grotesque effects.

After a comparatively lean period in the 1950s, there was a new wave of writing in the 1960s and 1970s, and in this period Anglo-Welsh authors became able for the first time to be published inside Wales itself. They organise with great resourcefulness their literary societies, clubs, discussion groups, night classes and conferences, so that they have all the energy and confidence of a school of writers. A striking feature of this school is their readiness to co-operate with Welsh-language writers, and a number of the Anglo-Welsh writers who are, by birth or learning, bilingual have produced a large variety of anthologies of Welsh literature in translation. Their journals are *Poetry Wales, Planet* and, longest-lived of all, *The Anglo-Welsh Review.* They have found it a struggle to establish their literature as a school or university subject, but they are inspired by the example of other literatures of the English-speaking world, notably that most respectable university subject, American literature.

In some ways the Anglo-Welsh authors are faced with a dilemma because of the erosion of so much of the distinctive character of Welsh life which provided them with an obvious vein to mine in the 1920s and 1930s, and because it is difficult for an author to decide whether his loyalty lies to the Welsh people or to English literature. So many of the current Anglo-Welsh authors, however, are patriotic and self-consciously Welsh writers that the future of the Anglo-Welsh school is assured at least for the coming generation.

CHAPTER 9

Land of Song, the Bard and Rugby

Land of song

'Land of song' or 'Land of the harp' is a common cliché about Wales, much more common than the obvious geographical cliché 'Land of the Mountains'. The Welsh national anthem, composed in 1856, having defined Wales as the 'Land of my fathers', goes on to say that it is the 'Land of bards and singers'. How did such clichés arise?

There is no clear evidence that in distant centuries Wales was more musical than other countries, though it had plenty of native music-making, influenced by the court and the gentry and by the Catholic church. The Welsh had their own instruments in the Middle Ages, nurtured by the bards. Some of the bards were proficient in poetry (*cerdd dafod*) and others were adept at music (*cerdd dant*, 'craft of the string'), a term which shows that although music was performed on a primitive oboe called a *pibgorn* (pipe-horn) and on a *crwth* or crowd (a bowed harp or viol), pride of place was given to the harp.

The original Welsh harp was a small instrument, its horsehair strings giving a buzzing tone like a spinet, but this was replaced in the late Middle Ages by the larger stronger Irish harp, often with metal strings and a plangent tone. The Irish harp was succeeded in turn by a version of the Italian baroque harp during the seventeenth century, this being the *telyn deires,* the triple harp, the instrument generally referred to since the eighteenth century as the Welsh harp. Throughout this early modern period Welsh harpists were admired and employed in England, many of them at court. Some of the medieval Welsh bardic harpistry was preserved by William Penllyn who won the music competition at the Caerwys *eisteddfod* of 1567, known to us in a copy made in the seventeenth century by a royal harpist, Robert ap Huw. Robert ap Huw's manuscript of music seems strange and remote, primitive and alien even compared to the music of the European Renaissance. With the decline of the bards and the anglicisation of gentry tastes after 1600, the ancient musical tradition disappeared. New instruments such as the fiddle flooded into Wales, and with them came a taste for Welsh provincial versions of English or French music, the dances of the Tudor and Stuart court, the lyrics of the English stage, to judge from the favourite tunes to which popular Welsh poets wrote their ballads such as 'Leave Land', 'Butter and Pease', 'Prince Rupert's March'. A huge quantity of native airs and tunes were written in the seventeenth and eighteenth centuries in imitation of the imported music, for example 'David of the White Rock' by a young Caernarfonshire harpist. Sometimes the title of the imported song was translated, its rhythm or mode transformed, so that its foreign origin was forgotten. The Welsh airs or Welsh folk songs, which we learn and enjoy today, in most cases date from this period.

During the eighteenth century Welsh music came under many contradictory influences. One was a cultural revival affecting not only Welsh history and literature, but also music. Patriots and antiquaries wished to recreate a less derivative musical culture, and revive what they thought was an ancient bardic musical tradition. Three musicians most responsible for recreating the notion that Wales was the land of the harp were John Parry 'Blind Parry', from the 1740s onwards, Edward Jones 'Bardd y Brenin', from the 1780s onwards, and John Parry 'Bardd Alaw' in the early nineteenth century. These three were energetic performers, collectors and editors of music, with positions of influence in London society, and succeeded in creating the image that Wales had a unique musical heritage, the baroque harp was truly the 'Welsh harp' and that the music stemmed in some indefinable way from the time of the ancient druids. From the descriptions of English travellers, we know that much music was performed in Wales, by harpers in the north and fiddlers in the south. In this period also the revived *eisteddfod* held musical competitions, and handsome prizes were given for harp playing and for the art of *penillion* singing, that is, singing to harp accompaniment. Much of the music performed was in all probability of recent origin, but the cultural propagandists of the eighteenth century created the notion of a Welsh national music.

The other, contradictory, influence upon Welsh music in this period was Methodism. From its origin in 1730s to about 1850 it was fairly hostile to the cultural revival, and to wean the Welsh away from their dependence on harping, fiddling and dancing, the

Methodists created their own popular music. They did not invent hymn-singing, but they discovered, just as revivalist sects were to discover in America, that the surest way to attack the emotions of common people and preach to the illiterate masses was through songs. About 1744, towards the end of the first phase of the revival, hymn singing became all important, and the Methodists found in one of their leaders, Williams of Pantycelyn, an indefatigable hymn writer. Pantycelyn's hymns, it was claimed, largely created the second phase of the revival in 1762 (see Chapter 7). Folk melodies, dances and song tunes, the latest hits among the groundlings of London's theatres, were all grist to Pantycelyn's mill. One of his characteristic tunes was 'Lovely Peggy — Moralis'd'.

During the eighteenth century there were a few professional musicians in Wales, and towards the end of the century some books to teach music in Welsh, but in the main, musicians were self-taught, and the style of congregational singing probably did not in any way resemble that of today. The evangelised congregations sang their hymns with passion and fervour and sometimes gathered together to sing non-stop for three days and three nights. There was nothing self-consciously Welsh about this congregational tradition, but undoubtedly we have in Methodism an important strand of the fabric of the 'Land of Song'.

The tradition created in the eighteenth century continued into the nineteenth. The *eisteddfod* and Welsh patriotism maintained the triple harp for several generations in the teeth of the advance of the French pedal harp, its last defenders being in fact outsiders in Welsh society, Augusta Waddington, Lady Llanover and the Romany-speaking family of John Roberts 'Telynor Cymru'. The same forces encouraged the collecting and composing of Welsh songs, and during the early nineteenth century, the bringing to perfection of the art of *penillion* singing. The origins of this art have yet to be discovered. Certainly in the popular *eisteddfod* meetings of the 1790s there were competitions for singing medleys of stanzas (*penillion telyn*) to harp accompaniment, and by the mid nineteenth century the art as we know it today had arrived. The harpist chooses a well-known melody, a hymn or a folksong perhaps, and after a few bars of the tune, the singer chimes in with his words, swiftly improvising a descant or counterpoint, sometimes syncopating his rhythm so as to cut across the harpist's beat, making sure he ends his verse at the end of the harpist's melody.

197

During the late eighteenth century the English theatre which had provided entertainment for the middle and upper classes in Wales had given the Welsh a taste for English concert music, and in the *eisteddfod* meetings from 1819 onwards London-based artistes gave many concerts throughout Wales, creating an untiring appetite among the Welsh for the music of composers such as Handel and Haydn. The music of the classical composers most enjoyed by them, however, was choral music. In Wales as in England there had always been choral music in large churches and cathedrals, but in Wales such choirs must have been few and far between. It appears also that the natural custom of Welsh congregations even into the 1840s was to sing in unison. By the middle of the century, however, a large number of singing teachers, instruments and music books had appeared all over Wales, and the common people demanded grandiose chapel buildings. Chapel galleries were excellent for separating the various choral voice parts; chapel buildings with their flat ceilings often had superb acoustics and there appeared a wide-spread enthusiasm for elaborate choral singing. In the religious revival of 1859 much emphasis was placed on congregational sing-ing. This was a result of the work of such men as John Roberts 'Ieuan Gwyllt', John Ambrose Lloyd and Edward Stephen 'Tanymarian', who collected and edited hymns and anthems, encouraged each chapel to hold its *ysgol gân* (singing school after the evening service) and its *cymanfa ganu* (singing assembly) meetings, and they publi-cised this choral culture in their many musical journals. People like Eleazar Roberts brought Curwen's tonic sol-fa into Wales from Liverpool in 1860, and this simple and effective method of teaching people to read music quickly spread like wildfire in Wales more than in any other country. The London Tonic Sol-fa College was seen as a poor man's university, and the various certificates of the college were displayed with pride, gilt-framed, on the walls of cottages the length and breadth of the land. The early Methodist opposition to musical instruments was overcome gradually, and by the late nineteenth century most chapels had organs or harmoniums, some even small orchestras, and so important did the music become that people worshipped in chapel not with their families but with other sopranos or tenors in the places assigned to them in the gallery.

The Welsh people in the second half of the nineteenth century began to hold innumerable *eisteddfod* meetings and these en-couraged the performing of works secular as well as sacred. The

198

eisteddfod adjudicator and the *cymanfa* conductor became the demi-gods of Welsh society. There were many Anglican choral and musical festivals in Wales in the same period, and if one adds all these influences together, it can easily be seen how Wales became by 1870 the land of the great choirs. The seal was set by the victories of the great choir of the conductor Caradog of Aberdare (*Côr Mawr Caradog*) at the Crystal Palace music festivals in 1872 and 1873.

The whole period from 1860 to 1914 forms a distinct period of Welsh chapel and *eisteddfod* music. Most of the composers were amateurs, although the most prolific of them, Joseph Parry (hero of Jack Jones's novel *Off to Philadelphia in the Morning*), was a professional and professor of music at the new college in Aberystwyth in 1874. The composers were, of course, open to outside influence — the Victorian music hall, Gilbert and Sullivan operas, American hymnology of the Sankey and Moody type, Rossini and Verdi — yet the demands and limitations of the composers' market gave Welsh music of this period a distinctive character.

There were many signs of change before 1914 in the world we have just described: professional concert halls appeared — Cardiff's Park Hall in 1885, for example — and Cardiff had its triennial festival in the 1890s where contemporary British composers such as Elgar introduced their works to the public. By contrast, the aesthetic cultural revival of the 1890s had its effect on Welsh music, with a fresh revival of interest in folk songs, and a Welsh Folk Song Society was founded in 1906. In the main, the greatest thrust in musical development was to draw the Welsh on all levels into the general musical development of Britain, and to break down the limited but distinctive chapel-based music of the Victorian era. On a serious level this change can be seen in the activity of Sir Walford Davies and his Welsh National Council of Music in 1919, his lectures and music festivals. Professional and instrumental music were advanced by the BBC Welsh Orchestra and the Welsh National Opera (both dating from 1945) and the Guild for the Promotion of Welsh music, founded in 1954. On a popular level, the decline of the initiative of village and chapel society and with it the decay of the Welsh language, meant that for the majority of Welsh people popular music became current Anglo-American entertainment. To the public of the 1920s and 1930s the music of the cinema, the wireless, the gramophone and the dance hall seemed a great improvement. It reflected the way in which Welsh native society had been drawn into

199

British society as a whole, and part of this movement of absorption has been the greater number of people from Wales making their mark as professional musicians, composers, instrumentalists, and in two fields with particular brilliance: operatic singing (Gwyneth Jones and Sir Geraint Evans) and popular singing (Shirley Bassey and Tom Jones).

The Welsh story, here as in other fields, is partly one of absorption and partly one of resistance, and it would be wrong to complete this section on music without mentioning at least two musical developments in the Welsh-speaking hinterland of Wales in the twentieth century. The earlier is the great revival of the art of *penillion* singing since the 1930s, the art becoming more elaborate and skilful, and (though this is contrary to the original principle of improvisation) being adapted for groups or choirs. Journals, societies, summer schools, courses and festivals have appeared to foster *cerdd dant,* a term now covering harp music and *penillion* singing. The development, reflecting the growth of self-conscious Welsh patriotism in the 1960s, is that of Welsh pop. The most famous pop singer of the 1960s and 1970s is Dafydd Iwan, but in his wake have appeared a host of singers, groups, companies and journals, a market specialising in Welsh-language concerts and records. This satirical and semi-political pop music should be differentiated from the wide market for 'popular music' records in Wales, for example, the widespread demand for records of Welsh male-voice choirs or the Welsh-language balladists such as Trebor Edwards, whose records sell many thousands each year. Indeed a glance at the popular shelves of record shops in Wales might lead one to suppose that little in Welsh popular musical taste had changed since 1900.

Land of the bards: the Eisteddfod

Since the *eisteddfod* is unique among European cultural institutions, it deserves a section to itself. The word means literally 'a session', and it refers to a session of cultural competitions. The first recorded session was simply called a court and it was held, at the behest of the ruler of south Wales, the Lord Rhys, at Cardigan in 1176. The bards, who were musicians as well as poets, took care to regulate their craft and keep unskilful rhymesters and buskers out, and this they did at various moots of which we know little. At an *eisteddfod* at Carmarthen around 1450 the bards agreed upon stringent regulations controlling the writing of Welsh poetry, both as regards metre and rhyme and as regards *cynghanedd* or alliteration. Poetry written (then or now) according to these regulations is called strict metre poetry. In the sixteenth century there were two important *eisteddfod* meetings at Caerwys in Flintshire in 1523 and 1567, and one of the Caerwys prizes, a miniature silver harp given for music, still survives at Mostyn near Caerwys. The sense of tradition was extremely strong at Caerwys, the bards claiming that their regulations were the Statute of Gruffydd ap Cynan, purportedly going back to about 1100.

Caerwys was a brilliant sunset glow, and night soon fell on the *eisteddfod* which disappeared after 1567; we have no certain knowledge of any *eisteddfod* until 1701. When the institution resurfaced, the last of the old bards had died, the musicians had all disappeared and the revived institution would hardly have been recognisable to the earlier generations. The *eisteddfodau* were advertised in almanacks, and are therefore known as 'almanack *eisteddfodau*'. They consisted of small groups of amateur versifiers and rhymesters enjoying a verbal battle over a few pints in a tavern.

From 1701 to 1789 the *eisteddfodau* were rather paltry affairs, but in 1789 three *eisteddfodau* were held, at Llangollen, Corwen and Bala, which were quite different and heralded the arrival of the modern institution. The organising genius was Thomas Jones, Jones the exciseman. The publicity, taste and standards, the prize money and medals, all came from the rich London Welsh; the public attended the adjudications, the transactions were published, there were bookstalls in the surrounding streets and Welsh interludes or plays in the evenings.

Almost at the same time, but quite separate, arose the *Gorsedd of Bards*. This was the invention of the fertile imagination of Edward Williams 'Iolo Morganwg' a Glamorgan stonemason, scholar and poet (see Chapter 8). Iolo Morganwg wanted to give Welsh society a permanent cultural institution, of which the *eisteddfod* meetings would be just one part. The nearest thing to this which Wales had had was the medieval Order of Bards. Like many Romantic scholars, he also believed that the Welsh bards had been the successors of the ancient druids. He also needed the patronage of the rich London Welsh and in 1792 on Primrose Hill in London he launched his new druidic order which he called the *Gorsedd* (throne) of bards. To give it publicity he created for it a liturgy and colourful ceremonial.

During the great wars with France from the 1790s to 1815, the *Gorsedd* and the *eisteddfod* languished, but with the return of peace, they were again in demand. From 1819 to 1821 four provincial societies were founded in Wales to publicise Welsh culture and hold *eisteddfodau*. One of the first of these provincial *eisteddfodau* was held at Carmarthen in 1819, at which Iolo Morganwg succeeded in persuading those attending to agree to incorporate his *Gorsedd* into the *eisteddfod*. The provincial *eisteddfodau* were held from 1819 to 1858 and during this period they became genuinely attractive to the common people. They brought in a number of features which still remain in the modern *eisteddfod*: the long prize essay, evening concerts by professional artistes, long patriotic or presidential speeches and competitions for crafts and trades. Lady Llanover's prize essay at the Cardiff *eisteddfod* of 1834 really launched the idea of a Welsh national costume for women, and the Abergavenny *eisteddfodau* held under Lady Llanover's aegis in this period greatly encouraged Welsh tweeds. The provincial *eisteddfodau* also developed a symbolic language of decoration for public occasions in Wales — insignia, mottoes, emblems — some of which is still used today.

For long fairly hostile to the *eisteddfod*, by the late 1840s chapel-goers embraced the institution, probably as a result of the furore of the Treason of the Blue Books. For example, the *eisteddfod* begun by secular patriots at the industrial centre of Merthyr Tydfil was taken over by teetotalist zealots, and in 1854 they offered a prize for a novel on the subject of 'The Reformed Drunkard', thus helping to launch the novel as a literary form in Welsh. The rapprochement between the chapel and the bardic institution paved the way for a truly national *eisteddfod*, an institution which became feasible by the late 1850s because of the widespread circulation of journals through Wales and the new railway network. The first of the modern annual national *eisteddfodau* took place at Llangollen in 1858, and although the organisers were romantic reactionaries in many cases, they were canny enough to bring the crowds in by what must have been amongst the earliest rail excursions. A remarkable series of national *eisteddfodau* held between 1858 and 1868, although marred by serious financial difficulties, laid the foundations of the modern *eisteddfod*.

The *eisteddfod* was the subject of intense public debate, some of the bards wishing to keep it as a preserve of poets, others, such as the educational pioneer Sir Hugh Owen, establishing a social science section for lectures and debates. The 1865 *eisteddfod* even had an industrial exhibition. Another feature of the modern institution emerges in this period, the use of the *eisteddfod* field as a place for annual general meetings of societies and a place for discussing public questions. It was at a meeting held during the 1863 *eisteddfod* that plans for a university college for the Welsh were drafted. The tendency of the middle-class patrons to use English in the *eisteddfod*, a language not understood by the majority of the audience, caused intense furore. Some of the prize essays of this period had an epoch-making effect, for example, those of the scholar–chemist from Merthyr, Thomas Stephens. In 1858 he submitted an essay to the Llangollen adjudicators demolishing the legend of Madoc's discovery of America in about 1170, a remarkable scientific examination of the sources. The adjudicators who were Romantic mythologists rejected the essay on the grounds that the prize could only be given to one who proved the Madoc legend true, not false. The fame of Stephens's essay, however, made him one of the most well-known Welsh scholars of his period.

From 1858 onward the national *eisteddfod* was greatly strengthened by the enormous spread of lesser *eisteddfodau*, underpinned in their turn by a myriad of competitive meetings that did not even claim the name of *eisteddfodau*. The Welsh became more adept at administration by the 1870s and 1880s and it is characteristic of the period that in 1880 a permanent body to administer the national *eisteddfod* came into being, The National Eisteddfod Association. The *Gorsedd* of bards had not been very active in the 1860s and 1870s but it too was carefully integrated into the national body, now with grandiose regalia designed by Sir Goscombe John and Sir Hubert von Herkomer. The *Gorsedd* became something of a poor man's university, with ordinary working men passing its examinations, adopting bardic names and wearing the blue, green and white robes of its varied orders of seniority. Most Welsh poets of the late nineteenth and early twentieth centuries took bardic names. The Reverend Howell Lewis took (from his birthplace Cynwyl Elfed) the bardic pseudonym 'Elfed'. Some of these bardic names were colourful, such as 'Eryron Gwyllt Walia' (Eagleman of Wild Wales), and these compensated for the dullness of the perpetual 'incognito' of the thousands of names such as John Jones which had become common in this period. Reactionary Romanticism then co-existed with progressive radicalism in the *eisteddfod*. It was less easy for it to co-exist with scholarship and academicism, and the scholars of the new University of Wales, while co-operating with the *eisteddfod*, condemned the *Gorsedd* as a fake. For many decades relations between the two institutions were cool, and it took many years to restore friendship.

Added to those debates was the argument over the language of the National Eisteddfod, the tendency being, as with all bilingual institutions in Wales, to slide gradually into English monolingualism. A resistance to this tendency can be seen in the 1890s, and it grew strongly in the 1920s and 1930s. It was only in 1950 that the so-called 'all Welsh rule' was imposed in the National Eisteddfod. Since in the same period the government passed a law allowing Welsh local authorities to make financial contributions to the institution through the rates, the National Eisteddfod is always a subject of public concern and debate, and some authorities in the south and east where Welsh is only spoken by a minority have questioned the all Welsh rule, and used it as a reason for withholding their support. In reaction the defenders of the all Welsh rule have become diehard in their attitudes.

From about 1880 to 1914 the holding of *eisteddfodau* became a national mania in Wales, and thousands were held up and down the country, thousands more all over the world wherever the Welsh emigrated, in Patagonia, Australia, Canada and above all, the United States of America. Since the end of World War I there have been a number of changes. The local *eisteddfod* has steeply declined because of a loss of vigour in the local chapel and community, because opportunities for leisure and hobbies have become more varied and because common people have found other ways of achieving distinction and status. On the other hand, several new 'semi-national' *eisteddfodau*, such as those of the Pantyfedwen Foundation in Cardiganshire, and national events such as the *eisteddfod* of the youth organisation *Urdd Gobaith Cymru*, or the international folk music and dance *eisteddfod* at Llangollen, have appeared. In most parts of Wales an *eisteddfod* is held in each school at some point during the year, often just before or on 1 March, so

St David's University College, Lampeter, Dyfed, the first university institution in Wales: the old buildings cut into a motte (on the left of the picture) of Norman construction

that *eisteddfota* (attending an eisteddfod) is part of the life of most Welsh people today.

The modern National Eisteddfod is therefore the result of many different influences, ancient and modern, and is all things to all men. It is held during the first week of August for a little over a week, one year in the south, the next in the north. The events are held in a vast prefabricated pavilion which stands in the centre of an open field, scattered around which are other lesser pavilions (for drama, litera-ture and other arts), and also rows of tiny booths selling wares, such as books and records, or simply advertising some good cause. Com-petitions go on throughout the week in the main pavilion, for brass bands and instrumentalists, singers, choristers, reciters of poetry and prose, the adjudication being given a few items later. Money prizes and medals are given. In the evening there are concerts, perhaps by the National Youth Orchestra of Wales, and after the concerts are over there may be a *noson lawen*, a merry night of informal music-making and entertainment. The ceremonials of the *Gorsedd* are held on the Tuesday and Thursday of the week. In the early morning the *Gorsedd* meets in a public park in a circle of stones, like a miniature Stonehenge, to proclaim its ritual and receive new members of the orders. On Tuesday afternoons the *Gorsedd* organises the ceremony of crowning the bard for the winning poem in the Welsh free metres, on Thursdays the ceremony of chairing the bard for the winning ode (*awdl*) in the strict metres, written accord-ing to the regulations revised at the Carmarthen *eisteddfod* of about 1450. Although these ceremonials are great crowd-pullers and are well known through radio and television to the world beyond the *eisteddfod*, many of the keen *eisteddfodwyr* (attenders at an *eis-teddfod*) will not even have entered the pavilion; instead they circulate the field endlessly, attending now an adjudication or an impromptu verse competition in the literary tent, now a short play in the drama tent, now buying the latest Welsh books and records from the little booths, now attending the annual general meeting of some organisation or an emergency meeting to protest about the latest national scandal, while in the evening they may never attend a concert, but go to a play in a local theatre or hall after which they may carouse in a private house or attend a satirical cabaret in some

University College, Cardiff: a more recent educational establishment with an architectural style of very different provenance temporary night club into the small hours. No alcoholic drink is allowed in the *eisteddfod,* but this does not appear to diminish the popularity of the institution. For most Welshmen, then, the 'National' refers to the *eisteddfod* and not to the Grand National steeplechase.

Land of rugby

It is assumed by people outside Wales that every Welshman is born with a rugby ball in his hands. It is certainly one of the most curious phenomena of Welsh history that an obviously alien import, the game of rugby football, should have been taken to heart so swiftly by the Welsh and turned into a self-consciously national sport. How did the Welsh spend their time before they began to play rugby? Although Wales before the Industrial Revolution was a country with a small population, scattered thinly over a difficult and hilly territory, it is agreed that the Welsh had a great variety of sports, in addition to the ancient pastimes of fishing and hunting.

As was the case in many parts of Europe, some of the ancient sports resembled some of the elements of rugby. George Owen, the late-sixteenth-century historian of Pembrokeshire, gives us a detailed description of *cnappan,* a communal sport where parish fought against parish at certain set dates, over vast areas of land, with as many as two thousand people taking part, some even on horse-back, the *cnappan* itself being a greased block of wood which was hurled in the air and fought for by the two armies of players. This game was played for centuries in west Wales. Moral and social reformers of the seventeenth and eighteenth centuries all bewailed the fact that the Welsh were obsessed with sports — boat racing at places on the coast such as Holyhead, horse racing inland, cock fighting and bear baiting, bowls and skittles, cross-country running, animal racing, forms of tennis such as fives against the walls of churches, forms of shot putting such as 'pitching stones'. In Anglesey and other parts of north Wales (where, later on, soccer became the favourite game) we have accounts of violent games of football where huge parish teams kicked footballs along the clifftops until the ball flew out into the sea. Some of the cross-country runners, such as Guto Nyth Brân (1700–37) who died after a twelve-mile race from Newport to Bedwas (Monmouthshire), entered into national folklore. In Glamorgan the popular game, even in the late nineteenth century, was a form of hockey called *bando* (bandy-ball) played between villages or two sides along the flat sandy beaches of the coast.

Such sports were associated with gambling and violence, sometimes with violent death, and generations before the coming of industry, were attacked by social and moral reformers; their work was made easier by the fact that the sports were associated with ancient calendar feasts and communal rituals at a time when the sense of local and community spirit was dying away. After the advent of the Agrarian and Industrial Revolutions, people had neither the time nor the space to practise their ancient sports. In Glamorgan, for example, the beach was the only flat place left on which to play *bando*.

The new sports, however, which came into Wales in the nineteenth century were not associated with popular violence, but with middle-class sportsmanship, health and discipline. Cricket came into some parts of Wales in the 1840s, for example, and took root in a few places such as Cardiff and Swansea. But it was not until the twentieth century that Wales produced even one major county team, Glamorgan, and Wales has no recognised national cricketing side. Rugby which is supposed to have been invented at Rugby School in England in 1823, came into Wales as a team game of the upper and middle classes in the 1840s. It appeared at Lampeter College in 1850, soon after at Llandovery College and among the middle classes of towns such as Neath by about 1870. Given the social circumstances of the time, games differed in their social status: for example, the native Welsh game of *chware-pêl* (hand-ball) was played by acknowledged experts among the working classes in the yards of taverns in industrial villages such as Nelson (Glamorgan), while only a few miles away the pupils at Lewis School, Pengam (an old private school) were playing fives according to the rules of English public schools. But in the 1870s, the crucial time for the emergence of modern sports in the industrial areas of Wales, factory owners and schoolmasters realised that team games of the type hitherto the preserve of the upper classes would be excellent for the morale and discipline of the workers. Whether the game to be encouraged was the dribbling code (soccer) or the handling code (rugby) was partly a matter of chance, depending on the tradition of the boarding school which was most admired, and on the fashionable game in the neighbouring areas in England. The owners of steel works at Aberavon (Glamorgan) encouraged the game of rugby

209

among their workers, forming the Aberavon Club in 1876. This was a death blow to the ancient community games of primitive football and *bando* in the district.

In the 1860s and 1870s there was a great rivalry between the two codes of football and, perhaps in order to gain status, the antagonists tried as quickly as they could to claim to be organising their respective code on a Welsh national basis. Soccer was first off the mark, the Football Association of Wales being founded at Ruabon (in the north-east borderland) in 1876 by Llewellyn Kenrick with the patronage of Sir Watkin Williams-Wynn. The South Wales Football Club (for rugby) was founded in 1875 but a union to cover the whole of Wales did not emerge until 1881. The dribbling code (soccer) was more common in the north-west of England and hence the stronger influence upon north Wales, while the handling code (rugby) was especially common in the west of England, and since from 1870 to 1914 a vast influx of immigrants came into the south Wales valleys from the west of England, rugby very quickly became established in south Wales, not merely because it was encouraged by owners or schoolmasters, but because it had its own momentum as a popular game. Clubs were formed early on in Carmarthen, Cardigan, Brecon and even in some towns in north Wales, but it was by the 1890s mainly the popular game of the south Wales industrial area from Llanelli to Newport. The industrial area of north-east Wales, where soccer became just as popular as rugby in the south, was tiny in comparison with the conurbations of Glamorgan and Monmouthshire.

In the last decades of the nineteenth century, industrial south Wales became an area of extraordinary economic expansion, and in its train came great self-confidence and a strong feeling that the area was the true Wales, that no other area could match it. The period was also one of revived Welsh consciousness. There was therefore a strong desire in the early 1870s to organise a specifically Welsh national league for sports, and by 1890 rugby enthusiasts wished to claim that rugby was the Welsh national game, despite its recent and alien origins. Chapel folk, remembering the violent and reckless sports of the old way of life, disapproved of the new passion for rugby, until it was proved to them after a decade or two, that it was a game of manliness and discipline. Welsh Americans did not see it fitting in to their romantic image of 'The Old Country' and made no attempt to import it into America. The Welsh religious revival of

1904–5 indeed had a strong, if temporary, effect in slowing the enthusiastic growth of the sport. Unfortunately for the revival, it happened to coincide with the chance appearance in Wales of one of the most brilliant national rugby sides ever produced. The Welsh national side (alone of the British Isles national sides) defeated New Zealand in 1905, in 1909 the Welsh team won its sixth Triple Crown victory (against England, Ireland and Scotland) and won Grand Slam victories (against France as well) in 1908 and 1909. The objections of the revivalists set aside, it seemed that Wales had suddenly become a partner nation in the British Empire: its economy was booming, its MPs were of crucial importance in the new Liberal government of 1906, and its national institutions (museum and library) were founded in 1907 (see Chapter 10). However much soccer might succeed in spreading through south Wales (as it did with rapidity after 1900), it did not seem to have the panache or the national victories which appeared for the Welsh on the rugby field just at the best possible moment. Without wishing to detract from the skill of the Welsh players, however, it should be pointed out that Wales, although a small country, was able to compete on something like equal terms with larger nations because in other countries rugby was only a minority sport.

Rugby, then, was simply the most famous and successful of a large number of sports to which the Welsh devoted themselves in the period 1870–1914. The very success which rugby had in identifying itself as the national game helps to explain why there was in Wales no equivalent of the attempt to revive Gaelic games in Ireland in this period. There was (and is) a localised Welsh version of baseball, somewhat resembling the American game, which arose in the Cardiff and Newport area around 1870, possibly coming in with immigrant workers from the west of England. A Welsh Baseball League came into being to control the game and a Welsh Baseball Union in 1921. Running and boxing and, for a short time, professional cycling and sprinting, were also popular sports, with pigeon and greyhound racing as the pastimes of the working man. Horse racing also came in for a short time, but never seemed able to take root, and the only major racecourses today in Wales are in the park of Piercefield near Chepstow and at Bangor on the Dee, both on the eastern borders. Soccer, which spread from north-east Wales and took root in the south with rapidity in the 1900s, giving rise to several successful professional sides, has also had a devoted following. The Cardiff City professional football side won the Football Association Cup in 1927. The Welsh Amateur Challenge Cup for soccer started in 1890 and is probably the oldest amateur soccer competition in the world. Amateur soccer found it easy to survive in Wales, but the growing professionalism of the game after about 1910 meant that when economic slump and depression hit Wales in the 1920s, many Welsh sides found it difficult to survive, many went under, and in subsequent decades there has always been a tendency for brilliant Welsh players to emigrate to rich clubs in other countries, which have sometimes been unwilling to release players to play for their national Welsh side. It is interesting to see that the upsurge in Welsh patriotism in the 1960s was not only accompanied by a great upsurge of interest in rugby and in huge success for the national side in that period, but also an upsurge of success for the Welsh national soccer side as well.

As if to mirror the greater variety and openness in Welsh society since 1945, it should be noted that there has been even greater variety in sports and athletics in the same period, with Wales having for almost all sporting activities its own local network of organisations, most of them having their headquarters in Cardiff. This variety of sporting activities has always been present in Wales to some extent, but during the age of the economic predominance of heavy industry 1870–1945 soccer and above all rugby dominated the scene. Since 1945 the Welsh sportsman is just as likely to be interested in canoeing, mountaineering and athletics as he is in soccer or rugby.

CHAPTER 10

The Growth of Welsh Institutions

As we are told that comparisons are odious, they have on the whole been avoided in this book, but one which springs to mind is that between Wales and Scotland. Looking back over the past two centuries, it is clear that Scotland's sense of nationality has depended much upon her institutions, the best known being her church and legal system. Wales, by contrast, in the seventeenth and eighteenth centuries had few institutions, and Welsh nationality was dependent on the Welsh language and its culture. During the past hundred years, however, at a time when the number of Welsh-speakers has dropped from about three-fifths to one-fifth of the population, the steady growth of Welsh institutions has made Wales resemble Scotland more and more in the structure of her nationality.

In the past the Welsh thought of themselves so much as a cultural or linguistic unit that they attached little importance to the survival of their own separate institutions. The Council of Wales and the Marches was abolished in 1689, the Courts of Great Sessions, the Welsh legal system, decayed and were abolished in 1830, and the Principality of Wales, as a fiscal or administrative unit of the crown, was in decline by the eighteenth century. After 1707 the word British which had often been used to denote things Welsh was appropriated to describe the newly formed state of the United Kingdom of Great Britain, and Parliament in 1746 declared that the word England in any legislation would be considered automatically to include Wales. If Wales was little more than a geographical expression, it needed no institutional structure. This situation was thus entirely different from that of Scotland, and if institutions were ever to emerge in Wales, they would have to come from below, from the life of the people. Before achieving any institutions the people would have to see the value of organisation, planning, co-operation and administration, and this is what gradually happened during the eighteenth century.

From the later 1730s, Griffith Jones's Welsh Circulating Schools accustomed people to the need for organisation and planning; from the early 1740s onwards the Methodist association in Wales showed that the Welsh had considerable aptitude for adminstration; and the clubs and voluntary societies, such as the Brecknockshire Agricultural Society founded in 1755 (one of the earliest of its kind in Britain) showed the value of co-operation in matters of enterprise and social improvement. But Wales had no capital city, hardly any towns to speak of, so the London Welsh gave a lead in the matter of structural development. It was they who founded in 1751 the first self-consciously Welsh society, the Honourable Society of Cymmrodorion, although it took its cue from the Society of Antient Britons founded as early as 1715. It was largely cultural in its interests, but also charitable and social, with a general concern for Welsh welfare in all its aspects, and a forum for discussing Welsh questions. The institution of the *eisteddfod* had been revived in 1701, but it was the encouragement and financial support of the London Welsh, especially of the Society of Gwyneddigion, which turned the *eisteddfod* into a national institution after 1789 (see Chapter 9). One of the few men of the period who envisaged a permanent all-embracing institution, a kind of ministry of Welsh culture to support Welsh life in all its aspects — language, culture, enterprise, learning — was Edward Williams 'Iolo Morganwg', and he only turned a small part of his dreams into reality: his guild of poets, The Gorsedd of Bards of the Isle of Britain (1792), was a mere shadow of the institution he planned (see Chapter 9).

With the return of peace in 1815, the notion of cultural associations became firmly established, and various institutions known as Cambrian or Cymreigyddion societies were founded throughout Wales. It was at the Carmarthen *eisteddfod* in 1819 held by the Cambrian Society of Dyfed that Iolo Morganwg's *Gorsedd* of bards was first directly associated with the *eisteddfod*. Iolo Morganwg was a Unitarian, but many of the leading lights of the new cultural associations were Romantic clerics, the Carmarthen *eisteddfod* being held under the aegis of Thomas Burgess, Bishop of St David's. It was Burgess who also gathered enough support to found in 1822 St David's College at Lampeter (Dyfed), the first university college built on Welsh soil. Up until then the only specifically Welsh university college had been Jesus College, Oxford, founded in 1571. The patriotic clerics and gentry of the 1840s also founded other institutions, the school at Llandovery College in 1848, the Welsh Manuscripts Society (1836), the Cambrian Archaeological Association (1846) and the Welsh Education Committee (1846).

At a social level below the Anglican clerics, the Methodists and dissenters spread their influence, especially during the first half of the nineteenth century. The Baptists and Independents were originally offshoots of English sects, but they gradually became locally based organisations, and the Calvinistic Methodists were purely Welsh in origin and structure. The running of these nonconformist causes, with their charitable societies, temperance assemblies, missionary meetings and publishing ventures, accustomed the common people to administration and the need for structure. The most influential body, Methodism, was also the most powerfully organised, and by 1870 Baptists and Independents and others were beginning to imitate the Methodists in their more centrally based administration, though reluctantly. St David's College, Lampeter, had the favour of church and state, and was able to grant degrees, but the nonconformists and dissenters had their own colleges and academies which people held in high respect; the Presbyterian College at Carmarthen and the Methodist College at Bala, were two among many.

Institutions of Victorian radicalism

Welsh radicalism, which triumphed between 1868 and 1922, was the result of the Welsh Methodists and dissenters becoming politically aware in the 1840s and 1850s, combined with the Romantic inheritance of the patriotic scholars, clerics and gentry of the early nineteenth century. Its institutions reflected two contradictory aims: one to preserve what was self-consciously or uniquely Welsh ('preservative' nationalism), and the other to obtain for the Welsh people those things which appeared to be of advantage to other peoples ('imitative' nationalism). In some institutions something wholly English might be copied or borrowed but given a Welsh stamp and a Welsh title. This ambiguous process is at work in most modern societies. Imitative nationalism, for example, is clearly seen in the work of Robert Jones 'Derfel' (R. J. Derfel), a long-lived and indefatigable Welsh radical publicist, who in the 1860s was demanding all kinds of national institutions for the Welsh such as a national art gallery, a national daily newspaper in Welsh and a national astronomical observatory. The Welsh language press teemed with periodicals, weeklies and monthlies, but no daily newspaper, and the English-language daily, the *Western Mail* did not begin its long career until 1869. The contradictory aims mentioned above were even seen in that most Welsh of institutions, the *eisteddfod*: revived as an annual national institution in 1858 at Llangollen, the *eisteddfod* was now a platform for traditional Welsh poetry and native music, such as *penillion* singing, now a stage for fashionable European musicians and, with its social science section, a forum for the discussion of current affairs in English on the model of the British Association. Its hard-headed utilitarian supporters and its Romantic *Gorsedd* bards reached a compromise, it was subjected to the Victorian desire for structure and institutions, and a National Eisteddfod Association was founded in 1880, thus forming the basis of its modern constitution.

Throughout the first half of the nineteenth century, the Welsh came to envy more and more the efficiency of the educational institutions of their neighbours, the English and the Scots, and the educational institutions of Wales are among the most characteristic we have inherited from the nineteenth century. One of the most interesting and complicated of these is the University of Wales. As a long-term result of the agitation in the 1840s over Welsh education, a movement was begun in 1863 to found a Welsh national university where nonconformists would be welcome — Lampeter and Jesus College being to all intents and purposes Anglican foundations. After years of debate and fund-raising (from rich capitalists, mines, factories and chapels), a large bankrupt hotel at Aberystwyth was found in 1870 as a home for the new college, which opened its doors as the University College of Wales in 1872. By 1880 its future was uncertain and a new public campaign arose to open colleges for north and south Wales, Cardiff opening in 1883 and Bangor in 1884. It was intended to close Aberystwyth; Aberystwyth's purposes had been practical and utilitarian, such patriotism as it had was largely imitative, but it had in a mere ten years become a national institution, a symbol of the resourceful self-improvement of radical Wales. The campaign to save the Aberystwyth college succeeded. The three university colleges of Wales taught for the London degree examinations, but such was the effectiveness of Welsh Liberal politicians and the patriotic enthusiasm of the 1890s, that in 1893 the colleges were brought together in one institution, giving its own degrees, the

University of Wales. Each college had its own independent structure, but their work was co-ordinated by a federal organisation as well. The University of Wales Registry was built in Cathays Park, Cardiff in 1904.

As a result of a government inquiry into Welsh education, the University was further expanded in 1920, with the founding of a new University College at Swansea, a University Press in 1922, a Board of Celtic Studies and various other boards. Further expansion took place in 1930 with the opening of the Welsh National Medical School in Cardiff, again an autonomous unit within a federal structure. As the result of the enormous expansion of British universities in the 1950s and 1960s, there was a powerful movement in Wales to defederalise the university, and make each college independent. Part of the furore was caused by the College of Advanced Technology in Cardiff aiming to set itself up as an independent university. The quarrel over university defederalisation was particularly bitter in 1963–4. In the event, the University structure was preserved, and the Cardiff college became the University of Wales Institute of Science and Technology (UWIST). In the early days of the University, St David's College at Lampeter regarded the obviously dissenting organisation with some disdain, answered with some coldness by the University. But by the mid twentieth century Lampeter was a college in decline. After a long process of accommodation between the two sides, Lampeter entered the University of Wales in 1972, 150 years after its original foundation.

It can be seen that the university is one of the most complex of Welsh national institutions, a great monument to the Victorian radical drive for educational improvement. Its original aim had been to give Welshmen all the advantages which Englishmen and Scotsmen then had to get on in the world. Despite these hard-headed utilitarian aims, it has also, through its Welsh departments or Board of Celtic studies, made a supremely important contribution to Welsh culture. Just as Aberystwyth had become within a very short time a national institution, so also the University of Wales itself by the 1960s had come to appear a national asset and a symbol of Welsh endeavour, to such an extent that its patriotic defenders succeeded in saving its federal structure against powerful counterforces.

Two further monuments to the Victorian radical drive for Welsh institutions are the National Museum and National Library, though these two bear witness to the way in which the earnest utilitarian radicalism of the mid century had been overlaid by a more cultural and Romantic patriotism by the 1880s and 1890s. Debated for many years, the projects for a national museum and library were resisted by the forces of unionism, since it was feared that such institutions would aid Welsh separatism, and that they would take away valuable finances from already existing institutions like the British Museum. Welsh economic power was considerable by 1900 and the political will was there, especially after the Liberal victory of 1906. In 1907 royal charters to found the museum and library were granted, the museum to be in Cathays Park, Cardiff, the library to be built in Aberystwyth. The greatest benefactors to the library, giving it land and the finest possible collections of books and manuscripts, wished the library to be built in Aberystwyth. The buildings were started within a few years, and the first portion of the library was opened in 1916. The museum was begun in 1910 but not opened until 1922. Both institutions have gone on expanding since then. The Museum, for example, has allied to it a number of other smaller Welsh museums; in 1947 it was given the castle of St Fagan's near Cardiff by the Earl of Plymouth, and here a Welsh folk museum was established where old buildings from all parts of Wales are reconstructed, Welsh dialects studied and recorded, Welsh music published and Welsh life compared with other societies in the world. More recently a Welsh industrial and maritime museum has been opened in Cardiff docks. The National Museum and National Library have helped to clothe with flesh the sublime structures dreamed up long ago by such patriots as Iolo Morganwg.

The drive for national institutions in Victorian and Edwardian Wales reflected, naturally enough, the main concerns of the period. Primary schools had been founded throughout Wales as a result of the Forster Education Act of 1870, but in 1889 Wales was given her own system of county schools, and in 1896 her own organisation to oversee both schools and examinations, the Central Welsh Board (1896–1949), well known to generations as the CWB. In 1907 came the Welsh Department of the Board of Education.

The same drive for structures and organisations was found in the economic and industrial field, with the founding of the Coal Owners Association of South Wales (1873), the South Wales Institute of Engineers (Cardiff), the North Wales Quarrymen's Union (1874) and the South Wales Miners' Federation (1898), this last being the celebrated 'Fed'. In the same period we have Welsh banks (such as the North and South Wales Bank), stock exchanges and coal exchanges. Also in this period we have the North and South Wales Liberal Federations and the Welsh National Liberal Council. Agitation over the Land Question (*Pwnc y Tir*) in the 1870s and 1880s led to setting up of an organisation, The Welsh Land League, in 1886, led by the redoubtable Thomas Gee of Denbigh. A quite different organisation dating from the more palmy days of Welsh agriculture is the Royal Welsh Agricultural Society, set up in 1904, though it is only in the past twenty years that it has centred its activities in one show ground, at Llanelwedd near Builth (Powys), the Royal Welsh. The Welsh element in the Liberal governments 1906–14, was especially strong, and it was Lloyd George's influence which led to the setting up of the nucleus of a future Welsh civil service through the foundation of Welsh departments of health and of national insurance in this period. The social concerns and anxieties of this period are reflected in some other characteristic Welsh national institutions: the Welsh National Memorial to Edward VII (1910) was a scheme to set up hospitals and sanatoria to rid Wales of the scourge of tuberculosis; in the same period we have the Welsh School of Social Service (1911) to encourage social work throughout Wales, and the Welsh Town Planning and Housing Trust which in 1916 became the Welsh Housing and Development Association.

One of the chief concerns of late-nineteenth-century radicalism was the disestablishment of the Anglican church in Wales. This campaign succeeded at last in 1914, the law coming into effect at the end of World War I. In 1920 the disendowed and disestablished church of Wales came into being, with a new constitution, a representative body and a governing body, and a new Archbishop of Wales at its head, an independent church yet part of the world-wide Anglican communion. The church could be said to have come into being most reluctantly, and in a sense is the last Welsh national institution created by Victorian and Edwardian radicalism.

The Welsh capital

Historically, one of the most obvious deficiences Wales suffered was the lack of a capital city. There was much uncertainty as to where Welsh organisations should meet or be based. Ludlow had served as a quasi-capital in the sixteenth and seventeenth centuries, London in the eighteenth century, and Welsh national meetings could be called in London, Bristol, Shrewsbury and Liverpool in the nineteenth and early twentieth centuries. The National Eisteddfod was peripatetic, a capital of the Welsh for one week of the year, this year in north Wales, the next year in the south. By the late nineteenth century institutions generally required buildings and a national centre was needed. By 1890 Cardiff had overtaken Merthyr and Swansea as the chief town of south Wales; indeed, it had swiftly become one of the richest cities in the British Empire, and its civic leaders began to see themselves as leaders of a Welsh capital. The Third Marquess of Bute, who had endowed the city with many handsome buildings since 1868, sold Cathays Park just before he died in 1900 to the town of Cardiff as a civic centre. Splendid avenues were laid out and grandiose Baroque buildings erected. Cardiff became a city in 1907, but did not succeed in making itself a capital city at this time. The intention of the citizens can clearly be seen, however, in the magnificent entrance hall of the City Hall (built in 1904) with its collection of sculptures of Welsh national heroes such as Bishop William Morgan and Llywelyn the Last. The National Museum and the University of Wales Registry were the first national institutions to be placed in Cathays Park, and this national character was confirmed by other structures such as the Welsh National War Memorial, erected in 1918, which is the centrepiece of the whole complex of Cathays Park. Just north of this memorial, the headquarters of the offices of the British government devolved to Wales, such as housing and local government, were completed in 1938. This is now the core of the Welsh Office building. Also in 1938, and next door to the Welsh Office, The Temple of Peace and Health, the headquarters of the Welsh National Hospital Board and the Welsh branch of the United Nations Associations was opened. This was the gift of Lord Davies of Llandinam, one of many organisations to be funded or founded by this family of rich Welsh industrialists; another institution founded by this family was the University of Wales Residential Centre founded at the home of Lord Davies's two sisters Gwendoline and Margaret Davies, at Gregynog near Newtown.

The rich and grandiose buildings around Cathays Park, then, symbolise the way in which Cardiff had become in fact if not in name the regional capital of Wales even before 1914; indeed, this development had a crucial influence upon the prosperity of the city, because while the revenues from coal exports fell from world record heights in 1911 to a nadir in the 1920s and 1930s, Cardiff expanded and to some extent prospered as an administrative and service centre for the whole of Wales. After the war, other organisations established their centres in Cardiff, and as the result of further agitation and campaigning, the city was eventually declared (by the Conservative government in 1955) the official capital of Wales. This was the belated recognition of a capital city which had grown up from 1890 to 1914.

Institutional development after 1920

By the end of the period of Liberal ascendancy in Wales (1868–1922) the institutional pattern had been set, and Welsh society had been transformed from a formless and unstructured mass of Welsh-speakers into a clearly defined region or province. Welsh institutions can be categorised into three kinds. First, is the Welsh branch of a British organisation, such as the Welsh National Insurance Commission. These bodies are not generally considered to be particularly Welsh, although they may, as the Wales Gas Board did after World War II, achieve the status of a quasi-national Welsh institution. The Wales Tourist Board, being concerned with the unique character of Wales, and because tourism is a subject which concerns everybody, has something of this character; so also the Welsh Water Board (with its headquarters appropriately enough at Brecon in mid Wales, the home of so many reservoirs), since water resources have come to be seen as a valuable national asset, and as so many Welsh reservoirs serve the great cities of England. There are very many bodies of this kind in Wales which have grown up since 1920 and they need not detain us here. They are of course extremely important but they have no uniquely Welsh character and do not need further explanation. Nor are we concerned here with such important institutions as the Royal Mint (north west of Cardiff) or Companies House (the registry of British companies, situated in Cardiff itself), which contributed to the prestige and prosperity of Cardiff as a capital, but can in no way be identified as specifically Welsh institutions.

The second type of organisation is a purely Welsh body or, if an offshoot of a British organisation, is for various historical reasons closely identified with Welsh sentiment and regarded by the people as a Welsh institution. The Welsh National Opera is a good example of this type of institution, begun in Cardiff in 1945, slowly expand-

ing at first with a largely amateur or part-time chorus, then expanding rapidly with government funds into a full-scale internationally
admired company performing all over Britain and abroad. Its home
base is the New Theatre, Cardiff. Although the company performs
grand opera in Italian, German or English, and only occasionally
produces operas by Welsh composers, it is seen as a great national
asset, with a considerable base of popular support. Its main financial
support comes from the Welsh Arts Council. From 1950 to 1967
there was a Welsh committee of the Arts Council of Great Britain,
but in 1967 this was reconstructed as an autonomous body, the
Welsh Arts Council, and for some years after 1967 there was a very
great increase in its funding, which made it by far the greatest patron
of the arts in Wales. The Arts Council, of course, is funded by the
British government, but the Welsh people have regarded themselves
for so long as a cultural unit, and cultural matters have always been
matters of concern in Wales, that the Arts Council has quickly
achieved the status of a national institution, its appointments and
spending programmes or cuts the subject of intense public debate.

This is just as true of a somewhat older institution, the British
Broadcasting Corporation in Wales, now BBC Wales. Broadcasting
in Wales began as early as 1923, and a BBC Welsh orchestra
appeared in 1928, but there was much resistance in London to the
setting up of a Welsh regional broadcasting service, and only after
intense lobbying from Welsh pressure groups was Wales separated
from the west of England and a Welsh Home Service started in 1937.
A bilingual service, with centres in Cardiff, Swansea and Bangor, it
quickly established itself in the hearts of the people as a national
institution. The same pattern repeated itself when television spread
from London to the regions in the 1950s and 1960s, both with
regards to the BBC and independent television services. In the field
of commercial or independent television Wales and the west of
England are served by Harlech Television (HTV) at present, but
there are separate services for Wales and England. HTV has now
constructed large new headquarters at Culverhouse Cross just
west of Cardiff. BBC Wales was constituted as a unit to serve Wales
only, with its headquarters in Llandaf, north of the city of Cardiff,
but with considerable studios in Bangor. Commercial radio stations
have also been established in various places in Wales such as Swansea
(Swansea Sound), and there is also a Welsh branch of the Independent Broadcasting Authority (IBA) with its headquarters in Cardiff.

The National Museum of Wales, Cathays Park, Cardiff

The Welsh Office, Cathays Park, Cardiff

Robert Stephenson's rail bridge across the Menai Strait, Gwynedd, now with an upper road deck

The most recent transport development in Wales, the M4, now complete almost to Cross Hands, Dyfed: the photograph illustrates some of the practical consequences of bilingualism

Since radio and television services have been provided in Welsh and English, broadcasting has been a matter of great and often acrimonious debate in Wales. The BBC provided two separate services, in Welsh and in English, on the radio, and in 1982 when the television's fourth channel became available, there was at last an opportunity to provide Wales with two television channels, one in Welsh and one in English. After an often bitter public debate over several years, and intense lobbying and discussion, the Welsh fourth channel was established in 1982, to which the BBC and commercial television both contributed programmes, a service which was welcomed by the Welsh-speaking public.

There has also been a gradual spread of regional administration in Wales, beginning with such bodies as the Welsh Department of the Board of Education and of the Board of Health and National Insurance in the years before World War I. The years of economic depression, the strain of World War II and the shortages of the postwar years, all combined to forward centralised planning and government controls, and so great was the machinery of control by the 1940s that some form of devolution became feasible and necessary. Branches or departments of London ministries and boards were set up in Wales in ever greater numbers after 1945. In the same period there was growing pressure upon London from Wales to produce some new form of regional administration, somewhat on Scottish lines (see Chapter 3).

Welsh-language institutions

The third type of institution in the modern pattern since 1920 is the specifically Welsh or Welsh-language institution. After the founding of the Cymmrodorion in 1751, and the spread of Cambrian and Cymreigyddion societies through Wales after 1815, numerous Welsh societies were set up for the general encouragement of Welsh arts and culture, both in Wales and wherever Welshmen settled (in England or overseas). There were also youth movements in Wales, such as the Band of Hope, usually offshoots of the Sunday school movement, from the mid nineteenth century. Baden-Powell's scout and guide movements also spread into Wales within a short time of their foundation, but in 1922 Wales achieved its own unique youth movement, *Urdd Gobaith Cymru* (Order of the Hope of Wales), founded by Sir Ifan ab Owen Edwards, the son of the great

225

Welsh educationalist, Sir Owen M. Edwards. Usually known simply as the *Urdd,* the organisation bears resemblance to many other youth movements, with its summer camps on Lake Bala and at Llangrannog on the Cardiganshire coast, its open air activities and its sports, and its local groups meeting at a club called an *Aelwyd* (hearth). In other ways it is uniquely Welsh, with its strong emphasis on speaking or learning Welsh, its *twmpathau dawns* (Welsh folk-dance evenings), its local and national youth *eisteddfodau* and its magazines. Fundamentally a voluntary body, the *Urdd* has worked in and through the state school system (many of the branches are school branches) and it has received much help from the state, as a recognised, and remarkably successful, youth organisation. It has branches in Cardiff, but its headquarters are at Aberystwyth, a pattern followed by many of the Welsh-language institutions. While recognising Christianity as the religious creed of the movement, the *Urdd* is nevertheless a secular institution, and is characteristic of the way in which Welsh life became secularised in the years after World War I.

One Welsh-language institution which arose directly from the *Urdd* was the Welsh School Movement, the movement to set up schools using the medium of Welsh although in partially or wholly English-speaking areas. The first of these was opened as a private venture by Sir Ifan ab Owen Edwards in Aberystwyth in 1939, and after the war similar primary schools were opened by local authorities in Llanelli and other places, the network of primary schools gradually giving rise to comprehensive or secondary schools. It should be noted that there were (and are) many schools in the rural north and west of Wales which have always taught partly or wholly through the Welsh language. Such schools are called 'naturally Welsh schools', thus underlining the highly self-conscious character of the Welsh schools (*Ysgolion Cymraeg*), non political in nature, but with a missionary zeal to defend the embattled Welsh language in the face of indifference and hostility. The spread of these schools through many areas of English-speaking Wales has in turn given rise to further institutions, the *Undeb Rhieni Ysgolion Cymraeg* (Union of Parents of Welsh Schools) in 1952 and the *Mudiad Ysgolion Meithrin* (Nursery Schools Movement) in 1971. The great majority of the Welsh-language institutions take their cue from the *Urdd,* being zealous, self-conscious but non-political in their mission. One most effective institution is the *Cyngor Llyfrau*

Cymraeg (Welsh Books Council) founded in 1962 with its head-quarters in Aberystwyth. The council is funded by local authorities and by the Arts Council, and helps Welsh publishers to edit, design and, above all, market books throughout Wales. For the council as for other Welsh-language institutions, Aberystwyth is the Cardiff of the Welsh-speaking hinterland of Wales.

Other Welsh-language institutions arise to fill some vacuum that is perceived in Welsh society, a good example being *Merched y Wawr* (Daughters of the Dawn). There had, over the past century or more, been many Welsh-language women's organisations, but they had always been sectarian or religious. *Merched y Wawr* arose in the village of Parc near Bala in 1966 from the desire to have a Welsh-language equivalent of the Women's Institute (an organisa-tion, by the way, which had had its very first institute in 1915 at Llanfair Pwll on the Isle of Anglesey), and to have a secular Welsh-language women's organisation. It has spread rapidly with branches all over Wales.

A number of other Welsh-language organisations, however, have arisen because of a growing sense of anger or desperation amongst Welsh-speakers at the decay or decline of the language or the structure of the Welsh heartland, and they are organisations of protest. Some of these institutions such as the Free Wales Army in the later 1960s were short-lived; others, longer lasting and more practical, are concerned to provide houses or jobs for local people in the Welsh heartland, such as *Adfer* (Restoration) or *Cymdeithas Tai Gwynedd* (Gwynedd Housing Society), others such as *Cofiwn* (Let us Remember) are historical and ceremonial, attempting to sharpen the nation's conscience by reminding them of past heroes or past sacrifices. The most imaginative and successful of the militant Welsh-language institutions is without doubt *Cymdeithas yr Iaith Gymraeg* (the Welsh Language Society) founded in 1962 partly as a result of a radio lecture by the veteran Welsh nationalist pioneer, Saunders Lewis. This is a militant organisation consisting of numer-ous small local cells of activists, with a headquarters again at Aberystwyth, devoted to furthering the use and raising the status of the Welsh language. The first sign of its activities seen by the public was the vast number of English-only road signs all over Wales which were obliterated with green paint. Members of the society (mainly young people) have over the past twenty years pestered and badgered the Welsh public into changing its attitudes towards the

227

inferior status of the language. For example, in 1967 a Welsh Language Act was passed which gave Welsh equal validity with English in Wales, though it did not permit full bilingualism in administration. Over the years the members of the society have been prepared to go to prison for breaking the law in the furtherance of their cause, and inevitably, perhaps, have caused a split in Welsh public opinion over the language issue. Its imaginative propaganda and its varied campaigns on social as well as purely linguistic issues, however, make the Welsh Language Society one of the most effective, active and interesting of all Welsh-language institutions. Proof of its continuing vitality is that although economic slump and a general sense of caution and political reaction have slowed or halted the creation of Welsh institutions since the mid 1970s, the Welsh Language Society was able to mount an effective propaganda campaign in the early 1980s to bring pressure on the Conservative government to allow the Welsh-language television channel to go ahead in 1982.

Conclusion

Out of native religious and educational institutions, there arose the drive for national structures and organisations in Wales, especially at the zenith of Welsh Liberalism from 1880 to 1920. In the same period Welshness changed from something allied with the chapel way of life, to something with an administrative or bureaucratic structure, and a pattern of institutional development was laid down which has developed, although fitfully, ever since 1920. Often Wales has had to struggle for its institutions because of the fear in the rest of Britain that they would lead to Welsh separatism. To some extent this is true; the urge for developing Welsh organisations has at times gone hand in hand with Welsh patriotism and nationalism, but it must also be remembered that this complex web of Welsh organisations, autonomous yet dovetailed into so many British or English institutions, has given an effective field of action for the Welsh governing classes and at the same time integrated them fairly harmoniously into the British system.

Perhaps the element which most bewilders the visitor to Wales is that in some of these institutions Wales is hardly a region (merely an appendage of Merseyside, the Midlands or the west of England), in others it is a clearly definable area of Britain, and in others a bafflingly separate country. In some institutions Wales's Britishness, regionalism and nationalism are all jumbled up together as, for example, in the University of Wales. The Welsh-language institutions, such as *Urdd Gobaith Cymru* or *Cymdeithas yr Iaith Gymraeg,* however, have a unique character and are increasing in importance and numbers in the deepening crisis of the language and the Welsh heartland of the past half century. It is to be hoped that through this examination of Welsh structures and institutions people may find modern Welsh society less bewildering and incomprehensible.

Appendix I
Welsh Names:
Keeping Up With the Joneses

Everyone knows that Jones is the commonest Welsh surname, and the apparent lack of variety of surname is the subject of numerous jokes and stories. There is far more to Welsh surnames than the Joneses, however, and the evolution of the characteristic Welsh surnames, their distribution throughout Wales and other countries such as the border country of England or Ireland and America, tells us a great deal about the history of the Welsh people.

For much of the Middle Ages European peoples did not use fixed surnames, but each person had a baptismal name, to which society then affixed some distinguishing name, a descriptive adjective showing the man's colour of hair or his trade, or perhaps his father's baptismal name. Such names were similar to what we now call nicknames, and they changed in each generation. Soon after the Norman Conquest, the people of England, probably under the pressure of their conquerors, began to adopt fixed surnames, and by the late fourteenth century virtually all the English surnames of today had appeared. The English had also adopted the practice whereby the wife and children take on the father's surname, passing it on to the next generation unchanged. These names, such as Brown, Smith, Field, Paterson (son of Patrick), are to be found among English settlers in 'colonial' Wales of the later Middle Ages, especially in the little towns founded by the English such as Conwy or Swansea. But they stand out by contrast from the bulk of the native Welsh population, who stuck to the Welsh system of naming.

The Welsh system was a patronymic one: a son's baptismal name was followed by his father's baptismal name, and sometimes the names of his other forefathers, the linking word being *ap* or *ab* (meaning son of). A man called Rhys would be known as Rhys ap Morgan, if Morgan was his father's name, and in any cases of diffi-

231

culty he would give out his full name, perhaps Rhys ap Morgan ap Dafydd ap Thomas ap Gruffudd ap Siôn and so on to about the ninth forefather. A girl would be named in the same way; Rhys' sister might be Gwladus uch Morgan, the *uch* being an abbreviation for 'ferch' (the daughter of). There were, of course, plenty of nicknames such as Benfras (fathead) or Bongam (crookback) and bards were often known by such names, eg Dafydd Benfras. Generally these nicknames referred to personal qualities or frailties, and not to professions or places or properties. The patronymic name system lasted in Wales for a remarkably long time and reflected the clear distinction the Welsh then had (and still have) between surnames and nicknames, a strong sense of kinship and perhaps the lack of a sense of individualism. Since Welshmen carried about with them their own genealogy going back about nine generations, they knew their blood links with hundreds of others.

Of course, the Welsh emigrated from Wales during the Middle Ages and we find Welch, Walsh and Welshman among English medieval surnames. Walsh is in fact one of the commonest surnames in Ireland, a sign of the great importance of Welsh troops in the medieval Norman conquest of Ireland. It is in Ireland that we find the earliest surnames from Welsh placenames, eg Barry, Cogan, Taafe (from the River Taff) and Prendergast.

The great period of adopting fixed surnames among the Welsh came from the fifteenth to the eighteenth centuries, partly as a result of the spread of English government and administration, and partly as a result of a change in fashion, the individual and his family becoming more important than the kinship group or community. Fixed surnames appeared among the Welsh in the Welsh Marches or in Gower and south Pembrokeshire or the Vale of Glamorgan before the end of the Middle Ages. They were only becoming the rule in Anglesey in the eighteenth century, and in some mountainous districts such as Snowdonia they were not adopted until the mid nineteenth century.

Over the same period, fashions in baptismal names became highly conventionalised, perhaps with a certain amount of pressure from the parish clerk to adopt simple Biblical names such as John, Thomas or David, and a few royal names such as Richard, Edward, William or Henry, in place of the huge variety of medieval Welsh names such as Llywarch, Gwalchmai, Tegwared, Gwasmeir and Gwasmihangel. The state in this period used a mixture of languages

— French, Latin and English — but it was official policy to write Welsh names as much as possible after the English fashion.

We have then the three main elements of Welsh surnaming coming together: the prejudice of the Welsh in favour of a patronymic system, the arrival of very simple baptismal names and English spelling. During the period under discussion the commonest name by far was some Welsh variant or other of the name John (eg Siôn, Ifan, Ieuan, Ioan, Iwan). The patronymic system favoured by the Welsh meant that the sons of these people called 'John' took their fathers' name as their surname. The Anglicised spelling meant that some English surname must be found to express 'Ap Siôn' that is, 'son of Siôn', and Jones was most favoured, the final 's' expressing the English genitive form. So although 'son of Siôn' and its variants gave rise to the surnames John, Johns, Shone, Evans, Bevan, Ewen and Jevons, by far the commonest was Jones.

There are, however, other kinds of Welsh surnames. Placename surnames which are so common in England are rare, but some do exist: Conwy from the town of that name, Lougher from Loughor in Glamorgan. The strangest placename surname is that of Winston, a direct translation of Trewyn near Abergavenny (Gwent), from which family Sir Winston Churchill was descended. There are also a few geographical surnames: Kyffin comes from *cyffin* meaning borderland; Blayney from *blaenau* meaning headwaters or heads of valleys; Yale from the lordship of Iâl in north-east Wales. (This was the area of origin of Elihu Yale the benefactor of Yale University in America.) Adjectival or descriptive surnames, which are so common in other cultures, are rare in Wales, although the Welsh are inveterate users of nicknames. There are, however, a number of such surnames which are fairly common: Vaughan from *bychan* meaning junior or younger; Lloyd or Floyd from *llwyd* meaning grey; Wynne or Gwynn from *gwyn* meaning white or fair; and Gough or Gooch from *coch* meaning red or red-haired.

Although Jones was by far the commonest surname, baptismal names such as David and William were also popular, and to express 'son of David' or 'son of William' the forms Davies and Williams were evolved. A considerable number of native Welsh names survived and therefore gave rise to patronymic surnames, in almost all cases in anglicised spellings, such as Morgan, Owen (from Owain), Llewellin (from Llywelyn), Griffiths (from Gruffudd), Meredith (from Maredudd), Leyshon (from Lleisian), Meyler (from Meilir),

Gwyther (from Gwythyr), Eynon (from Einion), Maddox (from Madog). Some of these native names became very famous surnames in English history; the noble Cecil family took its surname from an ancestor Seisyll of Alltyrynys, while the royal dynasty of Tudor took its name from an ancestor Tudur of Penmynydd.

Some Welsh surnames arose from an anglicised version of a Welsh name which was in turn a foreign borrowing: Roger became Rhosier in Welsh, and in time this gave the surname Rosser. Siencyn, Hopcyn and Watcyn were common baptismal names in south-eastern Wales in the late Middle Ages, and gave rise to the surnames Jenkins, Hopkins and Watkins respectively. The baptismal names are probably Flemish, not Welsh, in origin, but the surnames are Welsh. The process of anglicisation of names and surnames created a number of variants which seem on the surface to be quite un-Welsh. Llywelyn and Rhydderch are names which are difficult to anglicise, and must have been a continual headache to the clerks of the parish or the courts of law; Llywelyn becomes Lewellen, Fluellen, Welling, and sometimes Lewis. Rhydderch becomes Rothero and Roderick, and so on. At other times surnames arose from baptismal names which have totally disappeared from use in Wales: for example, the baptismal names Geli and Dyfnallt were common in the Middle Ages only in a few corners of south-western Wales. It is in those areas that we find the surnames Gealy and Devonald.

Welsh surnames did not merely arise from plain baptismal names, but also from dimunitive or pet forms. Watcyn (Watkins) was a diminutive form of Walter. A pet form of Gruffudd was Gutyn or Guto, and these forms gave rise to the surnames Gittins, Gittings and Gittoes. The commonest pet form of Maredudd was Bedo, and this gave rise to the surname Beddoes. The most common variant of the patronymic surname in Wales, however, was the way in which the particle ap or ab (son of) became attached to the name. Siôn ap Harri (John son of Henry) might become John Harris, John Harry, John Penry or most likely John Parry. Ap Hywel thus becomes Powell, Ap Rhydderch becomes Protheroe. In front of a vowel the ap was often ab, so ab Owen gave rise to Bowen, ab Einion to Beynon.

The taking of fixed surnames was seen first among the gentry, and gradually seeped down to the lower orders. Regardless of class or social status, however, the patronymic surname was the choice of the great majority from the Tudor dynasty itself down to the low-liest peasant. In the seventh and eighteenth centuries Puritanism tended to favour Old Testament baptismal names, and a large number of Welshmen were given the names Isaac, Levi, Abraham, Habakkuk and Shadrach. When the sons of these men came to take the fixed surname, they adopted these ancient Hebrew names as the family surnames, so making them Welsh surnames.

Forenames and surnames had become very stereotyped by the early nineteenth century, but even then there was much confusion within families over what constituted a surname; some sons would take the father's baptismal name, their brothers the grandfather's name, and yet other brothers might take the mother's surname or a mixture of father's and mother's surnames. This is how one finds in Wales quite unaristocratic families with hyphenated surnames such as Parry-Williams, Lloyd-Jones or Lloyd-George. The late-eighteenth-century romantic Welsh scholars began to resist the stereotyped names; Edward Williams was generally known by his adopted bardic name of Iolo Morganwg, and he called his son Taliesin Williams after the ancient poet Taliesin. William Owen-Pughe called his son Aneurin after the early poet Aneirin, and this change started a fashion for more varied and interesting baptismal names during the nineteenth century. Musicians or poets were generally known by their bardic names: Howell Lewis took the name 'Elfed' from his birthplace in Cynwyl Elfed, and was always known as Elfed or H. Elvet Lewis. Since native Welsh names were revived in the late nineteenth century, these were used in Wales in addition to the names common throughout the British Isles, with the result that in the twentieth century we have the curious phenomenon of a bewildering variety of baptismal names in harness with extremely stereotyped surnames. The recent tendency amongst Welsh-speaking families has been in some cases to revert to the earlier patronymic medieval kind of name: the historian Sir Owen M. Edwards called his son Ifan ab Owen Edwards. Others have gone further and been known simply as 'ap Thomas'. The pat-ronymic name is all very well for men, but it has never become a fashion to revive the *uch* for women, eg Marged uch Ifan (Margaret daughter of Evan). In the past two or three decades there has been a fashion amongst some men and women simply to drop the angli-cised surname, and to turn the parental name, or simply a second forename, into a surname, eg Heledd Wyn, Eilian Llwyd, Siôn

Dafydd, Elis Myfyr and so on.

The complex and elaborate naming system of the Welsh which arose in the earliest times and lasted in some cases even into the early nineteenth century, reflected the central concern of the Welsh for genealogy. The gradual spread of fixed surnames, first of all a fashion only among English settlers in medieval boroughs, then spreading through all ranks from the fifteenth to the eighteenth centuries, was a sign of the growing anglicisation of Welsh life and the domination of a centralised state. By a detailed study of Welsh surnames, by plotting from which part of Wales a particular surname is likely to come — for some of them are highly localised — it is possible to trace where in Wales the bearer of the surname has come from, either through in-migration in Wales, or to England, Ireland or America.

Appendix II
Common Placename Elements

Welsh placenames are frequently of considerable antiquity and particularly rich in historical allusion and topographic description. In order to assist the visitor to Wales, the meanings of common placename elements are given below. It should always be remembered that debased versions of many placenames still abound, so spellings may vary considerably, and also that the mutation of initial consonants in compound placenames introduces changes to the form of such names. The list cannot be exhaustive. Personal names are not given.

aber	confluence	*bron*	hill-breast, slope
afon	river	*bryn*	
allt	wooded slope	(pl *bryniau*)	hill
ar	on	*bwlch*	pass, gap
bach	small	*bychan*	little, small
ban		*cadair, cader*	seat, stronghold
(pl *bannau*)	peak, crest	*cae* (pl *caeau*)	field, enclosure
banc	bank	*caer*	
bangor	monastery	(pl *caerau*)	fort
bedd		*canol*	middle
(pl *beddau*)	grave	*capel*	chapel
bedwen		*carn*	
(pl *bedw*)	birch	(pl *carnau*)	cairn, rock
betws	chapel of ease	*carnedd*	
blaen		(pl *carneddau,*	
(pl *blaenau*)	head, end	*carneddi*)	cairn, barrow
bod	dwelling	*carreg*	
braich	ridge	(pl *cerrig*)	stone, rock
bro	region, vale	*castell*	castle

cefn	ridge	*erw*	acre
celli	grove, copse	*esgair*	long ridge
cemais	river bend	*ffin*	boundary
ceunant	ravine	*ffordd*	way, road
cil (pl *ciliau*)	corner, retreat	*ffos*	ditch, trench
cilfach	cove, creek	*ffridd*	
clawdd	dyke	(pl *ffriddoedd*)	rough grazing,
clogwyn	precipice		sheepwalk
clun	meadow, moor	*ffrwd*	
coch	red	(pl *ffrydiau*)	stream, torrent
coed	trees, wood	*ffynnon* (pl	
cors	bog	*ffynhonnau*)	spring, well
craig		*gallt*	slope, wood
(pl *creigiau*)	rock	*garth*	hill, enclosure
crib	crest, summit	*garw*	rough
croes	cross	*glan*	riverbank, bank
croesffordd,		*glas*	green, blue
croeslon	crossroads	*glyn*	deep valley, glen
crug		*goetre*	woodland
(pl *crugiau*)	knoll		dwelling
cwm	valley	*gwaun*	moor, mountain
cwrt	court		pasture
cymer		*gwern*	swamp
(pl *cymerau*)	confluence	*gwyn* (f *gwen*)	white
dan	under, below	*gwyrdd*	green
dau (f *dwy*)	two	*hafod, hafoty*	summer
derwen			dwelling, shieling
(pl *derw*)	oak	*haul*	the sun
diffwys	precipice	*helygen*	
dinas	hillfort	(pl *helyg*)	willow
diserth	hermitage	*hen*	old
dôl (pl *dolau,*		*hendre*	winter dwelling,
dolydd)	meadow		permanent home
drws	gap	*heol, hewl*	road
du (f *ddu*)	black	*hir*	long
dwfr, dŵr	water	*is*	below, under
dyffryn	valley	*isaf*	lower
efail	smithy	*isel*	low
eglwys	church	*llain*	narrow strip of
eithin	gorse	(pl *lleiniau*)	land

llan	church, enclosure	*newydd*	new
llannerch	clearing	*odyn*	kiln
llawr	flat valley bottom	*onnen*	
		(pl *onn, ynn*)	ash tree
llech	slab, slate	*pandy*	fulling mill
llechwedd	hillside	*pant*	hollow
llety	small house	*parc*	park
llethr	slope	*pen*	head
lluest	hut, cottage, shieling	*penrhyn*	promontory
		pentre	village
llwch		*pistyll*	waterfall, spout
(pl *llychau*)	lake	*plas*	hall
llwyd	grey	*pont*	bridge
llwyn	grove	*porth*	gateway, harbour
llyn	lake		
llys	court	*pwll*	pool, pit
maenol,		*rhaeadr*	waterfall
maenor	manor	*rhiw*	hill, slope
maerdre	hamlet attached to chief's court	*rhos*	
		(pl *rhosydd*)	moorland
maes		*rhyd*	ford
(pl *meysydd*)	field	*sain, sant, saint*	saint
mawr	big	*sarn*	
melin	mill	(pl *sarnau*)	causeway
melindre	mill village	*sych*	dry
melyn	yellow	*tafarn*	
merthyr	burial place	(pl *tafarnau*)	tavern
mign		*tal*	end
(pl *mignedd*)	bog	*tarren*	
moel	bare hill	(pl *tarenni*)	rocky height
morfa	marsh	*teg*	fair
mur		*tir*	land
(pl *muriau*)	wall	*tomen*	mound
mwyn	ore, mine	*ton*	grassland
mynachlog	monastery	*traeth*	strand, beach
mynydd	mountain	*trallwng*	wet bottom land
nant		*traws*	cross
(pl *nentydd,*		*tre*	hamlet, town
nannau)	brook	*tri* (f *tair*)	three
		troed	foot

tros	over	*uwch*	above, over
trum	ridge	*y, yr, 'r*	the
trwyn	point, cape	*ych*	ox
twyn	hillock	*yn*	in
tŷ (pl *tai*)	house	*ynys*	island
tyddyn, ty'n	small farm, holding	*ysbyty*	hospital, hospice
		ystrad	valley floor
uchaf	upper	*ystum*	river bend
uchel	high		

Chronological Table

WALES	ENGLAND, SCOTLAND AND IRELAND	THE WIDER WORLD
c75 BC Invasion of Britain by Belgae		
55–54 BC Arrival of Romans in Britain		
AD 40 Death of Cunobelinus (Cynfelyn)		41–54 Emperor Claudius
AD 43 Roman conquest began	43 Roman Conquest began	
47 Roman attack on 'Wales'		
51 Defeat of Caratacus (Caradog)		
61 Roman attack on Anglesey		
74–5 Roman conquest of 'S. Wales'		
78 Agricola's conquest of 'N. Wales'	80–85 Campaigns of Agricola	79–81 Emperor Titus
		81–96 Emperor Domitian
	c130 Wall of Hadrian	117–38 Emperor Hadrian
		138–61 Emperor Antoninus Pius
		193–211 Emperor Septimius Severus
		313 Christianity tolerated in Roman Empire
383 Withdrawal of legions from Britain by Magnus Maximus (Macsen Wledig)		
c400 Cunedda moves from Scotland to Wales	c410 End of Roman rule	410 Rome fell to Goths
	?432 St Patrick in Ireland	
c440 Vortigern and legendary arrival of Saxons in Britain	?449 Beginning of Anglo–Saxon settlements	
c500 Battle of Mount Badon	c500 Irish 'Scots' arrived in Scotland	476 End of Western Empire
547 Death of Maelgwn Gwynedd		547 Death of St Benedict
577 Battle of Dyrham cuts off Welsh from south-west Britons		

Europe and beyond	England	Wales
590–604 Pope Gregory the Great	597 Augustine landed in Kent	c588 Death of Saint David (Dewi Sant)
632 Death of Mohammed	616–32 } Ascendancy of Northumbria	c600 Bards Taliesin and Aneirin flourished
	654–85 }	615 Battle of Chester cuts off Welsh from Northern Britons ('The Old North')
732 Mohammedan invasion of France checked at Tours	663 Synod of Whitby	681 Death of Cadwaladr, last Welsh king of Britain
800 Coronation of Charlemagne as Emperor of the West	735 Death of Bede	c768 Welsh Church conforms to Roman usages
843 Treaty of Verdun: beginnings of France and Germany	793 Scandinavian raids on England began	c784 Offa of Mercia constructs Offa's Dyke
?872 Harald Fairhair unifies Norway	802–39 Egbert, king of Wessex, overlord of England	844–78 Rhodri Mawr, King of Wales
910 Abbey of Cluny founded	844 Union of Picts and Scots	c850 Viking attacks on Wales
911 Scandinavian duchy in Normandy	871–99 Alfred, king of Wessex	c900–50 Hywel the Good, King of Wales
987 Capetian dynasty began in France	878 Peace of Wedmore: half of England subject to Scandinavians	
1000 (?) Leif Erikson discovered America	954 England united under house of Wessex	
	c960 Edinburgh held by kings of Alba	
	995–1017 Scandinavian conquest of England	
	1014 Battle of Clontarf: defeat of Scandinavians in Ireland	

Wales	Britain / England / Scotland	Europe / Church
1039–63 Gruffydd ap Llywelyn unites Wales	1034 Strathclyde part of Scottish kingdom	1046–72 Norman rule established in Naples and Sicily
	1042–66 Edward the Confessor	1073–85 Gregory VII (Hildebrand) Pope
1075–96 Rhys ap Tewdwr rules south Wales	1066 Battle of Hastings	1077 Pope humiliated emperor at Canossa
1090 Normans begin to conquer south Wales	1066–87 William I	1098 Foundation of abbey of Cîteaux
	1087–1100 William II (Rufus)	1099 First Crusade
c1108 Henry I settles Flemings in Pembroke	1100–35 Henry I	1104 Archbishopric for Denmark (Lund)
1115–16 Normans take over dioceses of St David's and Llandaff	1117 onwards new religious orders introduced in Scotland	1115 Foundation of abbey of Clairvaux
c1120 Rome canonises Dewi Sant as St David		1122 Settlement of investiture controversy between pope and emperor
1136 Geoffrey of Monmouth publishes History of the Kings of Britain	1135–54 Stephen	
1137 Death of Gruffydd ap Cynan	1138 Scots defeated at battle of the Standard	
1137–70 Owain Gwynedd rules		1148 Second Crusade
1143 Cistercians found Whitland Abbey		1151 Archbishop for Norway (Trondheim)
		1164 Archbishopric for Sweden (Uppsala)
1170–97 The Lord Rhys rules south Wales	1154–89 Henry II	
1176 'Eisteddfod' at Cardigan Castle	1169 Norman rule in Ireland began	
	1170 Becket murdered	
	1175 English feudal over-lordship imposed on Scotland	
1188 Journey of Gerald the Welshman (Giraldus Cambrensis) and Archbishop Baldwin around Wales	1189 English feudal over-lordship surrendered	1189 Third Crusade
1196–1240 Reign of Llywelyn Fawr	1189–99 Richard I	
	1192 Scottish church's independence of England recognised	
	1199–1216 John	1198–1216 Innocent III Pope
	1215 Magna Carta	1209 Franciscan order founded

1246–82 Reign of Llywelyn ap Gruffydd, 'The Last Prince'	1216–72 Henry III	1211–50 Frederick II, Emperor
1267 Treaty of Montgomery, Llywelyn as Prince of Wales	1237 Treaty of York ratifies Anglo-Scottish border	1215 Fourth Lateran Council
1276–7 First 'War of Welsh Independence'	1265 Simon de Montfort's parliament	1216 Dominican order founded
1277 Humiliation of Llywelyn at Treaty of Aberconwy		1226–70 Louis IX (St Louis) king of France
1282–3 Second 'War of Welsh Independence'	1272–1307 Edward I	
1282 Death of Llywelyn at Cilmeri	1293 French war began	1274 Death of Thomas Aquinas
1283 Death of his brother Prince David; Edward I's castle-building programme in Wales begins	1295 'Model Parliament'	1291–1314 Philip IV (the Fair), king of France
1284 Statute of Wales by Edward I	1296 English occupation of Scotland	1292 Crusaders finally lost Jerusalem
1294–6 Revolts against English occupation	1297–8 Rising of Wallace and Moray	
1301 Edward makes his son Prince of Wales		
	1307–27 Edward II	1308 Pope moved to Avignon
	1314 Bannockburn	1315 Swiss preserve independence at Morgarten
1316 Rebellion of Llywelyn Bren	1316–18 Edward Bruce king of Ireland	1328–50 Philip VI, king of France
c1320–80 Dafydd ap Gwilym flourished	1320 Declaration of Arbroath	
	1327–77 Edward III	
	1328 Scottish independence recognised by England	
	1337 Beginning of Hundred Years' War	
	1346 Battle of Crecy	
	1348 Black Death	
	1356 King John of France captured at Poitiers	1358 Jacquerie in France
		1377 Pope returned to Rome
	1377–99 Richard II	

1381 Peasants' Revolt		
1384 Death of Wyclif		
		1378–1417 Schism between Roman and Avignonese popes
		1386 Swiss ensure independence by battle of Sempach
		1397 Norway, Denmark and Sweden united
1399–1413 Henry IV	1400 Revolt of Owain Glyndŵr (Glendower)	
1400 Death of Chaucer	1404 First of Glyndŵr's Parliaments	
1411 University of St Andrews	1409 Decline of Glyndŵr's support	
1413–22 Henry V	1413–15 Disappearance of Glyndŵr	1414 Council of Constance
1415 Agincourt		1415 Death of John Hus
1422–61 Henry VI		1431 Death of Joan of Arc
1450 Cade's Rebellion	1450–1 Carmarthen Eisteddfod: regulation of strict metre poetry	
1451 University of Glasgow		1453 Turks took Constantinople
1453 End of Hundred Years' War		
1455–85 Wars of the Roses		
1461–83 Edward IV	1461 Welsh at Battle of Mortimer's Cross	
1476 Caxton's printing press	1471 Edward IV's Council of Welsh Marches at Ludlow	1469 Marriage of Ferdinand and Isabella united Spain
1483 Edward V		1491 France acquired Brittany
1483–5 Richard III		1492 Columbus crossed Atlantic
1485–1509 Henry VII	1485 Henry Tudor lands in Pembroke, and marches to Bosworth	1494 French invasion of Italy
1495 King's College, Aberdeen		1497 Vasco da Gama reached India by Cape of Good Hope
1495 Perkin Warbeck's rebellion		1503–13 Pope Julius II
1503 James IV married Margaret Tudor		1510 Pope formed Holy League against France
1509–47 Henry VIII		1515–47 Francis I, king of France
1513 Flodden		1517 Luther's Theses
1515 Wolsey appointed chancellor	1523 First Caerwys Eisteddfod	1519 Charles V, Emperor
1533 England repudiated papal authority	1531 Execution of Rhys ap Gruffydd, fall of house of Dinefwr	1523 Sweden regains independence
1536–8 Dissolution of monasteries	1534 Rowland Lee, Bishop of Lichfield, President of the Council of the Marches	1524 Peasants' War in Germany
	1536 First 'Act of Union' of England and Wales	1529 First Siege of Vienna by Turks
	1543 Second 'Act of Union'	1534 Order of Jesuits founded

Wales	England / Scotland	Europe / World
1546 First printed book in Welsh: *Yn y Lhyvyr Hwnn*	1547–53 Edward VI	1541 Calvin in power at Geneva
	1549 First Prayer Book	1545–63 Council of Trent
	1553–8 Mary Tudor	1547–59 Henry II, king of France
	1558 Loss of Calais	
	1558–1603 Elizabeth	1556–98 Philip II, king of Spain
1562 Act of Parliament establishing Protestant liturgy in Welsh	1559 Acts of Supremacy and Uniformity	1559–60 Francis II, king of France (husband of Mary, Queen of Scots)
1567 Translation of Prayer Book and New Testament into Welsh; second Caerwys Eisteddfod	1560 'Reformation parliament', Scotland 1st Book of Discipline	1560–74 Charles IX, king of France
	1565 Queen Mary married Darnley	1562 Wars of religion began in France
1570 Brass and wire foundries at Tintern: beginnings of Welsh industrialism	1567 Mary deposed in Scotland	
1571 Jesus College, Oxford, founded for the Welsh	1568 Mary fled to England	1572 Massacre of St Bartholomew's Eve
	1569 Northern Rebellion	1579 Union of Utrecht: Beginning of Dutch independence
	1577–80 Drake circumnavigated the globe	1580 Portugal united with Spain
1582 Iron smelting near Neath	1582 University of Edinburgh	1588 Spanish Armada
1584 Martyrdom of Catholic Richard Gwyn	1586 League with England	1589 Henry IV, king of France
1588 Complete Welsh Bible translated by Bishop Morgan	1587 Execution of Mary, Queen of Scots	1598 Edict of Nantes; toleration for French protestants
1591 Martyrdom of Puritan John Penry	1592 Presbyterian government authorised in Scotland	
	1600 East India Company founded	
	1603–25 James I	1607 Virginia colonised
	1604 Hampton Court Conference	1608 Champlain founded Quebec
	1611 Plantation of Ulster	
	1616 Death of Shakespeare	
	1625–49 Charles I	1618–48 Thirty Years' War
	1628 Petition of Right	1620 Pilgrim Fathers
1630 Popular edition of the Welsh Bible	1633 Laud Archbishop of Canterbury	
1639 First Puritan congregation in Wales convened at Llanfaches, Gwent	1634–8 Ship Money dispute	
	1638 National Covenant	1640 Portugal regained independence
	1639–40 Covenanters at war with king	

1643–1715 Louis XIV King of France	**1640** Long Parliament met	**1644** First battle of the Civil War in Wales: Battle of Montgomery
	1642 Civil War began	**1645** Charles I recruits troops in Wales
	1643 Solemn League and Covenant	**1647** Fall of the last royalist fortress, Harlech Castle
		1648 Cromwell in Wales, Second Civil War
	1649 Charles I beheaded; Commonwealth proclaimed	
	1649–50 Cromwellian conquest of Ireland	**1650–3** Act for Propagation of Gospel in Wales
	1652–4 Dutch War	
	1653 Protectorate	
	1660 Charles II restored as king of England and Scotland	**1660** Restoration of the Council of Wales
	1665–7 Dutch War	
1667 Louis XIV began aggressive wars	**1665–6** Great Plague and Fire	
	1672–4 Dutch War	**1674** Schools of the Welsh Trust
1683 Second siege of Vienna by Turks		
1685 Revocation of Edict of Nantes	**1685** Accession of James VII and II	
1689 War of the League of Augsburg	**1688–9** Revolution: James VII and II superseded by William and Mary	**1689** Abolition of the Council of Wales
	1690 Presbyterianism restored	
	1690 Battle of the Boyne	
	1692 Massacre of Glencoe	
	1694 Bank of England founded	**1694** Death of last household bard 'Siôn Dafydd Las'
		1699 Society for the Promotion of Christian Knowledge
	1701 Act of Settlement	**1701** New eisteddfod advertised in Welsh Almanacks

1703 Foundation of St Petersburg		
1709 Peter the Great defeated Swedes at Pultava	1702–14 Reign of Queen Anne	1707 Celtic studies founded with Edward Lhuyd's *Archaeologia Britannica*
	1707 Union of England and Scotland	
	1702–13 War of Spanish Succession	
	1714–27 Reign of George I	1715 Society of Antient Britons, London
	1715 Jacobite Rebellion	
	1716 Septennial Act	1718 First printing works set up inside Wales
		1735 Conversion of Howell Harris
1740–86 Frederick the Great, king of Prussia	1721–42 Ministry of Walpole	c1737 Beginnings of Griffith Jones's circulating schools
1742–8 War of Austrian Succession	1738 Beginning of Methodism	1743 Methodist Association in Wales
	1745–6 Jacobite Rebellion	1751 Foundation of Cymmrodorion Society in London
		1755 Brecknockshire Agricultural Society founded
1756–63 Seven Years' War	1757–61 Chatham's first ministry	1757 Brecon to London stage-coach route opened; Isaac Wilkinson starts industry at Hirwaun
1760 British conquest of Canada		1759 Guest starts to develop Merthyr Tydfil industry
		1761 Death of Griffith Jones
		1762 Second Methodist Revival
	1764 Hargreaves invented spinning-jenny	1764 Anglesey Copper industry launched
	1769 Arkwright invented water-frame. James Watt's steam engine patented	1771 Gwyneddigion Society founded in London
1776–83 American Revolution	1770–81 Lord North's ministry	1777 Bacon develops industry in Merthyr
	1779 Crompton's 'Mule'	1782 Pennant inherits Penrhyn estate, Caernarfonshire slate industry launched

Wales	Britain	World
1785 Thomas Charles of Bala's circulating schools	1784–1801 Ministry of Pitt the Younger	1789 French Revolution began
1789 Sunday schools of Charles of Bala; three *eisteddfodau* held by Gwyneddigion	1785 Cartwright invented power loom	
1791–2 'Madoc Fever': enthusiasm for Welsh American Indians		1793 War between Britain and France
1792 Iolo Morganwg's Gorsedd of Bards held in London		
1793–4 Cardiff to Merthyr canal		
1794 Richard Crawshay buys iron works at Cyfarthfa; radical M. J. Rhys emigrates to USA		
1797 French revolutionary fleet lands at Fishguard		
1801 Census shows Welsh population is 587,000	1801 Union of Great Britain and Ireland	1804 Napoleon Emperor of the French
1804 Richard Trevithick starts the first locomotive on railway between Merthyr and Abercynon; *Cambrian* newspaper started		1805 Battle of Trafalgar
1811 Census shows Welsh population up to 673,000; separation of Welsh Methodists from Church of England	1807 Slave Trade abolished	1815 Battle of Waterloo. Belgium and Holland united. Norway and Sweden united
1816–17 Industrial unrest in Wales	1819 'Peterloo Massacre'	1821–9 Greek War of Independence
1819 Carmarthen eisteddfod and Gorsedd of Bards		

Wales	Britain	World
1822 Foundation of St David's College, Lampeter	1825 Stockton–Darlington railway	1825 Independence of Spanish American mainland complete
1830 Abolition of the Courts of Great Sessions		1830 Belgium independent
1831 Rising at Merthyr Tydfil	1832 First Reform Act. Death of Sir Water Scott	
	1833 Municipal Reform	
	1833 Abolition of slavery in British dominions	1837 Telegraphy invented by Morse
1839 Chartist attack on Newport	1838–50 Chartist Movement	
1839–44 The Rebecca Riots	1840 Penny postage introduced	
1841 Taff Vale Railway; death of John Elias 'The Methodist Pope'	1845–8 Famine in Ireland	
1844 Government inquiry into problems of south Wales	1846 Repeal of Corn Law	1848 Revolutions in France and other European countries
1846 Government commission investigates Welsh education		
1847 Publication of the 'Blue Books' on Wales		
1851 Religious census shows huge majority of nonconformists in Wales	1856 Bessemer's steel process invented	1854–6 Crimean War
1856 Welsh national anthem composed		1857 Indian Mutiny
1858 Llangollen national eisteddfod, starts pattern of annual national gatherings		
1859 Liberal victories at elections, evictions of tenants; Welsh religious revival		1861–5 American Civil War
1863 Committee to start campaign for Welsh University		
1865 Welsh colony in Patagonia founded		

World events	British political events	Welsh events
1868 Suez Canal opened	1867 Second Reform Act	1868 Liberal victories in Welsh seats in election
1870 Unification of Italy complete	1870 Education Act	
1871 German Empire established		1872 University College of Wales opens at Aberystwyth
		1874 North Wales Quarrymen's Union founded
		1876 Football Association of Wales (soccer)
		1877 Oxford Professorship of Celtic founded
		1881 Welsh Rugby Union founded
		1881 Welsh Sunday Closing Act passed
		1883 University College opened in Cardiff
	1884 Third Reform Act	1884 University College opened in Bangor
1885 Canadian Pacific Railway completed		1885 Welsh Language Society founded by Dan Isaac Davies
	1886 Irish Home Rule proposed. Liberal Party split	1886 'Tithe War' in north and west Wales; Cymru Fydd (Young Wales) movement
	1889 County Councils established	1889 Welsh Intermediate Schools Act
	1890 Parnell ruined	1890 Lloyd George elected MP; McKinley tariffs stop Welsh exports to USA
		1893–6 Royal Commission on Land in Wales
	1893 Irish Home Rule Bill rejected	1893 Charter of federated University of Wales
1895 Discovery of X-rays		1895 Collapse of Cymru Fydd movement
		1896–7 First Penrhyn stoppage (slate industry)
		1896 Central Welsh Board (for education)
1898 Spanish-American War		1898 South Wales Miners Federation founded
1899–1902 South African War		1900 First Labour MP, Keir Hardie, elected for Merthyr Tydfil
1903 Beginning of aeroplane flight		1904 Evan Roberts and religious revival in Wales
1904–5 Russo-Japanese War		1905 Welsh rugby victory over New Zealand
1905 Norway became independent		

World	Britain	Wales
	1906 Women's Suffrage Movement began	1907 Foundation of National Museum and National Library and Welsh department of Board of Education
	1909 Old-age pensions introduced	1910 Unrest in coalfield, Tonypandy riots
1911 Amundsen reached South Pole	1911 Parliament Act	1911 Investiture of Edward as Prince of Wales at Caernarfon Castle
		1911 Census shows Welsh population is around 2,400,000
1914–18 World War I		1914 Act to Disestablish the Church in Wales
1915 Panama Canal opened	1916 Easter Rebellion in Ireland	1916 Lloyd George as Prime Minister
1917 Russian Revolution		
1920 League of Nations formed	1921 Irish Free State established	1920 Constitution of the Church in Wales; University College opened in Swansea
	1922 Wireless broadcasting began	1921 Census shows Welsh population up to 2,656,000
1925 Fascist dictatorship in Italy		1922 Urdd Gobaith Cymru (Welsh League of Youth) founded
		1925 Welsh Nationalist Party founded
	1928 National Party of Scotland formed	1926 Troubles in Welsh coalfield, miners strike; General Strike
1929–39 Great Depression		1931 Census shows drop of Welsh population to 2,593,000
1933 Hitler became Chancellor of Germany	1936 BBC's first TV broadcast	1936 Nationalists burn bombing school in Lleyn
1936–9 Spanish Civil War		1937 BBC Welsh region opened
1939–45 World War II	1944 Education Act	1942 Welsh Courts Act
1945 UN Charter signed; first use of atomic weapons	1947 Coal industry nationalised	1946 St Fagan's Castle to be Welsh Folk Museum
1947 Partition and independence of India		1947 International Eisteddfod founded at Llangollen

Wales	Britain	World
1948 Council for Wales and Monmouthshire established; Welsh Joint Education Committee founded	1948 British Railways set up; NHS started	
1951 Government establishes Ministry for Welsh Affairs	1949 Gas industry nationalised	1949 NATO formed; creation of People's Republic of China
1955 Cardiff declared as official capital of Wales	1952 First atomic weapon tested	1950–3 Korean War
	1956 First atomic power station	1956 Suez crisis; Hungarian uprising
		1957 First space satellite (Sputnik); Treaty of Rome established EEC; independence for Gold Coast (Ghana)
1961 Census shows Welsh population is still below total of 1921 at 2,653,000		1962 Cuban missile crisis
1962 *Cymdeithas yr Iaith Gymraeg* (Welsh Language Society) and Welsh Books Council founded		
1964 First Secretary of State for Wales appointed		
	1965 Abolition of capital punishment for murder	1965–73 Large-scale US involvement in Vietnam War
1966 First *Plaid Cymru* MP elected to Parliament		1967 Six Day War
1967 Charter for Welsh Arts Council; Welsh Language Act passed; Crowther (Kilbrandon) Commission meets	1968 Ulster Civil Rights movement	1968 Invasion of Czechoslovakia
1969 Investiture of Prince Charles as Prince of Wales at Caernarfon Castle		1969 First men on the moon
	1970 First victory of SNP candidate at general election	

1973 Kilbrandon Commission recommends assembly for Wales; Wales TUC founded	1972 Direct rule in N. Ireland	1973 Yom Kippur War; oil crisis
1974 New Welsh counties and local government	1973 Kilbrandon Report; entry into EEC	1974 President Nixon resigned after Watergate scandal
	1974 Eleven SNP members of parliament	
	1974–5 Reorganisation of local government	
	1978 Bill for Scottish Assembly passed	
1979 Referendum on Welsh and Scottish Assemblies, Welsh assembly heavily defeated	1979 Referendum on proposed Assembly Bill repealed	1979 Revolution in Iran
1982 Welsh-language television channel opens (S4C)		1982 Britain and Argentina at war

Bibliography

Following are some suggestions for further reading for those requiring greater detail or depth on the subjects covered in this book. For convenience, they are ordered by chapter headings.

General

Board of Celtic Studies, *Bibliography of the history of Wales* (University of Wales Press, 1962, with later supplements)

Carter, H. (ed) *National Atlas of Wales* (University of Wales Press, 1980)

Dictionary of Welsh Biography (Cymmrodorion, 1959)

Davies, R. R., Griffiths, R. A., Jones, I. G., Morgan, K. O., (eds) *Welsh Society and Nationhood* (University of Wales Press, 1984)

Dodd, A. H., *Life in Wales* (Batsford, 1972)

Edwards, O. D., (ed) *Celtic Nationalism* (Routledge, 1968)

Fishlock, T., *Wales and the Welsh* (Cassell, 1972)

Foulkes, D., Jones, J. B., and Wilford, R. A., (eds) *The Welsh Veto: the Wales Act 1978 and the Referendum* (University of Wales Press, 1983)

Griffith, Ll. W., *The Welsh* (Penguin, 1950)

Hechter, M., *Internal colonialism: the Celtic fringe in British National Development* (Routledge, 1975)

Jones, R. B., (ed) *The Anatomy of Wales* (Gwerin Publications, 1970)

Lewis, R., *Second-class Citizen* (Gomer Press, 1969)

Morgan, P., *Background to Wales* (Christopher Davies, 1968)

Morgan, W. J., (ed) *The Welsh dilemma* (Christopher Davies, 1973)

Osmond, J., *Creative conflict — the politics of Welsh Devolution* (Gomer Press and Routledge, 1977)

Smith, D., *Wales! Wales?* (Allen & Unwin, 1984)

Stephens, M., (ed) *A Reader's Guide to Wales* (Libraries Association, 1973)

Williams, C. H., (ed) *National Separatism* (University of Wales Press, 1982)

Williams, G., *The Land Remembers: a view of Wales* (Faber, 1977)

Chapter 1: Land of My Fathers

Bowen, E. G., *Geography, Culture and Habitat* (Gomer Press, 1976)

Bowen, E. G., (ed) *Wales; a Physical, Historical and Regional Geography* (Methuen, 1957)

Brown, E. H., *The Relief and Drainage of Wales* (University of Wales Press, 1966)

Brown, E. H., Bowen, D. Q., and Waters, R. S., *The Geomorphology of Wales and South West England* (Methuen, 1977)

Thomas, D., (ed) *Wales: a New Study* (David & Charles, 1977)

Chapter 2: People and Language

Bowen, E. G., *Saints, Seaways and Settlements in the Celtic Lands* (University of Wales Press, 1977)

Jackson, K. H., *Language and History in Early Britain* (Edinburgh University Press, 1953)

Jones, R. B., (ed) *The Anatomy of Wales* (Gwerin Publications, 1972)

Stephens, M., (ed) *The Welsh Language Today* (Gomer Press, 1973)

Thomas, A. R., *The Linguistic Geography of Wales, a Contribution to Welsh Dialectology* (University of Wales Press, 1973)

Williams, D., *A History of Modern Wales* (John Murray, 1950)

Chapter 3: Wales and England

Evans, E. D., *A History of Wales, 1660–1815* (University of Wales Press, 1976)

Fox, C., *Offa's Dyke — a Field Survey* (Oxford University Press, 1956)

Lloyd, J. E., *Owain Glendower* (Oxford University Press, 1931)

Rees, W., *An Historical Atlas of Wales* (Faber, 1951)

Rees, W., *The Union of England and Wales* (University of Wales Press, 1948)

Thomas, H., *A History of Wales, 1485–1660* (University of Wales Press, 1972)

Chapter 4: Rural Wales

Davies, E. and Rees, A. D., (eds) *Welsh Rural Communities* (University of Wales Press, 1960)

Rees, A. D., *Life in a Welsh Countryside* (University of Wales Press, 1950)

Thirsk, J., (ed) *The Agrarian History of England and Wales*, vol. IV (Cambridge University Press, 1967)

Thomas, D., *Agriculture in Wales during the Napoleonic Wars* (University of Wales Press, 1963)

Williams, D., *The Rebecca Riots; a Study in Agrarian Discontent* (University of Wales Press, 1955)

Chapter 5: Industrialisation

Addis, J., *The Crawshay Dynasty* (University of Wales Press, 1957)

Dodd, A. H., *The Industrial Revolution in North Wales* (University of Wales Press, 1971)

Jenkins, J. G., *The Welsh Woollen Industry* (National Museum of Wales, 1969)

John, A. H., *The Industrial Development of South Wales, 1750–1850* (University of Wales Press, 1950)

Lewis, W. J., *Lead Mining in Wales* (University of Wales Press, 1967)

Lindsay, J., *A History of the North Wales Slate Industry* (David & Charles, 1974)

Chapter 6: The Radical Tradition

Davies, D. H., *The Welsh Nationalist Party, 1925–45* (University of Wales Press, 1983)

Howell, D. W., *Land and People in Nineteenth-century Wales* (Routledge, 1978)

Jones, D. J. V., *Before Rebecca* (Allen Lane, 1973)

Jones, G. J., *Wales and the Quest for Peace* (University of Wales Press, 1969)

Jones, I. G., *Explorations and Explanations: Essays in the Social History of Victorian Wales* (Gomer Press, 1981)

Jones, R. M., *The North Wales Quarrymen's Union* (University of Wales Press, 1981)

Molloy, P., *And they blessed Rebecca* (Gomer, 1983)

Morgan, K. O., *Rebirth of a Nation: Wales 1880–1980* (Oxford University Press and University of Wales Press, 1982)

——. *Wales in British Politics, 1868–1922* 3rd ed (University of Wales Press 1980)

Philip, A. B., *The Welsh Question: Nationalism in Welsh Politics 1945–70* (University of Wales Press, 1975)

Smith, D., (ed) *A People and a Proletariat: Essays in the History of Wales 1780–1980* (Pluto Press, 1980)

Williams, D., *The Rebecca Riots* (University of Wales Press, 1955)

Williams, G., (ed) *Merthyr Politics: the Making of a Working-class Tradition* (University of Wales Press, 1966)

Williams, G. A., *In Search of Beulah land* (Croom Helm, 1980)

——. *Madoc, the making of a myth* (Eyre Methuen, 1979)

——. *The Merthyr Rising* (Croom Helm, 1978)

——. *The Welsh in Their History* (Croom Helm, 1982)

Chapter 7: Church and Chapel

Bell, P. M. H., *Disestablishment in Ireland and Wales* (SPCK 1969)

Davies, E. T., *Religion and Society in Nineteenth-century Wales* (Christopher Davies, 1981)

——. *Religion in the Industrial Revolution in South Wales* (University of Wales Press, 1969)

Jenkins, D., *The Agricultural Community in South-West Wales at the Turn of the Twentieth Century* (University of Wales Press, 1971)

Jones, I. G., *Explorations and Explanations: Essays in the Social History of Victorian Wales* (Gomer Press, 1981)

——. and Williams, D., (eds) *The Religious Census of 1851: the calendar of returns relating to Wales* 2 vols (University of Wales Press, 1976, 1981)

Lambert, W. R., *Drink and Sobriety in Victorian Wales* (University of Wales Press, 1983)

Morgan, K. O., *Freedom or Sacrilege?* (Church in Wales, 1965)

Walker, D., (ed) *A History of the Church in Wales* (Church in Wales, 1976)

Williams, G., *Religion, Language and Nationality in Wales* (University of Wales Press, 1979)

————. *The Welsh Church from Conquest to Reformation* (University of Wales Press, 1962)

————. *Welsh Reformation Essays* (University of Wales Press, 1968)

Chapter 8: The Dragon's Two Tongues: Life and Letters

Caerwyn Williams, J. E., (ed) *Literature in Celtic Countries* (University of Wales Press, 1971)

Conran, A., *Penguin book of Welsh Verse* (Penguin, 1967)

Durcacz, V. E., *The Decline of the Celtic Languages* (John Donald, 1983)

Ford, P. K., (ed) *The Mabinogi and Other Medieval Welsh Tales* (University of California Press, 1977)

Gantz, J., (ed) *The Mabinogion* (Penguin, 1976)

Jackson, K. H., (ed) *A Celtic Miscellany* (Routledge, 1951; Penguin rev ed, 1971)

Jarman, A. O. H., and Hughes, G. R., (eds) *A Guide to Welsh Literature* (Christopher Davies, 1976)

Jenkins, G. H., *Literature, Religion and Society in Wales: 1660–1730* (University of Wales Press, 1978)

Jones, G., and Rowlands, J., *Profiles* (Gomer, 1980)

Jones, G., *The Dragon has Two Tongues* (Dent, 1968)

————. and Jones, T., (eds) *The Mabinogion* (Dent, 1949, 1976)

Jones, B., *A Bibliography of Anglo-Welsh Literature, 1900–1965,* (Libraries Association, 1970)

Jones, R. B., and Stephens, M., (eds) *Writers of Wales,* short biographies of authors; series includes Garlick, R., *An Introduction to Anglo-Welsh Literature* (1970) and Williams, G., *An introduction to Welsh Literature* (1978) (all published by University of Wales Press and Welsh Arts Council)

Jones, R. M., *Highlights in Welsh literature: Talks with a Prince* (Christopher Davies, 1969)

Morgan, G., *The Dragon's Tongue* (Triskel, 1966)

Morgan, P., *The Eighteenth-century Renaissance* (Christopher Davies, 1981)

Parry, T., (trans Bell, I.) *A History of Welsh Literature* (Oxford University Press, 1955)

Stephens, M., (ed) *The Arts in Wales 1950–75* (Welsh Arts Council, 1979)

259

———. (ed) *The Welsh Language Today* (Gomer Press, 1973)

Thomas, N., *The Welsh Extremist* (Gollancz, 1971)

Thorpe, L., (ed) *Gerald of Wales: Journey through Wales/Description of Wales* (Penguin, 1978)

Williams, J. L., *Bilingualism, a bibliography of 1,000 references with special references to Wales* (University of Wales Press, 1971)

Chapter 9: Land of Song , the Bard and Rugby

Corrigan, P., *One Hundred Years of Welsh Soccer: the official history of the Football Association of Wales* (Welsh Brewers, 1976)

Crossley-Holland, P., (ed) *Music in Wales* (Hinrichsen, 1948)

Ellis, O., *The Harp in Wales* (University of Wales Press, 1978)

Lerry, G. G., *The Football Association of Wales: Seventy-fifth Anniversary, 1876–1951* (Football Association, 1951)

Miles, D., *The Royal National Eisteddfod of Wales* (Christopher Davies, 1978)

Scholes, P. A., 'Wales', in *Oxford Companion to Music* (Oxford University Press, 1956)

Smith, D. and Williams, G., *Fields of Praise: the Welsh Rugby Union 1881–1981* (University of Wales Press, 1980)

Smith, J. S., *Impressions of Music in Wales* (Venture, 1948)

Thomas, G., *The Caerwys Eisteddfodau* (University of Wales Press, 1968)

Chapter 10: The Growth of Welsh Institutions

Andrews, J. A., (ed) *Welsh Studies in Public Law* (University of Wales Press, 1970)

Coupland, R. A., *Welsh and Scottish Nationalism* (Oxford University Press, 1954)

Daunton, M. J., *Coal Metropolis: Cardiff 1870–1914* (Leicester University Press, 1977)

Davies, D. H., *The Welsh Nationalist Party, 1925–45* (University of Wales Press, 1983)

Davies, J., *Cardiff and the Marquesses of Bute* (University of Wales Press, 1981)

Ellis, E. L., *University College of Wales, Aberystwyth 1872–1972* (University of Wales Press, 1972)

Evans, D. E., *University of Wales, a historical sketch* (University of Wales Press, 1953)

Francis, H. and Smith, D., *The Fed — the South Wales Miners' Federation, 1898–1978* (Lawrence & Wishart, 1978)

Hilling, J. B., *Cardiff and the Valleys* (Lund Humphries, 1973)

Hughes, G. T., Morgan, P., and Thomas, J. G., (eds) *Gregynog* (University of Wales Press, 1977)

Jenkins, R. T., and Ramage, H., *History of the Honourable Society of Cymmrodorion, 1751–1951* (Cymmrodorion, 1951)

Lloyd, D. M., (ed) *The Historical Basis of Welsh Nationalism* (Plaid Cymru, 1950)

Morgan, K. O., *Rebirth of a Nation: Wales 1880–1980* (Oxford University Press and University of Wales Press, 1982)

Peate, I. C., *Folk Museums* (University of Wales Press, 1948)

Philip, A. B., *The Welsh Question: Nationalism in Welsh Politics, 1945–70* (University of Wales Press, 1975)

Rees, J. F., (ed) *The Cardiff Region, a survey* (British Association, 1960)

——. *The Problem of Wales* (University of Wales Press, 1953)

Rees, W., *Cardiff, the History of the City* (Cardiff City Corporation, 1962)

Stead, P. P., *Coleg Harlech, the First Fifty Years* (University of Wales Press, 1977)

Appendix I: Welsh Names

Morgan, P. and Morgan T. J., *Welsh Surnames* (University of Wales Press, forthcoming)

Reaney, P. H., *A Dictionary of British Surnames* (Routledge, 1958)

Index

Aberavon, 209
Aberdare, 118, 124, 169
Abergavenny, 124, 202
Aberystwyth, 41, 51, 88, 123, 124, 216–17, 218, 226–7
Ablett, Noah, 144
Acreage Returns (1801), 103–5
Agrarian Revolution, 89–105, 209
Agriculture, 25, 34, 40, 41, 61, 84–108, 141
Air masses, 21
America, 88, 116, 135, 185, 188, 204
Amlwch, 111
Amman, Valley of, 116
Ammanford, 31
Aneirin, 178–9, 193
Anglesey, 19, 42–3, 45, 57, 62, 66, 80, 103, 105, 122, 150, 160–1, 208
Anglicanism, 145–6, 155–6, 167–77, 187, 215, 219
Anglo-Normans, 29, 30, 39–45, 46, 61–4, 85–6
Anglo-Saxons, 32, 35–6, 37, 39, 45–6, 178–9
Anti-Slavery Movement, 162
Ap Cynan, Gruffydd, 179; Statute of, 201
Ap Gwilym, Dafydd, 181–2
Ap Huw, Roberts, 195
Ap Iwan, Emrys, 169
Ap Llywelyn, Gruffydd, 39
Apostolic Church, 167
Archenfield, 73
Arenig Range, 17
Arthur, King, 179, 180–1
Association Football, 209–12
Australia, 204

Bacon, Anthony, 115
Bala, 88, 161, 201; Bulls of, 161
Band of Hope, 169, 225
Bangor, 28, 122, 216, 222
Bangor (on Dee), 211
Banks, 88
Baptists, 158–9, 160, 168, 215
Bards, 64, 178–83, 200–8; *Gorsedd* of, 201–8, 214, 216
Barlow Commission, 130
Barmouth, 97–8
Barnet, 87
Barry, 55, 124
Bassey, Shirley, 200
Bastides, 40, 44–5
BBC Wales, 222; Orchestra, 199, 222
Beaker folk, 33
Beaufort, Margaret, 69
Beaumaris, 44
Bedford, County of, 94
Bedwas, 208
Belfast, 58
Berkshire, 99
Bersham, 114, 116
Berwyn Mts, 16
Bessemer, Henry, 117
Bethesda, 112, 113
Bevan, Aneurin, 148
Bible, translation of, 183
Bilingualism, 46–57, 204, 222–5
Blaenafon, 111, 114
Blaenannerch, 166
Blaenau Ffestiniog, 112, 113
Blaenau Morgannwg, 13, 16
Blue Books, treason of, 138–40, 162, 163, 202
Board of Agriculture, reports of, 103

Board of Education, Welsh Department of, 218, 225
Board of Health and National Insurance, Welsh Department of, 225
Bois, Henri, 167
Borderland, 16, 39
Bosworth, 70
Boulder clay, 19
Boulton, Matthew, 114, 116
Brecon, 41, 73, 118, 210, 221; Agricultural society, 89, 100, 214; County of, 26, 73, 80, 97, 113, 129, 157
Brentwood, 87
Bridgend, 100–103, 131
Bristol, 30, 88, 92, 110, 220
Britannia Tubular Bridge, 122
Brittany, 23, 35, 70
Bronze Age, 24, 33–4, 35
Broseley, 114, 115
Brown Earth, 26
Brownrigg, William, 115
Brunel, Isambard Kingdom, 122–3
Builth, 219
Burgess, Bishop Thomas, 214
Bute, Marquis of, 122, 220

Cadair Idris, 16, 17
Cadwaladr, 70
Caerhun, 36
Caernarfon, 28, 44, 63, 73, 113; County of, 45, 62, 80, 82, 96–7, 105, 112, 190
Caersŵs, 36
Caerwys, 201
Calvinism, 157–8, 166, 177, 215
Cambrian, 15
Cambrian Archaeological Society, 215
Cambrian Mts, 13
Campbell, R.J., 166
Canada, 204
Canals, 118
Capital city, 32, 58, 81, 124, 148, 219–21
Cardiff, 32, 41, 58, 78, 81, 82–3, 117, 118, 122–3, 124, 125, 128, 130, 142,

148, 199, 202, 209, 211, 212, 216–7, 218, 219–29
Cardigan, 28, 200, 210; Agricultural society, 100, 103; County of, 45, 57, 62, 63, 72, 80, 96–7, 103, 107, 110, 111, 112, 113, 158, 162, 185, 204
Cardigan Bay, 13, 19, 21, 32, 55
Carmarthen, 63, 73, 82, 107, 122–3, 150, 200–1, 202, 207, 210, 214; County of, 45, 57, 62, 63, 72, 80, 103, 107, 110, 157, 158, 167, 185
Carreg Wastad, 90
Castles, 40–1, 44–5
Catholicism, 155–6, 157, 177
Cave art, 32
Celtic Saints, 38, 41
Celts, 24, 32–6, 37, 58–61
Central Welsh Board, 142, 218
Channel Islands, 110
Charles, Thomas, 161
Chartists, 137
Chepstow, 60, 122–3, 211
Cheshire, 62, 74
Chester, 40, 63, 122
Chirk, 118
Choral music, 198–9
Christianity, 37–8
Cirques, 19
Claudius, Emperor, 36
Climate, 18, 20, 21–5, 32–3
Clun, Lordship of, 73
Clwyd, County of, 80; Vale of, 13, 16, 29, 103, 105
Clwydian Range, 13
Coal, 16, 110–11, 125–33
Coal Owners Association of South Wales, 218
Coalbrookdale, 114
Coalfield, North Wales, 30–1, 51–2, 110, 113–7, 125–33; South Wales, 30–1, 51, 80, 83, 110–11, 113–7, 125–33
Colwyn Bay, 124
Companies House, 221
Conservative Party, 148–52
Conwy, 28, 29, 44, 118, 122
Conwy, River, 19, 80, 118

Copper, 111–12, 113
Cork, 123
Corn Laws, 90
Cornwall, 22, 23, 35, 111–12
Corris, 112
Cort, Henry, 115–16
Corwen, 80, 112, 201
Coventry, 88
Crane George, 116
Craven Arms, 123
Crawshay (family), 111, 115
Cricieth, 43, 44
Cricket, 209
Crumlin, 118
Cunedda, Sons of, 35
Cwmbrân, 131
Cyfarthfa, 111, 115
Cyfeiliog, Owain, 179
Cymmrodorion, Honourable Society of, 214, 225
Cynwal, William, 183
Cynwyl Elfed, 203

Darby, Abraham, 111, 114
Davies, E.T., 164
Davies, John, 183
Davies of Llandinam (family), 220
Davies, Sir Walford, 199
Dee, River, 30, 37, 118; Ports of, 112
De Fursac, Rogues, 167
Deganwy, 43
Deheubarth, 42, 43, 60, 63–4
Denbigh, 66, 73, 219; County of, 73, 80, 112
Derwenlas, 118
Deva, 36
Dinas Brân, 43
Dinorwic, 112
Diserth, 111
Distribution of Industry Act (1945), 131
Dolau Cothi, 37
Dolforwyn, 43
Dolgellau, 183
Dolwyddelan, 43, 44
Domesday Book, 24
Dowlais, 111, 114, 115
Dragon, red, 70

Drainage, 17–18
Dre-fach, 18
Drovers, 87–8
Drumlins, 19
Dyfed, County of, 13, 17, 22, 41, 57, 80, 83, 84, 214
Dyfi, River, 19, 21, 29, 118
Dovey Junction, 123–4
Dynefwr, 43

East Anglia, 89
Ebbw Vale, 148
Edinburgh, 58
Education Act (1870), 47–8, 78, 218
Edward I, 43–5, 61–4, 85
Edward III, 74
Edward VIII, Welsh National Memorial to, 219
Edwards, Archbishop A.G., 173
Edwards, Charles, 184
Edwards, Sir Ifan ab Owen, 225–6
Edwards, Jane, 191
Edwards, Sir Owen M., 189, 226
Edwards, Thomas Charles, 170
Edwards, Trebor, 200
Eglwys Bach, 166
Eisteddfod, 161–2, 169, 185, 186–7, 195–208, 214, 216, 220
Elgar, E., 199
Elias, John, 136, 160–1, 162
Elim Four Square Gospel Movement, 167
Elis, Islwyn Ffowe, 191
Elizabeth I, 183, 184
Ellesmere, 118
Ellis, T.E., 142
Enclosure, 94–9
Engineers, South Wales Institute of, 218
European languages, Indo, 32; Old, 32
Evans, Caradoc, 192
Evans, Christmas, 160
Evans, Sir Geraint, 200
Evans, Gwynfor, 82, 150
Evans, John, 156
Evans, John (of Eglwys Bach), 166
Evans, Theophilus, 185–6

Felindre, 18
Fforest-Fach, 131
Fforest Fawr, 97
Finney, C.G., 161
Fishguard, 28, 90
Flannel, 89, 113
Flint, 33, 66; County of, 62, 63, 70, 80, 112, 188, 201
Folklore, 19
Football Association of Wales, 210
Forest of Dean, 37, 111
Forestry Commission, 26
Forward Movement, 166
France, 23, 32, 69, 110, 125
Free Wales Army, 227
French wars, 89–92, 95–105, 116, 202
Froncysylltau, 118

Gallo-Brittonic, 35
Gaunt, John of, 69
Gee, Thomas, 139, 219
General Strike (1926), 146
Geoffrey of Monmouth, 180
Geology, 15–16, 17–18, 33
Giraldus Cambrensis, 84, 180–1
Glaciation, 18–21, 24
Glamorgan, Agricultural Society of, 100; County of, 51, 57, 62, 70, 72, 80, 81, 120–3, 105, 107, 110, 118, 129, 146, 165–6, 167, 208–9, 210; Vale of, 13, 16, 36, 41, 46, 103, 105, 129, 131
Glaslyn, River, 97–8
Gley soil, 25
Gloucester, 39, 40; County of, 51, 72, 74
Glyndŵr, Owain, 45, 64–9
Goidelic, 35
Goodwin, Geraint, 192
Gower, 13, 29, 41, 46, 103–4, 131, 156, 158
Great Revival, 156–60
Great Sessions, Courts of, 73, 137, 213
Great Western Railway, 122–3
Gregynog, 220
Grey, Reginald, 65
Griffiths, James, 149

Gruffydd, W.I., 189, 190
Guest, John, 114, 115
Guest, Lady Charlotte, 180
Guild for the Promotion of Welsh Music, 199
Guto Nyth Brân, 208
Gwendraeth, Valley of, 116
Gwent, 60; County of; 29, 80, 131, 156
Gwynedd, 41, 42, 43, 60, 63–4, 65, 66, 181; County of, 22, 80, 83
Gwyneddigion, Society of, 214

Hafod, 103
Halkyn Mt., 112
Hampshire, 115
Handel, G.F., 198
Hardie, Keir, 144, 173
Harlech, 44, 65, 97–8
Harlech Television, 222–5
Harp, 195–7
Harris, Howell, 156–8
Hastings, 39
Haverfordwest, 123
Hawarden, 52, 66
Haydn, J., 198
Hechter, M., 152
Henry III, 43
Henry IV, 65, 66–9, 70
Henry V, 69
Henry VII (Henry Tudor), 69–70, 74, 182
Henry VIII, 70–1
Hereford, 39, 40, 41; County of, 46, 60, 72, 73, 74
Highways Act (1862), 78
Hillforts, 34, 36, 37
Hiraethog, Mynydd, 13, 29
Hirwaun, 19, 111, 114, 118, 131
Holyhead, 122, 208
Home Rule, 82–3, 142, 148, 150
Homfray (family), 111, 115, 116, 122
Housing associations, 227
Hughes, John (Ceiriog), 188
Hughes, T. Rowland, 191
Hume, David, 91
Humphreys, Emyr, 193
Huntingdon, County of, 94

Hywel Dda, 39, 60, 71, 179

Ice Age, 18–21, 32; Little, 24
Ilston, 156
Independent Churches, 158–9, 160, 163, 168, 215
Industrial Revolution, 18, 30–1, 47, 113–28, 209
Insole, Goerge, 125
Ireland, 34, 35, 38, 56, 58, 92, 122, 142
Irish Sea, 18, 33, 38
Iron, 111, 114–7
Iron Age, 24, 32, 34–5
Ironstone, 16, 114, 117
Isca Silurum, 36
Isle of Man, 35, 38
Iwan, Dafydd, 200

Jeffreys, George, 167
Jeffreys, Stephen, 167
Jenkins, R.T., 190
Jesus College, Oxford, 214, 216
John, Sir Goscombe, 203
Jones, Bobi, 191
Jones, D. Gwenallt (Gwenallt), 190, 191
Jones, David, 193
Jones, E. Pan, 145
Jones, Edward (Bardd y Brenin), 196
Jones, Glyn, 192
Jones, Griffith, 157, 184, 214
Jones, Gwyn, 192–3
Jones, Gwyneth, 200
Jones, I.G., 164
Jones, M.O., 164
Jones, Michael Daniel, 139
Jones, Robert (Derfel), 215–6
Jones, Thomas (Exciseman), 201
Jones, Thomas Gwynn, 189
Jones, Tom, 200
Johnes, Thomas, 103, 104
Justices of the Peace, 74, 75–6, 77

Kames, 20
Kenrick, Llewellyn, 210
Kettle holes, 20

Labour Party, 82, 83, 134, 143–52, 173
Lampeter, 162, 214
Lancashire, 30, 109, 123, 124, 129
Land Question, 141, 145, 219
Landforms, 14–21
Landsker, 29
Las, Sion Dafydd, 183
Latin, 37, 45–6
Lead, 16, 111, 112, 113
Lewis, Howell (Elfed), 203
Lewis, Saunders, 190, 191, 227
Lewis School, Pengam, 209
Lhuyd, Edward, 186
Liberal Party, 134, 142–5, 148–52, 165, 170–3, 219
Liberation Society, 139, 165
Limestone, 16, 110, 112
Liverpool, 92, 123, 220
Llanbadarn, 38
Llanberis, 112, 113
Llanddeiniolen, 96–7
Llanddewi, 38
Llanddowror, 157
Llandovery, 88, 123; College, 209, 215
Llandrinio, 98
Llandudno, 124
Llanelli, 31, 111, 116, 117, 123, 128, 149, 210
Llanelwedd, 219
Llanfaches, 156
Llanfyllin, 80
Llangeitho, 158
Llangollen, 118, 201, 202, 204, 216
Llangurig, 123
Llanidloes, 109, 123
Llanilltud, 38
Llanover, Lady, 197, 202
Llansamlet, 110
Llantrisant, 125
Llewellyn, Richard, 193
Lloyd, John Ambrose, 198
Lloyd-George, David, 142–3, 145, 146, 170–3, 219
Llwyd, Alan, 192
Llwyd, Morgan, 184
Llŷn, 57, 190

Llywarch, 179
Llywelyn I, 43, 44, 62, 66, 220
Llywelyn II, 39, 43, 62, 66, 179
Local government, reorganisation of, 78–83
Local Government Act (1888), 78
Local Government Act (1972), 79–81
Local Government Boundary Commission, 81
London, 88, 122–3, 125, 201, 219–20
London and North Western Railway, 123
London Tonic Sol-fa College, 198
Loughor, 165–6
Ludlow, 71, 134, 219

Mabinogion, 180–1
Mabon, William Abraham, 144, 168
Machynlleth, 65, 80, 109, 124
Madoc, 135
Maenclochog, 112
Maesteg, 127, 167
Magnus Maximus, 180
Mallwyd, 183
Manaw Gododdin, 178
Manchester & Milford Railway, 123
Manors, 41
Marches, 39, 40, 62, 64, 70–3, 85–6, 88–9, 181
Margam, 19
Marshall, William, 91
Mary (Tudor), 77
Mawddach, River, 19, 29
May Day, 85
Mediterranean, 33
Meirionydd, District of, 57
Menai Strait, 122
Merioneth, 74; County of, 45, 62, 72, 80, 82, 88, 97–8, 112
Merseyside, 30, 52, 124
Merthyr Mawr, 100–103
Merthyr Tydfil, 78, 82, 111, 113, 114, 115–6, 118, 122, 124, 137, 160, 187, 202, 203, 220
Mesolithic, 23, 24, 33
Methodist College, Bala, 215
Methodism, 136, 138, 146, 156–77, 184, 185, 186, 187, 196–7, 215

Michaelston-le-Pit, 30
Middle Ages, 24, 64, 179
Middle East, 33, 37
Midlands, English, 30
Milford Haven, 13, 20, 123, 132–3
Milton, John, 185
Mold, 188
Monmouth, County of, 51, 73–4, 80, 103, 105, 118, 129, 146, 168, 208, 210
Montgomery, County of, 72, 80, 89, 98, 109, 113, 142
Moraines, 19
Morfa Dyffryn, 97–8
Morgan, Bishop William, 183, 220
Morgannwg, 60
Morris, Lewis, 185
Morris-Jones, Sir John, 189
Mostyn, 201
Motte-and-bailey castle, 40, 41
Mynydd Bach, 96–7
Mynydd Carn, 179

Nannau, 183
Nantlle, 112, 113
Narberth, 107
National Anthem, 13, 195
National Eisteddfod Association, 203, 216
National Health Service, 148
National Insurance Commission, 142
National Library, 142, 217–8
National Museum, 142, 217–8
National Youth Orchestra of Wales, 207
Nationalism, 65, 66, 82–3, 150–2
Native society, 60–1, 62, 84–5, 86
Neath, 110–11, 113, 118, 124, 209; Vale of, 116, 127
Nedd, River, 118
Nelson, 209
Neolithic, 24, 33
New Radnor, 74
New Zealand, 211
Newcastle, 125
Newport, 78, 117, 118, 128, 137, 142, 208, 210, 211
Newtown, 109, 123, 131, 144, 220
Neyland, 123

Normans, 29, 30, 39–45, 46, 61–4, 85–6
North and South Wales Bank, 218–19
North Wales Quarrymen's Union, 218
Northampton, County of, 94
Nottingham, 129

Offa's Dyke, 37, 39, 46, 58–60, 61
Oil refining, 132–3
Old Red Sandstone, 26
Onions, Peter, 115–6
Ordovician, 15
Orkney, 38
Orleton, 19
Owen, Daniel, 188
Owen, George, 208
Owen, Goronwy, 185, 187
Owen, Sir Hugh, 203
Owen, Robert, 144
Owen-Pughe, William, 187
Oxford, County of, 94
Oxford Movement, 138, 162–3

Paddington Station, 124
Palaeolithic, 23, 32–3
Panton, Paul, 103
Pantycelyn, 158
Pantyfedwen Foundation, 204
Parishes, 77–8
Parry, John (Bardd Alaw), 196
Parry, John (Blind Parry), 196
Parry, Joseph, 199
Parry, W.J., 168
Parry-Williams, T.H., 190
Parys Mountain, 111, 113
Patagonia, 51, 139, 204
Peace Society, 162
Peat, 23–4, 25
Pembroke, 69, 103–4; County of, 29, 62, 70, 72, 80, 107, 112, 113, 208
Penllyn, William, 195
Pennant, Richard, 112
Pennant, Thomas, 186
Pennsylvania, 116, 157
Penrhyn, 112
Penydarren, 115, 122
Pen-y-gaer 36

Penygroes, 167
Peter, David, 159
Peterston-super-Ely, 30
Pevensey, 39
Phillips, Morgan, 177
Phillips, Sir Thomas, 160
Piercefield, 211
Pitt, William, 90
Placenames, 237–40
Plagues, 24, 64
Plasgwyn, 103
Plateaux, 17–18, 29
Plebbs League, 144
Plymouth, 115; Earl of, 218
Podzol, 25
Pontypool, 118, 124
Pontypridd, 125, 127
Poor Law Act (1834), 106
Population, 48, 84; change, 48–51, 53–4, 79, 128–9
Port Dinorwic, 113
Port Penrhyn, 113
Port Talbot, 117, 128
Porthcawl, 124
Portmadoc, 97–8, 113
Powys, 41, 42, 43, 46, 60, 64, 179, 181; County of, 30, 80, 131
Powys Fadog, 43, 60, 73
Powys Wenwynwyn, 43, 60, 73
Prayer Book, translation of, 183
Presbyterian College, Carmarthen, 215
Preseli, Mynydd, 13, 16, 29
Prestatyn, 55, 60, 122
Price, Richard, 186
Price, Sir John, 182–3
Prichard of Llandovery, 184
Primrose Hill, 201
Prince of Wales, 43, 45, 62, 65
Principality, 62–4, 70, 74, 77, 213
Pritchard, T.J.Ll., 188
Promotion of Christian Knowledge, Society for the, 157, 184
Pryderi, 180
Prys, Edmund, 183
Pugh, John, 166
Pumlumon, 16, 112
Puritanism, 156, 170, 184, 188

Quakers, 157
Quakers' Yard, 122

Radnor, County of, 73, 80, 107, 113, 123
Raglan, 69
Railways, 118–24
Rainfall, 21, 22–5
Rebecca Riots, 107–8, 137–8
Rees, Thomas, 168
Rees, William, 139
Referendum, 82–3
Reform Act (1867), 140
Regional contrasts, 26–31
Rendel, Stuart, 142
Rhine, River, 34
Rhondda, 51, 125–7, 144
Rhuddlan, 44, 66; Statute of, 45, 62
Rhyl, 124
Rhys, Sir John, 189
Rhys, Keidrych, 192–3
Rhys, Lord, 200
Rhys, Morgan John, 136, 162
Rhys, Sir Sion Dafydd, 183
Richard II, 65
Richard III, 70
Richard, Evan Henry, 168
Roberts, Eigra Lewis, 191
Roberts, Elezar, 198
Roberts, Evan, 165–7
Roberts, John (Ieuan Gwyllt), 198
Roberts, John (Telynor Cymru), 197
Roberts, Kate, 190, 191
Roger of Montgomery, 41
Romans, 36–7
Ross-on-Wye, 23
Rowland, Daniel, 158
Rowland, Henry, 186
Rowland, John, 191
Royal Commission on Religion in Wales, 167–8
Royal Mint, 221
Royal Welsh Agricultural Society, 219
Ruabon, 210
Rugby football, 32, 208–12
Rural depopulation, 48, 55
Ruthin, 65, 66

Rutland, 94

St Asaph, 173
St Bride's Major, 30
St David, 38
St David's, 65, 214
St David's College, Lampeter, 162, 209, 214, 215, 216, 217
St Fagan's, 218
St Illtud, 38
St Padarn, 38
St Patrick, 38
Salesbury, William, 183
Sarn features, 19
Scilly, Isles of, 22
Scotland, 23, 35, 56, 58, 82, 150, 178, 213, 225
Scottish islands, 23
Secretary of State, 58, 81, 82, 148, 149
Seren Gomer, 136
Severn River, 29, 30, 37, 41, 60, 92, 98, 103
Seymour, Lord Robert, 103
Sheffield, 129
Sheriff, 74, 75
Shetland, 38
Shrewsbury, 40, 41, 88, 123, 179, 220
Shropshire, 46, 72, 73, 74, 111, 114, 115
Silures, 15, 36
Silurian, 15
Silver, 112, 113
Sinclair, Sir John, 91
Singing, 164, 195–200
Slate, 16, 112–3
Smith, Adam, 91
Smithfield, 87
Snowdonia, 13, 16, 17, 19, 29, 42, 55, 113
Social Gospel Movement, 166
Social Service, Welsh School of, 219
Soils, 25–6
Somerset, 51
South Wales Football Club, 210
South Wales Miners' Federation, 218
Southampton, 123
Spain, 32
Special Areas Act (1934), 129–30

Speenhamland, 99
Stafford, 114
Stephen, Edward (Tanymarian), 198
Stephens, Thomas, 203
Stoke-on-Trent, 129
Strata Florida, 123
Squatters, 94–6
Stephenson, Robert, 122
Stone, 16
Structure, 14–21
Sunday school, 161
Surnames, 213–6
Sussex, 110–11
Swansea, 38, 78, 110–11, 113, 116–17, 118, 121–3, 128, 131, 192, 209, 220, 222

Taff Vale Railway, 122
Talgarth, 157
Taliesin, 178, 193
Tawe, River, 19, 118
Teifi, River, 18, 80
Telford, Thomas, 118, 122
Temperature, 22–5
Temple of Peace and Health, 220
Tenby, 124
Thames, River, 24
Thomas, D.A., (Lord Rhondda), 144
Thomas, David, 116, 127
Thomas, Dylan, 192–3
Thomas, Gwyn (English-language writer), 192–3
Thomas, Gwyn (Welsh-language writer), 191
Thomas, R.S., 193
Thomas, William (Islwyn), 188
Tin, 116–17
Tithe War, 141
Tonypandy Riots, 144
Tourism, 55, 57
Traeth Mawr, 97–8
Transhumance, 84–5, 94
Transport, 92–4, 117–24
Tredegar, 168
Treforest, 130
Trefriw, 118
Tregaron, 88
Trevithick, Richard, 122

Tudor, Owen, 69
Turnpike trusts, 92–4, 107–8, 117
Tyneside, 129
Tywi, River, 19, 47, 92

Union, Acts of (1536–1543), 46, 69–75, 81, 86, 110, 134, 182
Unitarians, 160
University of Wales, 51, 141, 142, 216–17, 220, 229; constituent colleges, 216–17; Extra-Mural, 173; Institute of Science and Technology, 217; Medical School, 217; Registry, 217
Urdd Gobaith Cymru, 225–6, 229
Urien, Prince, 178
Usk, River, 30, 38, 41, 92, 103

Vegetation, 23–4, 25–6
Vergil, Polydore, 182
Vikings, 38
Vineyards, 23, 24
Von Herkomer, Sir Hubert, 203
Vyrnwy, River, 30, 98

Waddington, Augusta, 197
Wales Act (1978), 82–3
Wales and Monmouthshire, Council for, 81
Wales and the Marches, Councils of, 71, 74–5, 76, 134, 213
Wales Gas Board, 221
Wales Tourist Board, 221
Waterford, 123
Wat's Dyke, 60
Watt, James, 114, 116
Weather, 21–5
Welsh Affairs, Minister for, 58, 81, 148
Welsh Amateur Challenge Cup, 212
Welsh Arts Council, 222
Welsh Baseball Union, 211
Welsh Books Council, 227
Welsh Circulating Schools, 157, 184, 214
Welsh Education Committee, 215
Welsh Folk Museum, 218
Welsh Folk Song Society, 199

Welsh Housing and Development Association, 219
Welsh Intermediate Education Act (1889), 141-2
Welsh Land League, 219
Welsh language, 28–31, 32, 35–6, 45–57, 71, 145, 183, 204, 222–9; schools, 56, 226
Welsh Language Act (1967), 56, 228
Welsh Language Society, 82, 150, 227–9
Welsh Manuscripts Society, 215
Welsh National Council of Music, 199
Welsh National Hospital Board, 220
Welsh National Insurance Commission, 221
Welsh National Opera, 199, 221–2
Welsh National War Memorial, 220
Welsh Nationalist Party, 82, 148–52
Welsh Office, 58, 81, 149, 220
Welsh Sunday Closing Act (1881), 141, 165
Welsh Town Planning and Housing Trust, 219
Welsh Water Board, 221
Welshpool, 92
Wesley, John, 158
Wesleyans, 158, 160
West Indies, 88
Western Mail, 216
Whitefield, George, 158

Wilkinson, John, 114, 116
William Fitz Osbern, 41
Williams, Crwys (Crwys), 189
Williams, D.J., 190
Williams, Edward (Iolo Morganwg), 186–7, 201–2, 214, 218
Williams, Eliseus (Eifion Wyn), 189
Williams, John Ellis, 191
Williams, Wern, 160
Williams, William (Pantycelyn), 158–9, 184, 185, 197
Williams-Parry, Robert, 189, 190
Williams-Wynn (family), 134, 210
Winds, 22–5
Women's organisations, 227
Woollen Mills, 18, 88–9, 109, 113
Worcester, county of, 74
Workers' Educational Association, 173
Wrexham, 19, 112, 114
Wye, River, 30, 41, 60, 103
Wynne, Ellis, 185–6

Ynyscedwyn, 116
Yorkshire, 109, 129
Young, Arthur, 91, 100–3
Ysbyty Cynfyn, 104
Ystalyfera, 116
Ystradgynlais, 80
Ystrad Meurig, 123

Zimmern, Alfred, 146